WARRIOR PREACHERS

DAVID A. HARRELL

WARRIOR PREACHERS

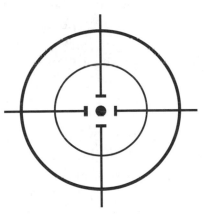

A SPIRITUAL CALL TO ARMS
IN AN AGE OF MILITANT UNBELIEF

Words of Appreciation

The apostle Paul constantly reminds Timothy that legitimate Christian ministry is hard spiritual warfare (1 Timothy 1:18; 6:12; 2 Timothy 2:3-5; 4:7). Pastors are not supposed to think of themselves as political spin doctors, public relations experts, or diplomats tasked with winning the world's favor and approval. We are to be warriors whose main objective is to "tear down speculations and every lofty thing raised up against the knowledge of God" (2 Corinthians 10:5). And we are shepherds whose duty includes guarding the flock against wolves and other threats. In other words, there's a militancy inherent in the pastoral job description that isn't stressed enough in our generation. David Harrell is a pastor who gets it, and he unfolds this motif brilliantly in Warrior Preachers. Whether you are a minister or a lay person who wants to support and encourage your pastor, this book will edify and encourage you.

JOHN MACARTHUR: PASTOR-TEACHER, GRACE COMMUNITY CHURCH; CHANCELLOR, THE MASTER'S UNIVERSITY AND SEMINARY

No sane person enjoys conflict, but no faithful minister of Jesus Christ can avoid it. Jesus said, "If the world hates you, know that it has hated Me before it hated you" (John 15:18). So we're not to be surprised at the world's militant opposition to the Christian message (1 John 3:13)—and we're not to try to avoid the conflict by softening our message, adapting it to worldly tastes, speaking to people's "felt needs," or bowing to the ever-changing rules of political correctness. Ministry is spiritual warfare. Dave Harrell has traced this theme through the Scriptures, and the result is this wonderful resource that will equip, encourage, and remind Christians (leaders and lay persons alike) that we need to be true, faithful soldiers for Christ.

PHIL JOHNSON: EXECUTIVE DIRECTOR, GRACE TO YOU

The church has faced dark days in the past, and it has always been led back to the high ground of biblical fidelity by strong men. It will be the same for the church today. A new generation of preachers, raised up by God, is desperately needed to help return the church to the solid footing of sound doctrine that produces holy living.

May God use this book to challenge you to stand strong as a "warrior preacher" in this hour of spiritual warfare.

Steven J. Lawson, President, OnePassion Ministries; Professor, The Master's Seminary; Teaching Fellow, Ligonier Ministries; Lead Preacher, Trinity Bible Church of Dallas

Warrior Preachers
A Spiritual Call to Arms in an Age of Militant Unbelief

© 2023 David A. Harrell
Shepherd's Fire Media
www.shepherdsfiremedia.org

The author expresses his appreciation to Joel C., retired Green
Beret and current special agent, for some aspects of Green
Beret training and deployment strategies mentioned from time
to time in the text.

Unless otherwise noted, Scripture quotations taken from the
New American Standard Bible® (NASB), Copyright © 1960,
1962, 1963, 1968, 1971, 1972, 1973, 1975, 1977, 1995 by The Lock-
man Foundation.
Used by permission. www.Lockman.org

ISBN: 978-1-7363143-9-5

Cover design and book layout: www.greatwriting.org

Printed in Colombia

The purpose of this book is:

To fortify and encourage pastors and church leaders who are committed to a God-centered, biblically integrated, and consistent ministry as they face the increased challenges of militant unbelief in our culture and apostasy in the church, and to enlist new recruits to join the fight.

Dedicated to the fearless warriors of the faith serving in obscurity and persevering with joy as they await our coming Savior and King, the Lord Jesus Christ.

Acknowledgments

I wish to thank Lennae Rickard and Pamela Ufen for employing their proofreading skills in the initial draft of this book. They are always faithful and joyful in their service to Christ and an inspiration to all who know them.

I also want to thank Carl Dobrowolski (and his staff with Goodwill Rights Management Corp.) for his ongoing consultation services and his enthusiastic support of what we are trying to accomplish through Shepherd's Fire Media in general and more specifically through this book, *Warrior Preachers*.

Finally, I am greatly indebted to Jim Holmes of Great Writing Publications for his editorial, design, and book layout expertise; more importantly, I'm thankful for his deep love for Christ and His Word that causes our hearts to beat together in spiritual oneness. Jim's theological acumen is also a welcomed asset that I have treasured in this project and other books I have written with his help.

Contents

Foreword

Dr. Steven Lawson

Now you followed my teaching, conduct, purpose, faith, patience, love, perseverance, persecutions, and sufferings, such as happened to me at Antioch, at Iconium and at Lystra; what persecutions I endured, and out of them all the Lord rescued me! Indeed, all who desire to live godly in Christ Jesus will be persecuted. But evil men and impostors will proceed from bad to worse, deceiving and being deceived. You, however, continue in the things you have learned and become convinced of, knowing from whom you have learned them, and that from childhood you have known the sacred writings which are able to give you the wisdom that leads to salvation through faith which is in Christ Jesus. All Scripture is inspired by God and profitable for teaching, for reproof, for correction, for training in righteousness; so that the man of God may be adequate, equipped for every good work.

2 TIMOTHY 3:10–17

We live in perilous times in which the moral foundations of this world are crumbling beneath our feet. The effects upon the culture—and especially the church—are seen everywhere. This gathering storm of spiritual warfare is rapidly escalating by the day. No realm of society is off limits to the advancing forces of darkness that are spreading their deceptive lies and wicked perversions at alarming speed.

This spiritual apostasy is exerting the greatest pressure upon the men who stand in pulpits around this world. Never has the challenge been greater—nor the cost higher—to preach the truth than in this present hour. These divinely appointed heralds are under fierce attack, as "seducing spirits and doctrines of demons" (1 Tim. 4:1) confront them at every turn.

Tough times demand strong preaching. The church desperately needs faithful pastors who will lift up their voice with increasing courage and declare the life-changing message of Scripture. Not only must they teach the truth, but they must also "contend earnestly for the faith" (Jude 3). These men must "put on the full armor of God" (Eph. 6:12) and "fight the good fight of faith" (1 Tim. 6:12).

This is no time for spiritual pacifists to claim exemption from active duty. There cannot be any conscientious objectors in this conflict between good and evil. There must not be passive men in pulpits, who preach tame sermons and offer trite talks. Instead, the times in which we find ourselves demand heroic figures of steely convictions, spiritual stalwarts who are anchored in the Word of God.

Now is the time for the strongest men to preach the strongest message in the context of the strongest ministries. The hour demands battle-tested leaders and heroic figures, men who are unwavering in their biblical convictions. We need those who are willing, if necessary, to stand *contra mundum*—against the world.

Preaching like this will require their willingness to suffer the pain of persecution. It will mean losing popularity and pleasures. It may mean the loss of family and friends. It could mean the loss of livelihood and health. It might even mean the loss of life. But all such losses are not worthy to be compared with the great gain of the approval of Christ and the joy of advancing His gospel.

In the face of such intense conflict, the times in which we live demand "warrior preachers." This term was coined in seventeenth-century Scotland to describe the preachers in the Covenanters movement. These fearless leaders stood firmly for the right to worship God according to biblical standards. They resisted the government authorities of their day, risking their very lives, in order to preach the full counsel of God. These men were unswayed by the spirit of the age, but instead remained deeply grounded in holy Scripture, no matter what price they would pay.

That is why David Harrell's book, *Warrior Preachers*, is so needed today. These pages issue a sobering call for pastors to be unflinching in their pulpit ministries during these desperate days. The church is always in need of such men, but never more so than today. As our world sinks into a deep abyss of depravity, we need men who are firmly rooted in the unchanging truths of Scripture. We need men who will not cower to the opposition as they proclaim the truth. We need men who will not retreat from the frontlines of spiritual combat, but who will hold their position. This well-written book will sound a battle call, stir your heart, and summon you to action for the sake of Christ.

The church has faced dark days in the past, and it has always been led back to the high ground of biblical fidelity by strong men. It will be the same for the church today. A new generation of preachers, raised up by God, is desperately needed to help return the church to the solid footing of sound doctrine that produces holy living.

We rejoice that God has guaranteed the final victory over the devil. In the meantime, the apostle John assures us in the midst of this battle that "greater is He who is in you than he who is in the world" (1 John 4:4). The path to this glorious triumph will only be realized through the sacrifice of godly men who "preach the word. . . in season and out of season" (2 Tim. 4:2). Such men will proclaim the truth when it is convenient and inconvenient, when it is well received and fiercely opposed. For these preachers, the church does always wait.

May God use this book to challenge you to stand strong as a "warrior preacher" in this hour of spiritual warfare.

Steven J. Lawson
President, OnePassion Ministries
Professor, The Master's Seminary
Teaching Fellow, Ligonier Ministries
Lead Preacher, Trinity Bible Church of Dallas

Introduction

Warrior Preachers:
A Spiritual Call to Arms in an Age of Militant Unbelief

"For your sake we are being put to death all day long; we were considered as sheep to be slaughtered." But in all these things we overwhelmingly conquer through Him who loved us.

ROMANS 8:36–37

An evil cloud of satanic darkness encompasses the world today. The fierce winds of deception are pummeling all that God deems righteous. The very foundations of basic civility and common sense are being shaken. And without question, the church of Jesus Christ is under siege! Only the most naïve, undiscerning, and biblically illiterate Christian can deny this. Like never before, a violent storm of persecution against authentic Christianity is gaining strength across the globe.

Because "the whole world lies in the power of the evil one" (1 John 5:19), the vast majority of the inhabitants of this planet live in fear and uncertainty. War, violence, immorality, poverty, famine, disease, drug addiction, drug and sex trafficking, illegal immigration, social justice, homosexuality, transgenderism, systemic racism, and economic instability are all subjects that have become so commonplace in public discourse that our society has been inoculated against their damning implications. Ethnic (racial) tensions are at an all-time high, while confidence in our political leaders is at an all-time low, especially in the United States. Very few people trust the media or even the medical and science experts who claim to have all the answers, and the majority of Americans believe the country is moving in the wrong direction.

As A.W. Tozer once said, "A scared world needs a fearless church." But this is not what we see today in our post-Christian culture. Most churches are fearful, not fearless, cowering to the pressures of the world, capitulating to the shrill voices of feminism and political correctness, and compromising God's truth to gain man's praise. As a result, they forfeit divine blessing, spiritual power, and moral authority. Worse yet, they place themselves in the pathway of divine judgment. Indeed, most churches today have "Ichabod" ("The glory has departed") written across their entryway, but remarkably, both their leaders and their members are clueless of their true spiritual condition in the eyes of God.

Because of this, most non-religious people have no confidence in the leaders of evangelicalism—and for good reason. Much of Christianity today is a counterfeit. Most Christians are "Christian" in name only. But since the birth of the church at Pentecost in the first century, authentic, biblical, New Testament Christianity has been very rare, whereas hypocrisy, self-deception, and false teachers abound. What is even more rare are fearless men of God who will boldly proclaim the unsearchable riches of Christ without compromising any aspect of the gospel—pastors who will unflinchingly "preach the Word . . . in season and out of season; reprove, rebuke, exhort, with great patience and instruction" as they are commanded to do (2 Tim. 4:2)—men of uncommon valor who can echo the testimony of the apostle Paul and boldly declare,

> For I am not ashamed of the gospel, for it is the power of God for salvation to everyone who believes, to the Jew first and also to the Greek. For in it the righteousness of God is revealed from faith to faith; as it is written, "but the righteous man shall live by faith."
> (Rom. 1:16–17)

> *What is greatly lacking in the church today are*
> *"warrior preachers"—a term used to described the*
> *Reformation preachers of seventeenth-century*
> *Scotland known as the Covenanters. . .*

Sadly, this is not the heartfelt testimony of most pastors and church leaders today. Far too many are more concerned with attracting a crowd than equipping the saints, while many others fear cancel culture more than God Himself. With the courage of a fainting goat, they collapse in panic when someone criticizes them for saying (or even believing) something society considers offensive, like the true gospel—the only truth that can save souls from the just wrath of a holy God.

What is greatly lacking in the church today are "warrior preachers"—a term used to describe the Reformation preachers of seventeenth-century Scotland known as the Covenanters—who, under threat of torture and death, sacrificed themselves to protect the treasure of the true gospel that exposed man's guilt and condemnation before a holy God, and proclaimed Christ's finished work on the cross as the only means of saving grace. These were the godly Puritans who rejected false doctrines and the popish relics of

Roman Catholicism, including the ritualistic, superstitious, and external religiosity also inherent in the Church of England. They were instead committed to holiness in the heart and to biblical preaching.

Warrior preachers then and now are biblical preachers; men who fear God, not man; men who never cower to critics and never avoid preaching a text that might offend; men who preach the whole counsel of God regardless of the response it might elicit; men who realize they are mere heralds of the King of kings, preaching the only message that can save sinners, sanctify saints, and bring glory to the One who purchased our redemption.

> *Warrior preachers today are men who will not capitulate to the culture, but will confront it. They reject the popular notion of evangelical pragmatism that regards friendship with the world as a better strategy for evangelism than preaching the gospel.*

Practically speaking, warrior preachers today are men who will not capitulate to the culture, but will confront it. They reject the popular notion of evangelical pragmatism that regards friendship with the world as a better strategy for evangelism than preaching the gospel. Furthermore, warrior preachers simply will not bow to the demonstrably false and divisive deceptions of Critical Race Theory that fuel the woke cult invading our schools, workplaces, and churches. Therefore, they will not preach the false gospel of social justice, nor will they yield to the gross immoralities and insane ideologies of the LGBTQIA+ revolutionaries seeking to indoctrinate and seduce our children. These are godly men, worthy to be called soldiers of the cross, known by all to be "a living and holy sacrifice, acceptable to God" (Rom. 12:1), faithful men with no desire for wealth, power, prestige, or worldly accolades.

These are "the King's Champions"—the title given to "Great-Grace" in Bunyan's *The Pilgrim's Progress*—the one who came to the rescue of "Little-Faith" and vanquished the thieves who preyed upon vulnerable pilgrims. These are indefatigable and fearless warriors of the faith who understand from Scripture and know from personal experience that "the weapons of our warfare are not of the flesh, but divinely powerful for the destruction of fortresses . . . destroying speculations and every lofty thing raised up against the knowledge of God" (2 Cor. 10:4–5). Would to God that He amass a vast army of valiant champions who, with the apostle Paul, can say, "Suffer hardship with me, as a good soldier of Christ Jesus" (2 Tim. 2:3).

> *Whether you're a preaching pastor in a church or whether you serve Christ in another area of Christian leadership, I invite you to measure your life and ministry according to God's standard.*

By drawing from the training, tactics, techniques, and procedures of the United States Army Special Forces "Green Berets" and the biblical and historical descriptions of valiant soldiers of the cross, this book intends to strengthen and encourage warrior preachers who are currently engaged in the battle, and to enlist new recruits to join the fight. As the subtitle of this book states, this is "A Spiritual Call to Arms in an Age of Militant Unbelief." I have deliberately chosen to cite very few examples of the kinds of wickedness we see flourishing in our culture to illustrate my concerns, which I have already done in my earlier book, *Why America Hates Biblical Christianity*.[1] Instead, I will focus more on biblical warnings and remedies that have seemingly been forgotten by many in church leadership—assuming such leaders knew them in the first place.

Whether you're a preaching pastor in a church or you serve Christ in another area of Christian leadership, I invite you to measure your life and ministry according to God's standard. Then, by His grace and power, I challenge you to enter the battle that has already been won by our glorious Savior and King, the Lord Jesus Christ—fully embracing the inspired words of that great warrior preacher, the apostle Paul, who said,

> "For your sake we are being put to death all day long; we were considered as sheep to be slaughtered." But in all these things we overwhelmingly conquer through Him who loved us. (Rom. 8:36–37)

1 David A. Harrell, *Why America Hates Biblical Christianity: Pursuing Christlikeness in Times of Mounting Hostility and Apathy* (Wapwallopen, PA: Shepherd Press, 2021).

1

The Warrior's Enemy

*Be of sober spirit, be on the alert. Your adversary, the devil,
prowls around like a roaring lion, seeking someone to devour.*
(1 Peter 5:8)

Our adversary is of a spiritual, immaterial substance, and so invisible
both in his nature and approaches, and doth often reach us a deadly
blow before we know it is he and in the very simplicity of our hearts
we run into the snare. . . . He is either weakening our comforts, or
enticing us to sin, or making us weary of the ways of God. If he cannot pervert us, and draw us by some gross sin to dishonour God, he
ceaseth not to vex us, and make our heavenly course uncomfortable to
us. The devil never ceases to pursue his designs, but observes all our
motions, all the postures of our spirits, when we are merry and when
we are angry, when we are laughing and when we are mourning. He
sees how the tree leans, and then joins his force to run us down.

THOMAS MANTON[2]

---

2 Thomas Manton, *The Works of Thomas Manton, Vol. 17* (Carlisle, PA: The Banner of Truth Trust,
first published by James Nisbet & CO. London, 1874), 76.

One of the greatest priorities for all military leaders is to know their enemy. Nowhere is this more evident than in the Special Forces units of the United States military. I have been privileged to glean much insight into this issue from a dear brother in Christ, Joel C., who has not only served with me as an elder, but has also served our country in combat as a Green Beret. Green Berets are the most elite branch of the U.S. Army and are defined by the Army as specially trained U.S. Army soldiers that are renowned for their ability to deploy in small teams, operate independently, and conduct their mission in austere environments. These Special Forces units perform seven doctrinal missions:

- Unconventional Warfare
- Foreign Internal Defense
- Special Reconnaissance
- Direct Action
- Combating Terrorism
- Counter-proliferation
- Information Operations[3]

The training and combat experiences described by my Green Beret fellow elder offer many helpful parallels for those who are willing to do battle with the guerilla warfare tactics of Satan and his minions—both demon and human—the vicious enemies of the kingdom of God.

⌀

Notwithstanding the rigorous selection and training process Green Berets must endure and pass in order to serve on a team (all of which will be discussed in subsequent chapters), when preparing

3 https://thelegionfund.org/5th/what-is-green-beret/

for a mission, they develop a four-part *PACE* plan (an acronym for *Primary, Alternate, Contingency*, and *Emergency*). An enormous amount of thought and training goes into this process in order to know the enemy and raise the probability of mission success when defending against it and waging war upon it. First, a *Warning Order* is issued to the Special Forces team to alert them that a mission is forthcoming. Next they receive a *Concept of the Operation* from the commanders that explains the goals of the mission—what success looks like, perhaps taking out a highly valued target or rescuing a hostage. Then, based upon intelligence (often acquired by the team itself), an *Operations Order* is developed by the team to break down the mission in minute detail. Once completed, it is sent back to the commander for approval.

The *Operations Order* is all encompassing. It includes who they are going up against, what the target is, and how to defeat it, all of which is based upon the enemy's typical TTP (*Tactics, Techniques, and Procedures*). They consider the enemy's *most likely* course of action and their *most dangerous* course of action. Everything is spelled out. Nothing is left to chance.

Next they make a sandbox of the target where they brief the commander about what the target actually looks like. For example, if it's a village, they must show were they will enter, where the helicopter will land, where the GMVs (*Ground Mobility Vehicles*) will be parked, where they will approach the target, who's going to be in the stack, who's going to be the breacher, and on it goes. And all of this is done just to get final approval for the mission.

Once approval to proceed is given, they begin to gather more intelligence of the target so they can construct one identical to it. They will learn its dimensions, they will know the construction of the gate and doors and what the locks are made of so they will know what kind of breaching charges to bring. They will determine how many enemy personnel are in the target area, where they are typically located, what kind of weapon systems they have, the nature of their surveillances and defenses, and the kind of reinforcements that might be available to them. All this will help them with their *Operations Plan* so they can determine things like what materials, supplies, weaponry, ammunition, transportation in and out, air support, and other troops in the vicinity they will need.

Next their builders construct an exact replica of the target where the team will practice their mission-related maneuvers dozens of times so that when they get on target and enter a village or a structure, they will feel like they've lived there all their life. They will know every alley, every roof, every room, every door, every window, every closet, and everywhere the enemy might hide. These drills also help them determine which team member is best suited for which position.

The Character of Our Enemy

Obviously, for the Green Beret, knowledge of the *Tactics, Techniques, and Procedures* of the enemy, combined with their *PACE* plan and intense training are all essential to the success of their mission. Imagine the heightened level of effectiveness in evangelical churches if they were equally committed to knowing and engaging our supernatural enemy described in Scripture as:

- Accuser of our brethren (Rev. 12:10)
- Adversary (1 Peter 5:8)
- Angel of the bottomless pit (Rev. 9:11)
- Belial (2 Cor. 6:15)
- Distressing spirit (1 Sam. 16:14)
- Dragon (Rev. 20:2)
- Enemy (Matt. 13:39)
- Father of lies (John 8:44)
- Liar (John 8:44)
- Lying spirit (1 Kings 22:22)
- Murderer (John 8:44)
- Prince of the power of the air (Eph. 2:2)
- Ruler of the darkness of this world (Eph. 6:12)
- Ruler of the demons (Matt. 12:24)
- Ruler of this world (John 14:30)

- Satan (1 Chron. 12:1; Job 1:6)
- Serpent (Gen. 3:4, 13–14; 2 Cor. 11:3)
- Spirit who works in the sons of disobedience (Eph. 2:2)
- Tempter (Matt. 4:3)
- The god of this age (2 Cor. 4:4)
- Wicked one (Matt. 13:19)

As the covert "ruler of this world" (John 12:31), Satan is a brilliant general (2 Cor. 2:11) that leads a highly organized demonic host (Eph. 6:12) in opposing the purposes and people of God. Although Christ's death on the cross "rendered powerless him who had the power of death, that is, the devil" (Heb. 2:14), currently he is allowed to continue his reign of terror; in fact, "the whole world lies in the power of the evil one" (1 John 5:19) and will continue to do so until Christ returns and judges Satan and his evil angels (Matt. 25:41; Rev. 20:10). As a master deceiver, he is capable of disguising himself as an angel of light (2 Cor. 11:13–15). Skilled in spiritual espionage he not only overpowers *unbelievers* (Eph. 2:2; 1 John 3:8–10; 5:19), blinding them to the truths of the gospel (2 Cor. 4:4) and holding them captive to do his will (2 Tim. 2:26), but he also attacks *believers*, especially those in leadership (2 Cor. 12:7). It is primarily through the leadership that he gains access to the church and destroys it (Eph. 6:11–17).

However, despite the supernatural power and diabolical purposes of such a formidable foe, many evangelical leaders do not realize what a high-value target they are in the eyes of the enemy, nor do they seem to care about the covert war being waged against them. Instead of knowing the *Tactics, Techniques, and Procedures* of the enemy and developing their version of a *PACE* plan to successfully combat them, the prevailing attitude tends to be one of *rapprochement*—which is at the heart of evangelical pragmatism. They say, "Let's find common ground with the world so they will like us; let's be like them so they will feel comfortable coming to our church." Because of this, most churches today are little more than a cross between a country club and coffee shop featuring live entertainment. They foolishly believe they must be conformed to the world in order to effectively sell their version of the gospel—a strategy that is hugely successful in filling churches with people who are spiritually dead and at enmity with God. As a result, their congregations are predominately non-believers— Christians in name only who consider the things of the Spirit of God to be foolishness and cannot understand them (1 Cor. 2:14). Whole churches are therefore bereft of biblical discernment and moral purity. With no commitment to personal holiness, it is rare to find even a modicum of Christlikeness among the members, rendering them powerless to be salt and light in a decaying and dark world.

As the covert "ruler of this world" (John 12:31), Satan is a brilliant general (2 Cor. 2:11) that leads a highly organized demonic host (Eph. 6:12) in opposing the purposes and people of God.

No wonder so many churches have no regard for the authority of Scripture that clearly condemns things like "evangelical feminism," women pastors, the LGBTQIA+ abominations, Critical Race Theory, Woke ideologies, the heretical Social Justice and Prosperity gospels. The evangelical world actually celebrates pastors who support the culture of progressive conformity that seeks to legalize unrighteousness and criminalize righteousness. For the most part, the modern church is not only indifferent toward the enemy; *it has become the enemy*—which was Satan's plan all along. Any honest evaluation of the prevailing attitudes, values, and lifestyles of many professing Christians will demonstrate how closely aligned evangelicalism has become to Satan's spiritual kingdom and his rule in the hearts of men. To be sure, Green Beret warrior preachers quickly detect these perils. They are men who are willing to sacrifice themselves for the cause of Christ, even if it means serving their whole life in utter obscurity; men who will fight for the truth and never yield ground to the enemy. Sadly, however, they are extremely rare and viciously opposed.

The Schemes of the Enemy

The *Tactics, Techniques, and Procedures* of the enemy can be clearly seen in the eventual demise of the church of Ephesus. Sadly, the clandestine tactics went undiscovered—which should be a warning to every believer. The apostle Paul's impassioned admonition to the first-generation elders were obviously ignored by the next generation. He had warned them to "be on guard for yourselves and for all the flock" concerning the "savage wolves [that] will come in among you, not sparing the flock, and from among your own selves men will arise, speaking perverse things, to draw away the disciples after them. Therefore be on the alert" (Acts 20:28–31). Having pastored the church for three years, Paul departed and Timothy took his place for about a year and a half. During that time, as predicted, the "savage wolves" emerged through the false teachings of two influential leaders, Hymenaeus and Alexander, who were probably elders that served alongside Timothy (1 Tim. 1:3, 20).

Every faithful pastor who has been plagued by rogue elders will understand the satanic nature of such a scenario and how devastating it can be personally and how damaging it can be to a church. Knowing the dangers of deception and of the character of those that teach them, Paul wrote his epistle to the Ephesians while in a Roman prison and closed it with a detailed exhortation saying, "Finally, be strong in the Lord and in the strength of His might. Put on the full armor of God, so that you will be able to stand firm against the schemes of the devil" (Eph. 6:10–11).

This warning brings clarity to the primary tactic of the enemy: "the schemes of the devil." The term "schemes" (Greek: *methodia*) speaks of clever, cunning, crafty deception, typical of a wild animal stalking its prey. Like a lion on the prowl, this predatory enemy lurks in the shadows of a church, studies the moral and spiritual weaknesses of its leaders, and determines the best course of action for a successful ambush; and then, when it is least expected, he strikes with deadly force. The apostle Peter experienced this firsthand on several occasions. Because of this he warned, "Be of sober spirit, be on the alert. Your adversary, the devil, prowls around like a roaring lion, seeking someone to devour. But resist him, firm in your faith" (1 Peter 5:8–9). Similarly, Paul warned the saints in Corinth to guard against anything that might produce disunity in the church, "so that no advantage would be taken of us by Satan, for we are not ignorant of his schemes" (2 Cor. 2:11). The term "advantage" (Greek: *pleonektēthōmen*) speaks of exploitation, like a greedy merchant that looks for every opportunity to beguile and deceive an unsuspecting consumer. Unfortunately, this is where most pastors and church leaders fail badly. In their overconfidence they feel *invincible* rather than *vincible*, they lose focus and fail to remain constantly vigilant against the cunning stratagems that target them specifically.

> *Like a lion on the prowl, this predatory enemy lurks in the shadows of a church, studies the moral and spiritual weaknesses of its leaders, and determines the best course of action for a successful ambush; and then, when it is least expected, he strikes with deadly force.*

My Green Beret brother told me how their training involved seemingly endless surprise enemy attack scenarios from every imaginable vector: a child on a crowded street approaching you with a grenade hidden in his or her clothing; IEDs hidden in what would appear to be a child wrapped in a blanket being cared for by a weeping mother in need, or one concealed in a dead donkey in the road that needed to be removed; or two men pretending to attack a woman in order to distract the soldiers long enough to allow the enemy to gain the advantage in a surprise attack; or an apparent rock slide on a road forcing their vehicle to slow down and take a slight detour into an ambush. The point of the training was simple: *stay alert!*

He said *most Special Forces fatalities occur at the beginning and at the end of deployment.* At the beginning of deployment, some can feel bulletproof and brash, excessively proud of their elite status, but they have no actual combat experience and are therefore not fully prepared mentally for the dangers around them. He made a statement in this regard that I will never forget: he said, "Overconfidence and a lack of focus is what gets them killed." He went on to add that the same dynamics can be at play with the soldiers ready to go home after a long deployment; resting on the laurels of their past successes can breed apathy and carelessness, causing them to take their mind off their mission as they blissfully contemplate their return home.

The Deadly Effects of Overconfidence

The parallels between these dangers on the battlefield and on the mission field are remarkable. I can't help but think of myself when I was fresh out of seminary. I had the training, the uniform, and the "gung ho" ministry attitude, confident in my own abilities—a legend in my own mind. But I had never been in combat. I had never truly suffered for Christ. I had never been in a ministry situation where survival was utterly dependent upon God's mercy. Yet how a man responds in combat is what truly reveals what kind of soldier he really is. I could preach about the schemes of the devil and the need to wear the armor, but I really had no idea what that really looked like in real life as pastor. I was not properly focused. I was not mentally prepared. I grossly underestimated the cunning deceptions of the enemy while at the same time I grossly overestimated my abilities to spot them and defeat them. Needless to say, I was wounded many times, ignorant of the schemes of the devil that targeted my own heart, my family, and my church. Perhaps you can identify with my testimony.

I had to learn to be suspect of my own spirituality; I had to learn to guard my heart from overconfidence and remember the words of the apostle Paul: "[L]et him who thinks he stands take heed that he does not fall" (1 Cor. 10:12). This is the stuff of a warrior preacher. He will never underestimate the vulnerability of his flesh to be deceived. He will warn himself and those under his care about the inevitability of spiritual defeat for those who are ruled by the desires of their flesh and fail to walk by the Spirit (Gal. 5:16)—those who refuse to submit to the Spirit's control of their life and whose lifestyle is habitually *negligent*, and even resentful of the simple commands of Scripture. This is what will help him remain vigilant in looking for those cunning deceptions that can trick him and his congregation into believing and acting in ways that are contrary to the Word and will of God. By God's grace and power, he will stay on the alert for subtle temptations and shrewd counterfeits designed to seduce him and his congregation into violating Scripture.

I cannot count the times I have heard pastors and elders grieve over some crisis in their life or church that they have foolishly brought upon themselves. Their sorrowful lament goes something like this: "I can't believe what has happened. It seemingly came out of nowhere." What they fail to realize is that because of their lack of watchfulness and discernment, they made themselves easy prey for the enemy who had them under surveillance from the outset of their ministries. Worse yet, they were oblivious to the fact that Satan and his minions are as patient as they are cunning, watching for vulnerabilities, tempting all of us to teach error and avoid truth, infiltrating our ranks with hypocrites, waging a propaganda campaign of deception and division, and laying IEDs of temptation in the well-traveled roads of habitual disobedience.

> *I cannot count the times I have heard pastors and elders grieve over some crisis in their life or church that they have foolishly brought upon themselves. Their sorrowful lament goes something like this: "I can't believe what has happened. It seemingly came out of nowhere."*

I have witnessed these strategies in my own life and in the church I pastor. Whatever the seduction, it appealed to my flesh and was always the result of ingenious trickery. "There is a way which seems right to a man, but its end is the way of death" (Prov. 14:12). All Christians, especially pastors, must begin with the presupposition that we are vulnerable, prone to being naïve, apathetic, self-righteous, and overconfident. We must heed the Lord's warning; "Keep watching and praying that you may not enter into temptation; the spirit is willing, but the flesh is weak" (Matt. 26:41). We must therefore learn to

. . .put on the full armor of God, so that you will be able to stand firm against the schemes of the devil. For our struggle is not against flesh and blood, but against the rulers, against the powers, against the world forces of this darkness, against the spiritual forces of wickedness in the heavenly places. Therefore, take up the full armor of God, so that you will be able to resist in the evil day, and having done everything, to stand firm.
(Eph. 6:10–13)

> . . . our combat is not merely a struggle against Satan alone, but against a highly organized supernatural empire that hates Christ and all who belong to Him.

The specifics of the armor he goes on to describe must become a part of who we are in order to be spiritually prepared and therefore "strong in the Lord" (a topic that will be addressed in chapter two). Here the apostle makes it clear that our combat is not merely a struggle against Satan alone, but against a highly organized supernatural empire that hates Christ and all who belong to Him. I must also add, however, that *our fallen flesh is also an enemy within*. Even if the devil and his forces ceased to exist, the unredeemed humanness in every believer is a formidable foe requiring us to be engaged in the work of mortification—putting to death the deeds of the body (Rom. 8:13), laying aside the old self (Eph. 4:22), putting on the new self (Eph. 4:24), and walking by the Spirit so we will not carry out the desire of the flesh that sets its desire against the Spirit (Gal. 5:16–17).

The warrior preacher will be aware of these foes and stand guard against them by the indwelling power of Christ, knowing that it is the enemy's great desire to draw his soul into sin through his devices.

Effective Strategies that Deceive Pastors and Destroy Churches

The seventeenth-century Puritan preacher and author, Thomas Brooks (1608–1680), was very familiar with Satan's devices, the first and foremost described as follows:

> *Device* (1). *"To present the bait and hide the hook*; to present the golden cup, and hide the poison; to present the sweet, the pleasure, and the profit that may flow in upon the soul by yielding to sin, and by hiding from the soul the wrath and misery that will certainly follow the committing of sin. By this device he took our first parents: Gen iii. 4, 5, 'And the serpent said unto the woman, Ye shall not surely die: for God doth know, that in the day ye eat thereof, then your eyes shall be opened; and ye shall be as gods, knowing good and evil.' Your eyes shall be opened, and you shall be as gods!' Here is the bait, the sweet, the pleasure, the profit. Oh, but he hides the hook—the shame, the wrath, and the loss that would certainly follow. There is an opening of the eyes of the mind to contemplation and joy, and there is an opening of the eyes of the body to shame and confusion. He promiseth them the former, but intends the latter, and so cheats them—giving them an apple in exchange for a paradise, as he deals by thousands now-a-day. Satan with ease puts fallacies upon us by his golden baits, and then he leads us and leaves us in a fool's paradise. He promises the soul honour, pleasure, profit, &c., but pays the soul with the greatest contempt, shame, and loss that can be."[4]

In keeping with Brooks' analogy of Satan *presenting the bait and hiding the hook*, I wish to submit what I perceive to be the top six TTPs (*Tactics, Techniques, and Procedures*) of the enemy that he uses to seduce pastors and church leaders into believing and acting upon fallacies that violate the Word and will of God which in turn leads them and their churches into error and the forfei-

---

4   Thomas Brooks, *The Works of Thomas Brooks, Volume One* (Edinburgh: The Banner of Truth Trust, Reprinted 2001), 12–13.

ture of divine blessing. While Satan's devices are legion—and the ones I mention will undoubtedly overlap one another in varying ways—these seem to be the most effective in destroying the lives of pastors and church leaders and filling churches with more goats than sheep. Every honest servant of Christ will admit to swallowing some of these baits, hook, line, and sinker. To whatever degree this may be true for you, I trust you will take heed to what is said and do so in the loving spirit it is intended, that in all things Christ might have the preeminence.

I wish to present these strategies by imagining how Satan might instruct his demonic commanders to carry them out. He would probably say something like this:

Fueling Pride

"Fuel his pride by causing him to believe he is more spiritual than he really is. Surround him with worldly sycophants who will stroke his ego and praise his external religiosity. Supply him with carnal evangelical gurus that will not only help him compromise his moral and doctrinal convictions, but also mitigate the severity and scope of the sin in his heart and in his church. Feed his insatiable appetite for affirmation that he habitually displays by his attention-seeking posts and "selfies" on social media. Influence undiscerning people to respond favorably, even glowingly, to his self-promoting pontifications on Facebook. Lavish him with praise whenever he embraces some cultural abomination that will protect him from censorship yet make others comfortable in their sin. Make him hyper-vigilant in spotting the speck in his brother's eye so he will not see the log in his own; and if he ever does feel guilty about his own sin, quickly douse every burning ember of conviction with so great a deluge of God's grace—the presumption of God's grace, that is—that he will quickly dismiss it as inconsequential. And by all means, cause him to focus on the *indicatives* of Scripture and ignore the *imperatives*. Fool him into believing such a position is a praiseworthy rejection of *moralism* that only sees the Bible as a list of dos and don'ts, rather than a story of what God has done in Christ. His fallacious and self-serving reasoning

will not only give immediate cover for his secret sins, but will also fuel the antinomian and libertine lusts of his flesh going forward. Mold him into such a prestigious Pharisee that he will revel in his fame and his conscience will be seared as with a branding iron."

Denying the Value of Holiness

"Convince him that a personal pursuit of holiness in which he privately and habitually communes with God in prayer and Bible meditation is unnecessary. Delude him into believing that any secret devotion to God is a relic of pietistic, parochial fundamentalism that frustrates grace and must be rejected as moralistic. Make him think the idea of disciplining himself for the purpose of godliness is only for the weak and immature, or better yet, for the legalistic moralist trying to impress God and merit salvation. Distract him with hobbies, entertainment, ministerial duties, and trivial pursuits—anything that will make him feel too tired and too busy to spend time alone with the Lord in private worship and praise. We must do everything we can to deprive his soul of spiritual nourishment, because this will cause him to forsake his love for Christ and go in quiet search for other lovers that will bring him pleasure for a season. By preventing him from being a man of prayer and the Word, he will be ineffective in the pulpit, and his flock will become like him. Make him such a stranger to the God he claims to worship that his heart will become hard, his love will grow cold, his speech will be careless, his character will be weak, his shepherding will be non-existent, and his preaching will be unbiblical, superficial, man-centered, ineffective, and dishonoring to God—although he will not admit to any of this and argue to the contrary."

Enjoying Secret Sins

"Make him comfortable with secret sins that will grow into public scandals. Convince him that God is not all that holy and he is not all that sinful; mislead him into believing that because God is love, He accepts everyone just the way they are. Help him excuse his sin by assuring him that he's more *deprived* than *depraved*, and that

God is far more concerned about his *happiness* than his *holiness*. Seduce him with pornography, entice him with immoral entertainment, tempt him with fleeting pleasures, and surround him with ungodly people—preferably those who are Christian in name only who will make him comfortable in his sin. Don't merely satisfy his prurience; inflame it! Make him believe that because he does not commit the worst sins, he's not all that guilty of the least sins. This will help convince him that his righteousness outweighs his unrighteousness on God's scale of justice. Delude him into defining sin as mere mistakes that rob him of fellowship with God and steal away his happiness. This will further corrupt his heart and pervert his understanding of the gospel. Prevent him from understanding the attributes of God and the doctrines of grace, repentance, and regeneration; otherwise he might question his own salvation. With these seductions, over time, his habitual sinfulness will silence his accusing conscience and he will be ruled by his flesh. Ultimately the malignity of his sin will define his character and destroy his life and testimony—but he will never see it coming."

Promoting Worldliness

"*Deceive him into believing the church must become like the world in order to win it.* Convince him that friendship with the world is the key to evangelistic success. Expose him to the worldly-wise philosophies of evangelical pragmatism so he can learn how to appeal to the felt needs of the spiritually dead that want to be entertained and pampered. Make him labor to understand contemporary culture more than Scripture. Trick him into thinking his church must become more attractive and relevant to the culture by reinventing itself and adjusting its gospel message to be less offensive to the sensitivities of those who are at enmity with God. Persuade him to be less dogmatic, more therapeutic, and tolerant of what the world believes—even if it is blatantly unbiblical. Compel him to believe there are such things as carnal Christians, or LGBTQ Christians, or progressive Christians that embrace the woke deceptions of political and religious liberalism. Expose him to the clever ways he can distort the true gospel by incorporating the wicked ideologies of the culture into a different gospel that cannot save. Mold him into a showman skilled in theatrics, able to attract large crowds. Tempt him to be more concerned with *methods* than *motives*. Make him focus more on personal image and pleasure than personal holiness; cause him to love the world so much that he thinks, looks, dresses, acts, and talks like those who hate Christ—and his church will follow suit. Tempt him to promote himself and crave the applause of men. Teach him the latest theories of psychology and sociology and to scoff at the authority and sufficiency of Scripture. Entice him to lock arms with unbelievers in various religious and social enterprises and be sure he rejects all biblical admonitions to be separate from the world. Prevent him from practicing compassionate church discipline in an effort to restore sinning members because it is "unloving." Together, these strategies will fill his church with pseudo-Christians, feed his lust for prestige, power, and money, and forfeit divine blessing. But because his church is successful in the eyes of the world, he will foolishly believe God is at work."

Promoting False Conversions

"Mislead him into believing man's only problem is his will, therefore a sinner can be induced into making a decision for Christ by argumentation. Delude him into believing that regeneration can be proven by physical effects like approaching an imaginary altar and repeating a sinner's prayer. Make him believe that the Spirit's work in regeneration is to merely persuade the sinner to resolve to become a Christian. Make him skilled in manipulative techniques to get unbelievers to make a decision to accept Jesus into their heart. But to do this, you must make him reject the biblical doctrine of total depravity—that man's nature is so corrupt that God must first renew a sinner's mind and nature before he can respond to the gospel in repentant faith. Convince him that fallen man is not spiritually *dead*, but only *sick*, and he is therefore able on his own to cooperate with God in salvation. Fool him into thinking regeneration is not the sole work of the Spirit that raises a sinner from spiritual death to life, but a combined effort of the sinner and the Spirit. He must be convinced that *God's will to save*

is ultimately subject to *man's will to believe*, therefore man, not God, is sovereign over salvation. This will prevent God from being accurately depicted as the omnipotent Sovereign actively drawing to Himself sinners He has elected by His grace to worship Him forever. Instead, God will be portrayed as a frustrated and helpless deity pacing the throne room of heaven, biting His nails, hoping sinners will hear Him knocking on the door of their heart and let Him in. Through 'decisionism' he will trivialize heartfelt repentance and replace the Spirit's work of regeneration. This will then widen the narrow gate and broaden the narrow road with an 'easy believism' gospel that bears no resemblance to genuine repentance and saving faith. Moreover, by confusing emotionalism and mere professions of faith as works of God, false professions will be the norm; and without genuine saving faith, churches will be populated with people who are Christian in name only, incapable of truly understanding the Word of God or living for His glory. Better yet, they will perish in their sin."

Elevating the Subjective over the Objective

"*Make him elevate experience over the authority of Scripture in order to promote a false gospel that promises health, wealth, and happiness.* This will appeal to the naïve and ignorant masses that crave these things. With the allure of material possessions and physical healing, they will not endure sound doctrine but accept rank heresy, false prophecies, private revelations, self-styled prophets, counterfeit miracles, and religious hypocrisy. Cause the pastor to be obsessed with the person and work of the Holy Spirit rather than Christ. This will fuel the lust of sinners for supernatural power and lead them into a fool's paradise of subjectivity that rejects the Scriptures. In so doing they will rebuff the very Spirit who wrote it, although their greed will not allow them to see it. Help him distort the nature and purpose of spiritual gifts so his followers will exalt themselves and enjoy an illusion of spirituality and power. Moreover, deceive him into believing that the miracle of the new birth in regeneration is insufficient; that being *in Christ* is not enough. This will cause them to seek a secondary, post-conversion experience of 'Spirit baptism' that will supposedly elevate an ordinary Christian into an elite status, validated by the ability to speak in tongues, which is nothing more than glossolalia—ecstatic gibberish of the ancient Greco-Roman mystery religions that will bear no resemblance to the actual New Testament gift. This will also help him promote self-willed, self-indulgent, irreverent, whimsical, and unbiblical worship that will utterly quench the true work of the Spirit to convict the world of sin, righteousness, and judgment and put the glory of Christ on display through His Word and His church. The appeal of this false gospel will be so powerful to the spiritually dead that they will pack stadiums and give all they own to learn how to manipulate a god of their own making to satisfy their lusts."

"Take Heed To Yourselves"

While Satan's strategies used toward you may differ than those just mentioned, be assured, you are a high-value target if you are in church leadership. Your failure can have a domino effect with many others. The godly English Puritan pastor and theologian, Richard Baxter (1615–1691), offers an excellent overview of these dangers that every pastor and church leader would do well to hear and heed:

> Take heed to yourselves, because the tempter will make his first and sharpest onset upon you. If you will be the leaders against him, he will spare you no further than God restraineth him. He beareth you the greatest malice that are engaged to do him the greatest mischief. As he hateth Christ more than any of us, because he is the General of the field, and the "Captain of our salvation," and doth more than all the world besides against the kingdom of darkness; so doth he note the leaders under him more than the common soldiers, on the like account, in their proportion. He knows what a rout he may make among the rest, if the leaders fall before their eyes. He hath long tried that way of fighting, "neither with small nor great," comparatively, but these; and of "smiting the shepherds, that he may scatter the flock." And so great has been his success this way, that he will follow it on as far as he is able. Take heed, therefore,

brethren, for the enemy hath a special eye upon you. You shall have his most subtle insinuations, and incessant solicitations, and violent assaults.

As wise and learned as you are, take heed to yourselves lest he overwit you. The devil is a greater scholar than you, and a nimbler disputant; he can "transform himself into an angel of light" to deceive, he will get within you and trip up your heels before you are aware; he will play the juggler with you undiscerned, and cheat you of your faith or innocence, and you shall not know that you have lost it: nay, he will make you believe it is multiplied or increased when it is lost. You shall see neither hook nor line, much less the subtle angler himself, while he is offering you his bait. And his baits shall be so fitted to your temper and disposition, that he will be sure to find advantages within you, and make your own principles and inclinations to betray you; and whenever he ruineth you, he will make you the instrument of your own ruin. Oh, what a conquest will he think he hath got, if he can make a minister lazy and unfaithful; if he can tempt a minister into covetousness or scandal! He will glory against the church, and say, "These are your holy preachers: you see what their preciseness is, and whither it will bring them." He will glory against Jesus Christ himself, and say, "These are thy champions! I can make thy chiefest servants to abuse thee; I can make the stewards of thy house unfaithful." If he did so insult against God upon a false surmise, and tell him he could make Job to curse him to his face (Job 1:2), what would he do if he should indeed prevail against us? And at last he will insult as much over you that ever he could draw you to be false to your great trust, and to blemish your holy profession, and to do him so much service that was your enemy. O do not so far gratify Satan; do not make him so much sport: suffer him not to use you as the Philistines did Samson—first to deprive you of your strength, and then to put out your eyes, and so to make you the matter of his triumph and derision.[5]

---

5   Charles H. Spurgeon, *Lectures To My Students*, (Peabody, MA: Hendrickson Publishers, Third Printing, October 2012), 16–17.

Satan's Primary Objective

You might be asking, "I wonder where I am most vulnerable to Satan's devices?" I believe the answer is the same for every believer: *it is in the realm of our love for Christ.* Can anyone among us say we love Him as we should? I think not. Nor will we until we see Him face-to-face in glory. So it is here where we must begin our self-examination, because this is every believer's Achilles heel. Therefore it is here where the devil and his minions will aim their arrows.

We can see this illustrated in the progressive demise of five out of seven churches described in Revelation 2 and 3. There the Lord addressed all seven churches specifically, but each church is representative of every church throughout the church age. Two of the churches (Smyrna and Philadelphia) were faithful and pure and received no rebuke from the Lord. Four of the seven were in varying stages of spiritual deterioration (Ephesus, Pergamum, Thyatira, and Sardis) and one was completely dead (Laodicea). All five received the Lord's rebuke and a call to repentance.

What is particularly noteworthy as it relates to Satan's schemes is that each of the first four churches the Lord rebuked had a decreasing number of believers in them, with the final church (Laodicea) being utterly apostate with virtually no believers.

Like the four stages of cancer that can lead to death if left untreated, each of the primary sins the Lord rebuked reveal the specific stage of their spiritual disease brought on by Satan's schemes.

STAGE ONE: *Ephesus* (the mother church of all the others) unwittingly abandoned her original love for Christ: "Therefore remember from where you have fallen, and repent and do the deeds you did at first; or else I am coming to you and will remove your lampstand out of its place—unless you repent" (Rev. 2:5).

STAGE TWO: *Pergamum* tolerated false teachers that compromised with the culture and ignored the biblical warnings against worldliness: "Therefore repent; or else I am coming to you quickly, and I will make war against them with the sword of My mouth" (Rev. 2:16).

STAGE THREE: *Thyatira* tolerated a woman false teacher who called herself a prophetess, causing them to descend even further in the depths of satanic deception that led to their participation in sexual immorality: "I gave her time to repent, and she does not want to repent of her immorality. Behold, I will throw her on a bed of sickness, and those who commit adultery with her into great tribulation, unless they repent of her deeds. And I will kill her children with pestilence, and all the churches will know that I am He who searches the minds and hearts; and I will give to each one of you according to your deeds" (vv. 21–23).

STAGE FOUR: *Sardis* had an outward reputation of being alive, but the Lord said, "You are dead" (Rev. 3:1). Though they did have "a few people who have not soiled their garments and walk with Me" (v. 4), it was a church made up primarily of ungodly, worldly, heretics that had abandoned the apostolic teachings: "So remember what you have received and heard; and keep *it,* and repent. Therefore if you do not wake up, I will come like a thief, and you will not know at what hour I will come to you" (v. 3).

DEATH: *Laodicea* was the "lukewarm" church that made God vomit (Rev. 3:15–16). The term "lukewarm" doesn't mean they were mediocre Christians. It means they fit neither category of being "hot" (a true Christian) or "cold" (one who rejected Christ). Although they were unregenerate, they did not openly reject Christ. They were hypocrites, pretenders that made a mockery of the gospel. A lukewarm Christian is no Christian at all. The Laodiceans were financially prosperous, yet they were smug, self-righteous hypocrites, as lost as the most depraved atheist. For this reason the Lord warned them to "be zealous and repent. Behold, I stand at the door and knock; if anyone hears My voice and opens the door, I will come in to him and will dine with him, and he with Me" (vv. 19–20).

Sadly, this has been the historical progression of evangelicalism in America.

But what is important to understand is that no church is impervious to these temptations. The progressive demise begins with an *imperceptible diminished love for Christ,* which then leads to *worldliness*, which produces *immorality*, which requires *heresy*, and ends in *apostasy*.

The church at Ephesus flourished under the shepherding of faithful pastors. Unlike many churches today, the people who were part of that local body did not come to be entertained or enjoy the benefits of a religious social club. They came to worship in spirit and in truth and exhaust themselves for the sake of the gospel, regardless the cost.

In Revelation 2:2–3, Christ commended them for their tireless labor in building the kingdom of God and for their courageous determination to persevere against all odds. He praised them for their godly discernment and refusal to tolerate the corrupting influence of evil men and false teachers. The faithful Ephesians were not self-seeking spectators; they were self-sacrificing soldiers of the cross. Their doctrinal and moral purity was excellent in every way. From all outward appearances they were a model New Testament church—the kind of church any mature believer would want to be a part of—and certainly one the Lord Himself commended!

> "Churchianity" can easily replace Christianity. Our deceitful hearts do not naturally drift toward a growing love for Christ. Instead, like a rudderless ship, they succumb to the prevailing winds of the world that carry us away from the safe harbor of intimate fellowship with the Lover of our soul.

Notwithstanding their virtues, beneath their exemplary externals existed a deadly defect they could not see, a fatal flaw that was well camouflaged by religious zeal, moral purity, and doctrinal orthodoxy. But their shortcoming did not escape the penetrating eye of divine omniscience; nor did it evade His loving rebuke. They had "left [their] first love" (v. 4). Their passionate love for Christ that once burned hot—like the fervent, chaste, and pure love of the newly wedded bride—had been reduced to smoldering embers; it was smothered by four decades of mechanical orthodoxy and dutiful devotion.

The indictment must have been devastating when they first received it: "But I have this against you, that you have left your first love." But the sting of the lash falls on all our backs. "Churchianity" can easily replace Christianity. Our deceitful hearts do not naturally drift toward a growing love for Christ. Instead, like a rudderless ship, they succumb to the prevailing winds of the world that carry us away from the safe harbor of intimate fellowship with the Lover of our soul and ultimately destroy us on the hidden reefs of apathy and sin's corruption.

Our gentle Savior and Lord of the church knew this. So He commanded them to do three things: *remember, repent,* and *return.* "Remember from where you have fallen" (v. 5). We must all *remember* the time when we first fell in love with the Lord and were overcome by His mercy and grace, when we first fell in love with His Word and His people and His promises! Then we must *repent* of our perfunctory piety, our dispassionate traditions, our phony sentimentality, and *return* to "the deeds [we] did at first" (v. 5)—those self-sacrificing acts of love and devotion to Christ and His people, and our zealous commitment to evangelism and discipleship!

> The Lord is not looking for a church committed to redeeming the culture or social justice, nor will He bless a church that is morally and doctrinally pure but has a diminishing love for Him.

A strong warning followed the Lord's rebuke: "I am coming to you and will remove your lampstand out of its place—unless you repent" (v. 5). The Lord is not looking for a church committed to redeeming the culture or social justice, nor will He bless a church that is morally and doctrinally pure but has a diminishing love for Him. He blesses those who not only guard the flames of their hearts' affections for Him, but also fuels them with adoring worship and fans them into a roaring inferno through faithful obedience—all of which Satan abhors! Paul expressed his concern in this regard when he said to the saints in Corinth, "For I am jealous for you with a godly jealousy; for I betrothed you to one husband, so that to Christ I might present you as a pure virgin. But I am afraid that, as the serpent deceived Eve by his craftiness, your minds will be led astray from the simplicity and purity of devotion to Christ" (2 Cor. 11:2–3).

Blinding Men to the Truth

As stated earlier, Satan's devices are legion. However, his primary objective is always the same: *to blind men to the truth of the gospel and prevent them from seeing the glory of Christ*. Paul made this clear when he said, "And even if our gospel is veiled, it is veiled to those who are perishing, in whose case the god of this world has blinded the minds of the unbelieving so that they might not see the light of the gospel of the glory of Christ, who is the image of God" (2 Cor. 4:3–4). Although believers are by definition those who embrace the gospel and see the glory of Christ, we would be fools to think the enemy retreats when we come to saving faith. Quite the contrary is true. He intensifies his attacks in three ways: first, he *distorts* the gospel; second, he *disputes* the person and work of Christ; and third, he *distracts* us from beholding the glory of Christ to such a degree that we no longer find our greatest joy and satisfaction in Him.

> *[The devil] is not only determined to prohibit God from being glorified by the adoring worship of His bridal church, but he also knows that such worship is directly proportional to the bride's apprehension of the glory of her bridegroom.*

Think of it this way: if the foremost commandment is to love the Lord your God with all your heart, and with all your soul, and with all your mind, and with all your strength (Mark 12:29), as Jesus says, then it stands to reason that our adversary the devil will do all he can to prevent this. He is not only determined to prohibit God from being glorified by the adoring worship of His bridal church, but he also knows that such worship is directly proportional to the bride's apprehension of the glory of her bridegroom. We see this affirmed throughout Scripture. As we behold the beauty of His infinite perfections and contemplate His love for us, our soul becomes so satisfied in Him that it has no desire for the fleeting pleasures of sin and becomes increasingly resistant to temptation. Satan must prevent this! He despises the sanctifying work of the Spirit knowing that "we all, with unveiled face, beholding as in a mirror the glory of the Lord, are being transformed into the same image from glory to glory, just as from the Lord, the Spirit" (2 Cor. 3:18). And because we are being perfected in the image of Christ, "we know that when He appears we shall be like Him, because we shall see Him as He is" (1 John 3:2).

> *As in the case of the blind beggar who was utterly destitute and helpless, every sinner is the same, spiritually speaking. Were it not for a merciful God who sought us out and stooped down to give us spiritual sight, we would still be walking in darkness.*

To truly see Christ is to love Christ! In fact, this is the animating force in our sanctification that is first initiated in the miracle of re-generation. We see this pictured when Jesus gave physical sight to the blind beggar in John 9:1–12. While this miracle was ultimately intended to validate Jesus' claim to be the Son of God and picture Him acting in sovereign grace to save Israel—who had been so in-fluenced by Satan that they were blind to their guilt and bondage to sin—it also pictures the individual ruin of man's fallen nature rebelling against Jesus, the spiritual "light of the world" (John 8:12). The narrative describes Jesus taking the initiative to show mercy to "a man blind from birth" (v. 1). Those born blind from birth give no value to sight because they have no idea what they're missing. Likewise, the spiritually blind have no capacity to see the wretchedness of their condition nor the imminent danger they are in; worse yet, they cannot see their desperate need for the Savior or the glory of His person and work. None of us could have ever seen our sin or the Savior apart from divine initiative, because "there is none who seeks after God" (Rom. 3:11), so God must *seek* after us (Luke 19:10) and *save* us. Jesus said, ". . .unless one is born again, he cannot see the kingdom of God" (John 3:3).

As in the case of the blind beggar who was utterly destitute and helpless, every sinner is the same, spiritually speaking. Were it not for a merciful God who sought us out and stooped down to give us spiritual sight, we would still be walking in darkness. But Sa-tan's devices against us will try to obscure these soul-exhilarating truths. He knows the more we behold Christ the more we become like Him! The light of the loveliness and purity of Christ exposes the filth of our sin and makes us all the more amazed by His grace.

The eminent seventeenth-century Puritan theologian and academic administrator at the University of Oxford, John Owen (1616–1683), expressed it this way:

> Let us live in the constant contemplation of the glory of Christ, and virtue will proceed from Him to repair all our decays, to renew a right spirit within us, and to cause us to abound in all duties of obedience. . . . It will fix the soul unto that object which is suited to give it delight, complacency, and satisfaction. . . . When the mind is filled with thoughts of Christ and his glory, when the soul thereon cleaves unto him with intense affections, they will cast out, or not give admittance unto, those causes of spiritual weakness and indisposition. . . . And nothing will so much excite and encourage our souls hereunto as a constant view of Christ and His glory. [6]

A Final Word of Encouragement to the Warrior Preacher

To be sure, there is no greater privilege in the Christian life than contemplating the glory of the person and work of the Lord Jesus Christ. This must be the very air we breathe if we are to be effective warriors for Christ that are able to defeat the enemy. We would all do well to learn from the angels who "long to look" upon the mystery of the incarnation of Christ (1 Peter 1:12). We see this illustrated in the position of the cherubim in the Holy of Holies in the Temple, who with outstretched wings stood over the Ark of the Covenant and beheld the mercy seat. Theirs was a posture of reverent awe as they gazed upon that golden lid that separated the violated Law within from the Holy presence that hovered above; that place where the just wrath of God was symbolically propitiated—the mercy seat being a type of Christ in the discharge of His priestly office.

Would that we be like the cherubim and fix our gaze upon Him

6   John Owen, *Meditations and Discourses on the Glory of Christ*, in *The Works of John Owen*, Vol. 1, *The Glory of Christ*, (Ednburgh: The Banner of Truth Trust), 460–61.

and behold "His glory, glory as of the only begotten from the Father, full of grace and truth" (John 1:14). May we be like the apostle Paul and say, "I count all things to be loss in view of the surpassing value of knowing Christ Jesus my Lord, for whom I have suffered the loss of all things, and count them but rubbish so that I may gain Christ" (Phil. 3:8). The constant beholding of the glory of Christ by faith is the habit of every mature believer and the greatest tonic to soothe an aching soul that longs for heaven. May every servant of God be disciplined to this end and dedicated to helping others do the same, remembering that "though you have not seen Him, you love Him, and though you do not see Him now, but believe in Him, you greatly rejoice with joy inexpressible and full of glory, obtaining as the outcome of your faith the salvation of your souls" (1 Peter 1:8–9).

Chapter 1 Questions

1. Can you honestly say you are at war with the kingdom of darkness for the glory of Christ and His kingdom?

2. Have you given careful thought to the enemy's "Tactics, Techniques, and Procedures" and how they impact your life personally and influence your church?

3. Would those who know you best describe you as a man who boldly confronts the wickedness of the culture or a man who seeks rapprochement with it in an effort to gain favor with the world?

4. Are you on guard against spiritual overconfidence and have therefore learned to be suspect of your own spirituality?

5. Where are you personally most vulnerable to Satan's clever schemes that prevent you from growing in personal holiness?

6. Are you constantly on the alert to spot shrewd counterfeits and false doctrines that can trick you and your congregation into believing and acting in ways contrary to the Word and will of God? Can you and your congregation articulate them specifically, and do you have a strategy to eliminate them?

7. Which of the six examples of the "Effective Strategies that Deceive Pastors and Destroy Churches" mentioned in the chapter best describes you and your church?

8. Do your religious zeal, moral purity, and doctrinal orthodoxy camouflage your diminished love for Christ?

9. Is contemplating the glory of the person and work of the Lord Jesus Christ the very air you breathe as a warrior preacher, or is this foreign to you?

2

The Warrior's Armor

Be strong in the Lord and in the strength of His might.
Put on the full armor of God, so that you will be able to stand firm
against the schemes of the devil.
(Ephesians 6:10–11)

The Christian's strength lies in the Lord, not in himself. The strength of the general in other hosts lies in his troops. He flies, as a great commander once said to his soldiers, upon their wings; if their feathers be clipped, their power broken, he is lost; but in the army of saints, the strength of every saint, yea, of the whole host of saints, lies in the Lord of hosts. God can overcome his enemies without their hands, but they cannot so much as defend themselves without his arm.

WILLIAM GURNALL[7]

7 William Gurnall, *The Christian In Complete Armour: A Treatise of the Saints' War Against the Devil* (Carlisle, PA: The Banner of Truth Trust, 1995), 18.

As I indicated in chapter one, very few pastors and church leaders ever consider themselves to be high-value targets of the enemy and therefore tend to have a cavalier attitude toward spiritual warfare and how to defend themselves against it. They fail to take seriously the fact that the world is a battleground between two opposing kingdoms: Satan and his demonic horde; and God and His holy angels. It is therefore easy to understand why so many congregations are equally apathetic and overpowered by wickedness in the culture Satan rules. With smug overconfidence, the divine warnings are cast aside, and the congregations find themselves unprotected against the cunning devices of our adversary, the devil. Consequently, evangelicalism has been so decimated by compromise, doctrinal error, worldliness, and moral failure, that most churches bear little resemblance to the New Testament standard—but they cannot see it.

> *The warrior preacher will infuriate the enemy*
> *by refusing to run away and with his brazen*
> *counterassaults into the kingdom of darkness.*

Such indifference has also fostered a general disregard for the spiritual armor God has made available to us and commanded us to wear. Because in some sense many pastors are no threat to the enemy and have no need for protection, they are already defeated and have unwittingly joined forces with the enemy.

But the warrior preacher will infuriate the enemy by refusing to run away and with his brazen counterassaults into the kingdom of darkness. As he skillfully wields the sword of gospel truth, sinners are rescued and saints are sanctified by the power of the Spirit through His Word. These are the King's champions—bold and uncompromising men of exceptional valor who aggressively engage the enemy in "the destruction of fortresses . . . destroying speculations and every lofty thing raised up against the knowledge of God" (2 Cor. 10:4–5). These are the mighty warriors of the cross that could never survive, much less be victorious, apart from the armor of God which they gladly wear every day of their life.

Green Beret Protection

Hearing the testimony of the combat experiences of my Green Beret brother in Christ, I couldn't help but notice many similarities with respect to pastoral ministry, especially as they relate to the profound importance of being properly protected in combat. For a soldier, knowing how to avail himself of the various safeguards available to him is truly a matter of life and death, and the parallels for effective ministry are similarly important. Here's what he said when I asked him about body armor and other means of protection available to the Special Forces:

> The regular army body armor is very heavy and bulky, and covers all vital areas, including the femoral arteries at the groin area. However, lighter and less cumbersome armor is used for Special Forces teams because the need for agility is the essential form of protection for special operations missions. We need to move very quickly (not just on the feet but with arms and hands) and maneuver in tight areas at times. The armor is limited to most vital areas; head and torso only (but not the sides) and the groin area is not covered. Technique, experience, and agility take the place of missing armor.

> *Everyone is highly trained, and you can trust each one in tense combat situations; they are highly capable, they know their job and are good at it, plus we've rehearsed a lot.*

I didn't worry as much about armor as I did agility, mostly because I knew God was sovereign and I was unkillable until God called me home. Also, as a team, we don't leave things to chance, and you trust your teammates to have your back. Everyone is highly trained, and you can trust each one in tense combat situations; they are highly capable, they know their job and are good at it, plus we've rehearsed a lot.

Other forms of protection include knowing the differ-ence between *cover* and *concealment*. You may *conceal* yourself behind shrubs, but there is no protection if you're seen. On the other hand, *cover* is solid, like a huge boulder. You are not seen; or if you are discovered, the cover cannot be penetrated. We always look for cover when under attack. And we *never* retreat! To do so puts us at greater risk by allowing the enemy to put their heads up and fire unabated without resistance while our backs are to them. So we never retreat. If we are ambushed, we seek cover or just get down. Immediately we assess the enemy. We then begin to put down an overwhelming volume of fire to pin them down. While we do that, one of the squads (a team is two squads) will do a wide flanking maneuver. When the flanking squad is in place, we (A Squad) will advance toward the enemy, putting out high volume of fire, while the flanking B Squad does the same from the side. There is a lot more that goes into this, but the idea is we never retreat; we always gain fire superiority and move in on and kill the enemy.

Now, there are times when you are way, way, way outnumbered, and that's when you call for air cover. While this is not armor, it is protection. We've been saved many times by air cover. When we are cut off, surrounded, or out of ammo from a sustained firefight, we call in air cover. They drop all manner of ordinance (bombs) to open a way of escape through the ring of enemy forces. We have to know where we are at all times so we can call in the appropriate coordinates and know the way home. But the key to this is knowing with absolute certainty where you are and where the enemy is. People have died by not making this critical distinction. Navigational skills are absolutely essential.[8]

Like our elite forces, the warrior preacher must have a warrior mindset, fully prepared to engage the enemy, be skilled in agility, able to move and think quickly, having the muscle memory of godliness in his heart that moves his will to act in truth and righteousness regardless of circumstance. He must share the Green

---

8 Joel C., from private correspondence.

Berets' attention to detail and think through all the potential variables of how the enemy might respond so that "nothing is left to chance." And like them, he must be a part of a team that is highly skilled and trustworthy; members of a plurality of godly elders who meet the qualifications of 1 Timothy 3:1–7 and Titus 1:6–9; men empowered by the indwelling Christ; brothers who will never retreat because they trust God and act according to the strength of His might, not their own. These are the elite soldiers of the Most High, men with the gift of discernment who know the precise coordinates of everything in the combat zone and, through fervent prayer, who call in the air cover of the Almighty to eliminate the threat of those who would seek to harm Christ's church.

Triumphant Resources in Christ

While the training, expertise, and combat resources available to our elite forces are impressive, they pale into insignificance when compared to the armaments that are ours in Christ. Satan's diabolical schemes to thwart the purposes of God are far too ingenious and clandestine for pastors and church leaders to effectively oppose apart from divine protection. The sophisticated hierarchies of demonic forces are far too lethal and strategic in their warfare for any believer to defend himself against apart from God's help. The warrior preacher will readily acknowledge this. He will understand that he has no defense against the powers of darkness on his own; he must have the supernatural empowerment that comes only from the One with whom he has been brought into union, the Lord Jesus Christ. For this reason we are commanded to "be strong in the Lord and in the strength of His might" (Eph. 6:10). Because we are no longer subject to the tyrannical rule of the prince of the power of the air but belong to Christ, we can appropriate "His might" described as

> the surpassing greatness of His power toward us who believe. These are in accordance with the working of the strength of His might which He brought about in Christ, when He raised Him from the dead and seated Him at His right hand in the heavenly places, far above all rule and au-

thority and power and dominion, and every name that is named, not only in this age but also in the one to come. (Eph. 1:19–21)

Because pastors and church leaders are high-value targets of the enemy, it is imperative for them to lay hold of the spiritual resources Christ supplies in order to be strengthened by Him. We see this, for example, in the Lord's promise and strong admonition to Joshua when He said,

> No man will be able to stand before you all the days of your life . . . I will be with you; I will not fail you or forsake you. Be strong and very courageous; be careful to do according to all the law which Moses My servant commanded you; do not turn from it to the right or to the left, so that you may have success wherever you go. (Josh. 1:5–6)

We also see this promised in the apostolic injunction in Ephesians 6:10 where we are commanded to "be strong in the Lord." This is crucial if we are to prevail against the enemy, and the only way to appropriate "the strength of His might" is by wearing the armor He provides—what Paul calls, "the full armor of God, so that you will be able to stand firm against the schemes of the devil" (Eph. 6:11). As we will see from the sustained imagery of the heavily armed Roman foot soldier, the armor available to the believer must be viewed as *God's own armor*. Said simply, *we must have God as our Shield and Defender at all times, lest we fall victim to the enemy.*

This level of self-awareness will make a wise minister appreciate the supernatural safeguards God has provided and motivate him to take full advantage of them, "for the weapons of our warfare are not of the flesh, but divinely powerful for the destruction of fortresses" (2 Cor. 10:4). This is what makes a warrior preacher.

Protections Against Trickery and Subterfuge

Having warned us of the immense danger of Satan's empire, Paul says, "Therefore, take up the full armor of God, that you may be able to resist in the evil day, and having done everything, to stand firm" (Eph. 6:13). The "evil day" refers to "this present evil age" from which we have been rescued (Gal. 1:4)—an age that will continue until Christ's return. This is the warrior preacher's battleground. Only by availing ourselves of God's protective resources and making all the necessary preparations to be fully armed for battle are we able to *stand firm* against Satan's diabolical deceptions. His trickery and subterfuge can render those in church leadership, especially pastors, indifferent to the very devices that produce disillusionment and frustration in ministry, that inflame their lusts for that which is evil, that rob them of usefulness and joy, and ultimately cause them to forfeit divine blessing and eternal reward—although they can neither see the trickery nor identify the subterfuge. Worse yet, in their blindness they will actually deny the obvious when confronted with it. I have witnessed this more times than I care to count.

> Only by availing ourselves of God's protective resources and making all the necessary preparations to be fully armed for battle are we able to *stand firm* against Satan's diabolical deceptions.

As we shall see, the divine resources necessary for us to "stand firm" are spelled out through the use of four participles, namely, "*having girded* your lions with truth," "*having put on* the breastplate of righteousness" (v. 14), "*having shod* your feet" (v. 15), and "*having taken up* the shield of faith" (v. 16) (emphasis mine). Only then are we fully prepared to resolutely hold our ground against the diabolical onslaughts of the enemy. We see a similar command conveyed by the use of four present imperatives in 1 Corinthians 16:13 that must always define the state of our character: "Be on the alert, stand firm in the faith, act like men, be strong." This speaks of men who refuse to capitulate to Satan's sophisticated system of evil. Unhappily, these attitudes are distressingly absent among evangelical leaders today. Flippancy, comedy, and superficiality have replaced the solemnity, reverence, and careful exposition of divine truth that characterized the biblical prophets and preachers who knew what it was to *stand firm* and *be strong*.

It is also worth noting that we are not commanded to go on the offensive by pretending to rout the enemy through exorcisms. We do not bind or rebuke Satan; we simply stand firm and resist his attacks knowing that "greater is He who is in you than he who is in the world" (1 John 4:4). Our only advance against the enemy is through preaching the gospel and thereby rescuing sinners from the domain of darkness and transferring them into the kingdom of God's dear Son (Col 1:13). We go on the offense by refusing to capitulate to the strident voices of opposition in our churches that reject essential doctrines and by ignoring the violent threats of a godless culture. But while we boldly advance upon the enemy through the natural expressions of biblical ministry, we are never commanded to attack Satan and his demons directly. Instead, we are commanded to "put on the full armor of God, so that you will be able to stand firm against the schemes of the devil" (Eph. 6:11).

James offers the same admonition by using the word "resist" when he says, "Submit therefore to God. Resist the devil and he will flee from you" (James 4:7). Likewise, Peter says, "Be of sober spirit, be on the alert. Your adversary, the devil, prowls about like a roaring lion, seeking someone to devour. But resist him, firm in your faith" (1 Peter 5:8–9). This is what Jesus did when He was tempted in the wilderness by the devil. By wielding "the sword of the Spirit, which is the Word of God" (Eph. 6:17), He effectively parried the blows of satanic temptation and stood His ground. As a result, Satan departed in defeat (Luke 4:13).

> *Our only advance against the enemy is through preaching the gospel . . .*

It is therefore of utmost importance that every believer understand the nature of the believer's armor, especially as it relates to those who serve Christ in leadership capacities—pastors in particular. Having counseled literally hundreds of men in these positions, I can safely say that each of the men who suffered some kind of personal or ministerial defeat did so for the same reason: *they didn't wear their armor.*

The Belt of Truth

First, Paul says, "Stand firm therefore, having girded your loins with truth" (Eph. 6:14). Here Paul uses the imagery of a Roman soldier's beltlike girdle, similar to a leather apron that hung under the armor and protected the lower abdomen and thighs. When preparing for battle, the soldier would tuck his tunic into his leather girdle to prevent the enemy from seizing any loose ends of his garment in hand-to-hand combat. So to gird one's loins signifies the need for *readiness in battle*, preparation for up-close and personal hand-to-hand combat. No doubt Paul reaches back to Isaiah's figurative description of the Messiah's readiness to rule in His coming kingdom where the prophet says, "Also righteousness will be the belt about His loins, and faithfulness the belt about His waist" (Isa. 11:5). It is this same *righteousness* and *truth* that our returning King will wear in battle that is currently available. But at the heart of Paul's imagery concerning "having girded our loins with truth" is the idea of *spiritual preparedness for combat*.

Peter employs the same imagery as one who knew firsthand what it was to be overconfident, unprepared, and unprotected. For this reason, motivated by the fullness of grace that will be ours when Christ returns, he says, "Prepare your minds for action" (1 Peter 1:13). It can also be translated "Gird up the loins of your minds," that is, *Be intentional in your thinking and put forth the necessary effort to discipline your thought life to make ready for mortal spiritual combat.* He continues his exhortation saying, "Keep sober in *spirit,* fix your hope completely on the grace to be brought to you at the revelation of Jesus Christ" (v. 13). Then, in light of the need to stay preoccupied with the soul-exhilarating joy of such a glorious promise, he exhorts us to live "as obedient children" (v. 13); and here's how: "Do not be conformed to the former lusts which were yours in your ignorance, but like the Holy One who called you, be holy yourselves also in all your behavior; because it is written, 'You shall be holy, for I am holy'" (vv. 13–16).

With respect to the believer's armor, we cannot "be strong in the Lord" and operate "in the strength of His might" (Eph. 6:10) and therefore "be able to stand firm against the schemes of the devil" (v. 11) unless we "[gird our] loins with truth" (v. 14). Elsewhere in this epistle Paul uses the term "truth" (Greek: *alēthia*) as a defining mark of the renewed mind, "which in the likeness of God has been created in righteousness and holiness of the truth" (v. 22). This was brought about by the truth of the gospel (1:13; 4:15, 21, 24), and for this reason we are exhorted to "[lay] aside falsehood, speak truth each one of you with his neighbor, for we are members of one another" (v. 25). Lying encompasses things like cheating, exaggerating or embellishing the truth so that it is no longer true, making false or foolish promises, betraying a confidence, and making false excuses.[9] We are also exhorted to guard against unrighteous and prolonged anger that can turn to bitter resentment (v. 26), and to avoid harming others through stealing but rather to give to those in need (v. 28). Then he adds this:

> Let no unwholesome word proceed from your mouth, but only such a word as is good for edification according to the need of the moment, so that it will give grace to those who hear. Do not grieve the Holy Spirit of God, by whom you were sealed for the day of redemption. Let all bitterness and wrath and anger and clamor and slander be put away from you, along with all malice. Be kind to one another, tender-hearted, forgiving each other, just as God in Christ also has forgiven you.
> (Eph. 4:29–32)

While this list is by no means exhaustive, it helps us understand what Paul means when he exhorts us to "Stand firm therefore, having girded your loins with truth" (Eph. 6:14). This is essential in pastoral ministry and will be the defining mark of a true soldier of the cross, "for the fruit of the Light *consists* in all goodness and righteousness and truth" (Eph. 5:9). Without a decisive commitment to *knowing the truth, living the truth, and preaching the truth*, we, along with those we serve, will be "carried about by every wind of doctrine, by the trickery of men, by deceitful scheming" (Eph. 4:14). Paul warned that "the Spirit explicitly says that in later times some will fall away from the faith, paying attention to deceitful spirits and doctrines of demons" (1 Tim. 4:1), but it will be the

---

9 Note on Eph. 4:25, *The MacArthur Study Bible* (Nashville, TN: Word Publishing, a Division of Thomas Nelson, Inc. 1997), 1810.

warrior preacher who will "contend earnestly for the faith which was once for all handed down to the saints" (Jude 3) and "fight the good fight of faith" (1 Tim. 6:12)—cultural resistance being the sure sign he is engaging the enemy.

The Breastplate of Righteousness

Next, Paul reveals the second essential piece of armor. We are to "put on the breastplate of righteousness" (Eph. 6:14). His language reflects the military metaphor in Isaiah 59:17 describing the armor of the Lord when He takes vengeance on His enemies at His second coming: "He put on righteousness like a breastplate, and a helmet of salvation on His head; and He put on garments of vengeance for clothing and wrapped Himself with zeal as a mantle." The breastplate was the heart protector for a Roman soldier, usually made out of hammered bronze fitted to the body, or chain mail, or sometimes leather with overlapping animal hooves or horns or metal. This crucial piece of armor would protect the vital areas of the torso from the thrusting force of a sword or spear in hand-to-hand combat, as well as the penetration of arrows. It typically extended from the base of the neck to the top of the thighs, and it was designed to allow for maximum protection without sacrificing mobility in the arms and waist.

> *The breastplate was the heart protector*
> *for a Roman soldier.*

In the context of the believer's armor, the "breastplate of righteousness" is best understood as *a decisive commitment to personal holiness*. It cannot refer to the imputed righteousness of Christ because that is the eternal possession of every believer at the moment of salvation, for indeed we are "justified as a gift by his grace" (Rom. 3:24; *cf.* 10:4). *Justification is that divine gift whereby God, through His grace, imputes the righteousness of Christ to believers, legally declares them to be righteous in His sight, and then treats them as such.* Therefore, this cannot be equated with a piece of armor a believer must put on. However, this transforming gift is not merely some initial blessing that stands alone. Rather, it is a blessing that encompasses all God gives His redeemed people. Justification impacts every area of our life. It is the bedrock upon which our salvation is permanently and immovably anchored.

Because of Christ's own righteousness imputed to believers, we are forever united to Him in His death and resurrection, and as a result of this union we are able to live *holy lives* (Rom. 6:1–14, 22). And this is what Paul is referring to in his expression, "the breastplate of righteousness." *Holy living is the evidence of our justification—not the ground—and the purpose of our salvation*: "For we are his workmanship, created in Christ Jesus for good works, which God prepared beforehand, that we should walk in them" (Eph. 2:10). The verdict of our acquittal through Christ's death and the imputation of His righteousness provide the necessary basis for us to "put on the new self, which in the likeness of God has been created in righteousness and holiness of the truth" (Eph. 4:24). In light of all that is ours in Christ, Paul says, "Therefore, having these promises, beloved, let us cleanse ourselves from all defilement of flesh and spirit, perfecting holiness in the fear of God" (2 Cor. 7:1).

> *Because of Christ's own righteousness imputed to believers, we are forever united to Him in His death and resurrection, and as a result of this union we are able to live holy lives (Rom. 6:1–14, 22). And this is what Paul is referring to in his expression, "the breastplate of righteousness."*

It is tragic to see how many pastors, church, and seminary leaders do not wear the breastplate of righteousness. Stories regarding sexual predators and abusive clergy in evangelical churches are far too common, although their denominational leaders often cover them up to protect themselves from lawsuits and public humiliation—a level of depravity that shows no concern for the safety of other potential victims. For example, the Executive Committee of the Southern Baptist Convention maintained a secret list of more than 700 pastors and other church-affiliated personnel accused of sexual abuse. The list was released in May of 2022 "in response to a historic report from investigative firm Guidepost Solutions into SBC leaders' failure to address sexual abuse for more than two decades."[10]

Certainly those who habitually behave so wickedly have no basis to claim genuine saving faith and will never enter the kingdom (1 Cor. 6:9–10), but they also prove the power of the flesh and thus the need to "flee immorality" (1 Cor. 6:18). For this reason, the warrior preacher must never take off his "breastplate of righteousness"—even in his imagination. We must "[put] aside all malice and all deceit and hypocrisy and envy and all slander" (1 Peter 2:1). This is how we stand firm and resist the enemy. With Paul, we must be able to say to our congregation, "For our proud confidence is this: the testimony of our conscience, that in holiness and godly sincerity, not in fleshly wisdom but in the grace of God, we have conducted ourselves in the world, and especially toward you" (2 Cor. 1:12).

I have lived long enough to watch fellow seminarians start out well but end in disaster, men who became increasingly comfortable with private sin and worldly deceptions that were cleverly masked by a satanic culture.

I have lived long enough to watch fellow seminarians start out well but end in disaster, men who became increasingly comfortable with private sin and worldly deceptions that were cleverly masked by a satanic culture. Consequently, they quenched the Spirit in their lives, and some even lost their marriages and ministries. Some fell victim to the deceptions of the left wing woke movement and embraced the aberrant social justice gospel. Others befriended heretics who lured them into the doctrinal errors of the "seeker sensitive" movement; their churches grew rapidly, but so did their love for the world and for a more "religiously correct" gospel. Other men became bullies and abused their flocks; yet others became wilting lilies that withered under unfair criticism while others pandered secret sins of immorality until their indulgence became public. One defeated brother lamented, "I failed to do what Paul did when he said, 'I discipline my body and make it my slave, so that, after I have preached to others, I myself will not

---

10   https://www.msn.com/en-us/news/us/southern-baptist-convention-leaders-publish-long-se-cret-list-of-accused-ministers/ar-AAXMn5b?ocid=uxbndlbing

be disqualified'" (1 Cor. 9:27). Oh, the power of Satan's seductions to appeal to the flesh, and oh, the ravages of sin!

What a contrast to warrior preachers who live "by the word of truth, by the power of God, by the armor of righteousness on the right hand and on the left" (2 Cor. 6:7)—men who not only know the objective truth of Scripture and are greatly strengthened by it, but who also live consistently with it. These are the King's champions who manifest the glory of Christ in their attitudes and actions, men of sterling integrity and moral purity, men devoted to all that is true, men who are dependable and upright in thought and deed. They take seriously the command to "discipline yourself for the purpose of godliness" (1 Tim. 4:7). These are men so committed to the glory of Christ that they eliminate all the loose ends of their life—all the extraneous, superfluous, and unrighteous characteristics that are contrary to godliness. They pursue personal integrity at all cost, and abhor hypocrisy more in their own life than what they see in others; and with the psalmist they declare, "Behold, You desire truth in the innermost being, and in the hidden part You will make me know wisdom" (Ps. 51:6).

*These are men so committed to the glory of Christ
that they eliminate all the loose ends of their life—
all the extraneous, superfluous, and unrighteous
characteristics that are contrary to godliness. They
pursue personal integrity at all cost.*

This describes that choice servant of God who takes seriously Paul's admonition to Timothy when he said, "No soldier in active service entangles himself in the affairs of everyday life, so that he may please the one who enlisted him as a soldier" (2 Tim. 2:4; *cf.* Heb. 12:1). Failure to wear the breastplate of righteousness will certainly result in the forfeiting of blessing and the loss of eternal reward, but God has promised to bless the godly; "For it is You who blesses the righteous man, O LORD, You surround him with favor as with a shield." (Ps. 5:12); "He who pursues righteousness and loyalty finds life, righteousness and honor" (Prov. 21:21); "Happy is he who keeps the law" (Prov. 29:18).

No matter how popular and prestigious, no matter how educated and winsome, pastors whose lives are living contradictions to holiness have no basis to claim they are divinely called and gifted under-shepherds of the Lord Jesus Christ, and they have no business being in ministry. Such a man is either a hireling who has no care for the sheep (John 10:11–13), or a ferocious wolf in sheep's clothing who seeks to exploit them by evil and deceit (Matt. 7:15). Sadly, both are commonplace in evangelicalism today. Worse yet, most people in the pews are too undiscerning to see it.

The Shoes of Preparation of the Gospel of Peace

In addition to "having girded your loins with truth, and having put on the breastplate of righteousness," Paul continues his list of spiritual resources we are to permanently wear if we are to be strengthened by Christ: "and having shod your feet with the preparation of the gospel of peace" (Eph. 6:15). Battle-ready footwear was essential to the Roman soldier, as it is to every man engaged in combat. They typically wore *caliga*, a half-boot which protected their feet on long marches[11] that were often thickly studded with sharp nails.[12] Many of the successes of the armies commanded by Julius Caeser and Alexander the Great are attributed to the quality of their military footwear that made it possible for them to travel quickly over great distances and surprise their enemies, while at the same time holding their ground in battle.

But the emphasis in Paul's unusual imagery is not on the kind of footwear the believer is to wear, but on *having one's feet fitted with readiness of the gospel of peace* which is necessary to obey the exhortation to "stand firm" (v. 14). Two interpretations seem possible here, although both are highly nuanced and overlap each other so significantly that they can each be considered two sides of the same coin. Paul has obviously borrowed the language of Isaiah 52:7: "How lovely on the mountains are the feet of him who brings good news, who announces peace and brings good news of happiness, who announces salvation, and says to Zion, 'Your God reigns!'" Certainly the feet of those running swiftly to bring good

---

11   P.T. O'Brien, *The letter to the Ephesians* (Grand Rapids, MI: W.B. Eerdmans Publishing Co., 1999), 475.

12   Josephus, *Jewish Wars* VI. i. 8, at https://www.biblical.ie/page.php?fl=josephus/War/WE06

news have a special kind of beauty. For this reason, Paul hearkens back to this same text to describe the messengers of the gospel (Rom. 10:15).

But a question arises when considering Paul's use of the term "preparation" (Eph. 6:15), also translated "readiness" (NIV, ESV). In relation to the genitival expression, "of the gospel," there is a debate whether it is a *genitive of origin*, or an *objective genitive*.[13] That is to say, does the "preparation of the gospel of peace" refer to a specific kind of preparation (readiness) *granted by the gospel of peace*, or does it refer to a preparation (readiness) *to proclaim the gospel of peace*? If the former, then "the preparation of the gospel of peace" signifies the firm-footed courage and zeal for battle that comes from knowing one is at peace with God and can therefore stand firm against any and all attacks of evil, knowing that God is on one's side. If the latter, it signifies a *readiness to proclaim* the gospel of peace, especially in light of the fact that the meaning of the term rendered "prepared" is also used metaphorically to signify readiness in battle.[14]

Now, the former interpretation (the genitive of origin) certainly fits the immediate context of *standing firm and resisting in the evil day.* Why yield ground to an enemy that has already been defeated? Why fear when God is on our side? In keeping with the metaphor, as Christians our spiritual footing is crucial if we expect to *"stand firm"* (vv. 11, 13, 14). Furthermore, since Paul is not talking about preaching, but about standing firm in spiritual battles (i.e., hand-to-hand combat, not evangelizing the lost), it is reasonable to therefore assume this is a reference to *the Christian's assurance of reconciliation*, that as believers we are at peace with God through justification (Rom. 5:1) and therefore well outfitted to fight the good fight of faith. We have confidence that God is evermore on our side, and with this assurance we will not give ground to the enemy, for it is Christ's complete atonement that has forever reconciled us to God, and it is Christ "who is able to keep [us] from stumbling, and make [us] stand in the presence of His glory, blameless with great joy" (Jude 24). Without this soul-strengthening assurance, the sorrows of life would be like burning coals

---

13   Ibid., 475.

14   Ibid., 476.

on bare feet. But to comprehend the legal peace of justification by faith is a blessed protection that enables us to stand firm according to the daily strength He supplies.

However, a second interpretation of Paul's phrase is also possible. This view argues that it seems *unreasonable* to assume that standing firm eliminates the need to also advance upon the enemy by carrying the message of the gospel into his territory to rescue sinners. Thus *having your feet prepared with the readiness derived from the gospel of peace* (objective genitive) could also signify an enthusiastic eagerness to proclaim the gospel. This is in keeping with Paul's earlier words concerning the gospel preparedness of Christ: "And He came and preached peace to you who were far away, and peace to those who were near" (Eph. 2:17; *cf.* Col. 4:6).

This interpretation is certainly in harmony with Isaiah's reference concerning "the feet of him who brings good news, who announces peace and brings good news of happiness, who announces salvation" (52:7). It is also consistent with the implied advance upon the enemy described in 2 Corinthians 10:3–5: "For though we walk in the flesh, we do not war according to the flesh, for the weapons of our warfare are not of the flesh, but divinely powerful for the destruction of fortresses. We are destroying speculations and every lofty thing raised up against the knowledge of God" (2 Cor. 10:3–5). Moreover, this view is in keeping with Paul's request for prayer made at the conclusion of his exhortation regarding the believer's armor, "that utterance may be given to me in the opening of my mouth, to make known with boldness the mystery of the gospel, . . . that in proclaiming it I may speak boldly, as I ought to speak" (Eph. 6:19–20).

To be sure, the apostle's feet were "shod . . .with the preparation of the gospel of peace" (Eph. 6:15). He was not only ready and willing to stand firm against all odds *because of the gospel of peace* that placed the Omnipotent Sovereign of the universe at his side in battle, but on that basis he was also *ready and willing to go on the offense and proclaim the gospel of peace* in enemy territory. Both interpretations have application for the warrior preacher and both must motivate him accordingly.

There is nothing more pathetic and dishonoring to God than a cowardly pastor whose feet are *not* "shod . . . with the preparation of the gospel of peace." At first he may only yield small portions of ground to the enemy—a little compromise here and a little there— never anything too noticeable. But as he loses his gospel footing, he will not only fail to advance in evangelism and discipleship, but his cowardly capitulation will continue to yield ground until he is ashamed of the true gospel. Gradually, his love for Christ will decrease and his love for the world will increase. His burden for the lost will diminish and his selfish ambitions will multiply. His confidence in the authority of God's Word will gradually vanish, while his confidence in human wisdom will steadily replace it. Evangelicalism's integration of secular psychology as a necessary supplement to what is perceived to be an insufficient Scripture is but one example.

> *There is nothing more pathetic and dishonoring to God than a cowardly pastor whose feet are not "shod . . . with the preparation of the gospel of peace." As he loses his gospel footing, he will not only fail to advance in evangelism and discipleship, but his cowardly capitulation will continue to yield ground until he is ashamed of the true gospel.*

Sadly, this describes the majority of evangelical pastors today, although they will deny it. Why? Because they have been deceived into believing a different gospel—one they are convinced is true (2 Tim. 3:14). With bare feet, they march on an easy and well-traveled thoroughfare where Satan has cleared away all obstacles that might bruise, cut, trip, or hinder his foot soldiers—a way that is not only painless and pleasurable, but also lined on both sides with cheering supporters equally deceived. Paul described them as those "who will not endure sound doctrine; but wanting to have their ears tickled, they will accumulate for themselves teachers in accordance to their own desire, and will turn away their ears from the truth and will turn aside to myths" (2 Tim. 4:3–4). Such is the power of satanic deception.

The Shield of Faith

Paul continues his exhortation by saying, "In addition to all, taking up the shield of faith with which you will be able to extinguish all the flaming arrows of the evil one" (v. 16). Here the apostle, writing by the inspiration of the Holy Spirit, draws upon the full-body protection of the Roman heavy infantrymen manning the front lines of battle. They carried a large oblong shield (Greek: *thureon*) that comes from the word "door." It was made of wood or metal with a heavily oiled leather covering capable of extinguishing flaming arrows ignited by pitch. It was typically two and one half feet in breadth by four and one half feet in height, often curved on the inner side and secured by leather straps. It was designed to protect the full body (a soldier's average height was around 5'7) while at the same time allow for long spears, pikes, sarissas, or similar pole weapons to protrude from them while in a phalanx formation (a tightly packed, rectangular formation capable of even withstanding a massive chariot attack).

The apostle's spiritual application is obvious: even as these massive shields protected Roman soldiers in combat, so too our faith in God protects us, extinguishing "all the flaming missiles of the evil one."

Without this shield, infantrymen were defenseless. For this reason Paul begins with the phrase, "in addition to all," meaning, "over all" so as to cover all that has been put on before.[15] The apostle's spiritual application is obvious: even as these massive shields protected Roman soldiers in combat, *so too our faith in God protects us, extinguishing "all the flaming missiles of the evil one."* But given the staggering amount of ungodliness manifested in the church, I fear many Christians, including many pastors and church leaders, seldom take up this shield.

Contrast this with Jesus' simple yet profound gospel command: "Repent and believe in the gospel" (Mark 1:15). To repent is to essentially change one's mind and purpose, to turn from one direc-

---

15   R. Jamieson, A.R. Fausset, & D. Brown, *Commentary Critical and Explanatory on the Whole Bible, Vol. 2* (Oak Harbor, WA: Logos Research Systems, Inc., 1997), 357.

tion and go in another. True repentance is therefore a God-induced hatred of sin, a loathing over it so powerful that a person desperately embraces the truth of the gospel of Christ as his only hope of salvation, and decisively commits to turning from sin, denying himself, and following Christ—even if it costs him his life. How often do we see this in evangelical leaders? Genuine repentance will also produce obedience to the second part of Jesus' command: "Believe in the gospel"—that is, not merely know the truth about Christ; Judas was convinced that Jesus was the Christ (Matt. 27:3–5) and demons believe in Jesus and shudder (James 2:19), but are without salvation.

True belief is therefore saving faith. It moves beyond basic knowledge and mental assent concerning the truth about Christ, and arrives at the glorious destination of grace whereby one personally trusts *in* Christ and depends *on* Christ for forgiveness of sins and reconciliation to a holy God. While faith begins with knowledge and assent, it goes much further; it animates the will to be utterly reliant on Christ as one's only hope of salvation and only source of sanctification. John Murray insightfully said this:

> Faith is knowledge passing into conviction, and it is conviction passing into confidence. Faith cannot stop short of self-commitment to Christ, a transference of reliance upon ourselves and all human resources to reliance upon Christ alone for salvation. It is a receiving and resting upon him.[16]

Scripture teaches that without faith it is impossible to please God (Heb. 11:6); we are justified by faith (Rom. 5:1); the just shall live by faith (1:17); Jesus is the author and finisher of our faith (Heb. 12:2); we are to examine ourselves to see if we are in the faith (2 Cor. 13:5); we are to fight the good fight of faith (1 Tim. 6:12); and stand firm in the faith (1 Cor. 16:13); and we can rejoice knowing the testing of faith produces endurance (James 1:3).

The biblical concept of faith can be seen in the Hebrew root word for "faith" (Hebrew: *'āman*), which has the basic idea of *firmness* or *certainty*, as in an infant being supported by the strong arms of a parent. From this basic idea comes the concept of *being*

16   John Murray, *Redemption Accomplished and Applied* (Grand Rapids, MI. / Cambridge, U.K.: William B. Eerdmans Publishing Company, 1955), 118.

certain about, or *being assured.* Therefore the Hebrew concept of "faith" carries the idea of *resting upon that which is absolutely dependable.* This is also the basis of the biblical word for *belief* and shows that biblical faith is an assurance, or a certainty, in contrast with modern concepts of faith as something possible, hopefully true, but not certain.[17] This means the shield of faith signifies an absolute, unwavering conviction that God (the Object of faith) is completely trustworthy and therefore worthy of our complete confidence in all He has promised. This spiritual reality then animates the will to obey all that He has commanded.

Another Hebrew word translated *"trust"* (Hebrew: *bātah*) has the basic meaning of *to feel safe, be confident, or to rely on.*[18] It suggests that we are helpless and in danger and must seek a hiding place, a place of safety, as in Psalm 91:1-2: "He who dwells in the shelter of the Most High will abide in the shadow of the Almighty. I will say to the LORD, 'My refuge and my fortress. My God in whom I trust!'" (Ps. 91:1-2). In this sense, the Almighty Himself is our shield of faith.

> *The shield of faith signifies an absolute, unwavering conviction that God (the Object of faith) is completely trustworthy and therefore worthy of our complete confidence in all He has promised.*

In the New Testament, faith (Greek: *pistis*) has the basic idea of a *firm persuasion, a conviction based upon unshakable truth.* It is always used of faith in God, or Christ, or spiritual truth. We see this, for example, in Hebrews 11:1: "Now faith is the assurance of things hoped for, the conviction of things not seen." The term "assurance" translates the Greek word, *hypostasis,* a compound word made up of *stasis,* "to stand," and *hypo,* "under."[19] It is also translated "substance" (KJV), signifying essence, foundation, or confident assurance. It refers to a bedrock foundation upon which a solid

---

17 Entry: *'āman* in *Theological Wordbook of the Old Testament,* (Chicago, IL: The Moody Bible Institute, 1980), 116, 51.

18 Entry: *bātah* in *Theological Wordbook of the Old Testament,* (Chicago, IL: The Moody Bible Institute, 1980), 101, 233.

19 John MacArthur and Richard Mayhue: General Editors, *Biblical Doctrine: A Systematic Summary of Bible Truth* (Wheaton, IL: Crossway, 2017), 598.

structure must be built. The writer continues by saying, "Faith. . . is the conviction of things not seen." The meaning of the word "conviction" (Greek: *elenchos*) is *evidence,* or *the proof test of the reality of "things not seen."* So together these phrases help us understand that our faith—that firm conviction based upon unshakable truth upon which we rely—is a certain hope that God will fulfill all He has promised. MacArthur adds, "Far from being nebulous and uncertain, faith is the most solid possible conviction. Faith is the present essence of a future reality."[20]

So when Paul exhorts us to "take up the shield of faith with which [we] will be able to extinguish all the flaming missiles of the evil one" (Eph. 6:15), he's commanding us to *maintain a confident assurance in things we cannot see physically but can see clearly through the eyes of faith.* The writer goes on to characterize faith in Hebrews 11 through several well-known examples:

- By faith Noah, being warned by God about things not yet seen, in reverence prepared an ark for the salvation of his household (v. 7).

- By faith Abraham, when he was called, obeyed by going out to a place which he was to receive for an inheritance; and he went out, not knowing where he was going . . . for he was looking for the city which has foundations, whose architect and builder is God (vv. 8, 10).

- By faith even Sarah herself received ability to conceive, even beyond the proper time of life, since she considered Him faithful who had promised (v. 11).

- By faith [Moses] left Egypt, not fearing the wrath of the king; for he endured, as seeing Him who is unseen (v. 27).

Every faithful soldier of Christ must maintain a confident assurance in the perfections of God's character, in the person and work of Christ, and in the body of doctrine He has revealed in His Word. This is the heart of a warrior preacher. He must ignore the seductive powers of erotic media and the damning demands of culture,

---

20　John MacArthur, *The MacArthur New Testament Commentary: Hebrews* (Chicago, IL: Moody Press, 1983), 288.

including influential voices within his own church. He must never forget that God blesses those who hear His Word and obey it (Luke 11:28). By taking up this supernatural shield of faith, he will be protected from Satan's deadly darts specifically designed to destroy him, for faith is "the victory that overcomes the world" (1 John 5:4). Moreover, in the heat of the battle he will be comforted knowing, "The steadfast of mind You will keep in perfect peace, because he trusts in You" (Isa. 26:3).

The Helmet of Salvation

Borrowing once again from Isaiah 59:17, Paul exhorts the believer to "take the helmet of salvation" (Eph. 6:17). No soldier would go into battle without head protection, and here Paul exhorts the believer to *protect his mind by understanding and appropriating the magnificent realities of salvation* previously discussed in his epistle. He has made it clear that our salvation is wholly a work of God; that "He chose us in Him before the foundation of the world" (1:4) and "predestined us to adoption as sons through Jesus Christ to Himself, according to the kind intention of His will" (v. 5); "in Him we have redemption through His blood, the forgiveness of our trespasses according to the riches of His grace" (v. 7); "we have obtained an inheritance, having been predestined according to His purpose who works all things after the counsel of His will" (v. 11); and we "were sealed in Him with the Holy Spirit of promise, who is given as a pledge of our inheritance, with a view to the redemption of God's own possession, to the praise of His glory" (vv. 13–14).

He did all this despite the fact that we were "dead in [our] trespasses and sins" (2:1) and "walked according to the course of this world, according to the prince of the power of the air, of the spirit that is working in the sons of disobedience" (v. 2). Nevertheless, "God, being rich in mercy, because of His great love with which He loved us, even when we were dead in our transgressions, made us alive together with Christ (by grace you have been saved), and raised us up with Him, and seated us with Him in the heavenly places, in Christ Jesus" (vv. 4–6). While there are many other passages in Scripture that demonstrate what God has done in accomplishing our redemption, these alone are enough *to prove that our salvation was ordained in eternity past according to His unin-fluenced will to bring glory to Himself.* Our salvation is all of grace from beginning to end, "For we are His workmanship, created in Christ Jesus for good works, which God prepared beforehand, that we should walk in them" (v. 10).

A superficial, minimalistic grasp of soteriology leaves both the pastor and his congregation vulnerable to the deceptions and accu-sations of the enemy; yet sadly this is all too common. Just ask the average Christian to explain some of the soteriological concepts re-vealed in Scripture that have been given them for their edification, encouragement, and protection, and you will quickly discover they wear no helmet.

> A superficial, minimalistic grasp of soteriology leaves both the pastor and his congregation vulnerable to the deceptions and accusations of the enemy; yet sadly this is all too common.

Practically speaking, especially as it relates to pastoral ministry, any helmet of salvation not made out of the impenetrable truths of the doctrines of sovereign grace—often described pejoratively as "Calvinism"—is incapable of protecting a believer from the ene-my's deadly blows of deception. Perhaps a few examples of Satan's common assaults on salvation might prove helpful. These are il-lustrated by deceptions pastors might believe who are deficient or errant in their understanding of salvation ("WITHOUT A HELMET") versus those who can answer biblically ("WITH A HELMET").

WITHOUT A HELMET: *Man is not so depraved as to be unable to co-operate with God in salvation; so you must induce sinners to make a decision for Christ through reasoning and emotional appeals.*

WITH A HELMET: Wrong. Man's sinful nature is so corrupt that all that he *does* and all that he *is* is fundamentally offensive to God, rendering him incapable of acknowledging his sinfulness and con-sequent condemnation. Apart from regenerating grace that spans that great chasm between man's depravity and the righteous de-mands of the law, no one would be saved. Like the invisible wind that blows when and where it wills, it is the Spirit alone that imparts spiritual life to the spiritually dead, and He does so through the proclamation of the Word of God. Therefore, since the gospel is the power of God unto salvation, I will preach Christ and Him crucified in all its purity and power and I will trust the Spirit to effectually call sinners to new life according to the sovereign decrees of divine election that cannot be resisted. The initiative, the power, and the glory are His and His alone.

WITHOUT A HELMET: *Your sins suggest you have never been born again, so you better find new rules to earn God's love so you can be saved and stay saved.*

WITH A HELMET: Regrettably it is true—I continue to sin. I'm not what I want to be and I'm not what I should be; but praise God, *I'm not what I used to be*! I know nothing good dwells in my flesh, and, despite my longing to obey God perfectly, I practice the very evils I hate, making me a prisoner of the law of sin that still operates in my body. But thanks be to God through Jesus Christ, I have been saved from the penalty, power, and one day the very presence of sin. As my substitute, Christ actually bore my sins—past, present, and future—in His body on the cross and satisfied the offended holiness of God on my behalf, and it was there that I gained my salvation, which caused my Savior to declare, "It is finished!" Therefore I rejoice, knowing there is now no condemnation to those who are in Christ Jesus. Moreover, when I sin—which I do more than I even know—I have an advocate with the Father, Christ Jesus; and when I confess my sins, He is faithful and just to forgive my sins and cleanse me from all unrighteousness. As to finding new rules to earn God's love, in truth there is nothing I can do to merit salvation; it is by grace alone, through faith alone, in Christ alone. Legalism only offers an illusion of spirituality. It also blurs the distinction between justification and sanctification, and it undermines Christ's atoning work on my behalf by assuming I must add my good works to what He has accomplished in order for me to merit salvation. Because the just shall live by faith, I will live confidently in God's grace.

WITHOUT A HELMET: *Since Christ has fully satisfied the demands of the Law on your behalf, stop frustrating God's grace with your attempts to pursue holiness; cease with your piety, and start celebrating the freedoms you have in Christ.*

WITH A HELMET: While it is true that my sins—past, present, and future—have been paid in full on the cross and in my justification I have been declared righteous and I am therefore forever clothed in the imputed righteousness of Christ, this does not mean that I am not obligated to the moral principles of God's standard for righteousness. Sanctification includes submission to the lordship of Christ and is the obvious proof of justification; therefore conformity to the moral principles of God's law is the *fruit*, not the *root* of holiness. Those who have no desire to walk by the Spirit and who make no progress in practical holiness have no basis to claim they are new creatures in Christ, characterized by both washing and renewal. Instead, theirs is a dead faith that cannot save. I will not let sin be master over me, for to do so would enslave me to that which caused such unimaginable suffering and death for my Savior. Instead, I will gladly become obedient from the heart, having been freed from sin and now being a slave to righteousness.

WITHOUT A HELMET: *Since God is sovereign over salvation and only His elect will be saved, stop worrying so much about evangelism as if He needs your help.*

WITH A HELMET: While it is the Spirit's work to convict and draw God's elect to salvation, He has made it clear in His Word that this ministry is accomplished through human instruments who passionately pursue the glory of God. True disciples of Christ are "fishers of men," obedient to His command to go and make disciples of all nations and to teach them to observe all that He has commanded. The Spirit-empowered preaching of the Word will either harden or soften hearts and it will not return to God empty, but shall accomplish His intended purposes. For indeed, all Scripture is breathed out by God and profitable for teaching, for reproof, for correction, and for training in righteousness. For this reason, I will gladly "endure all things for the sake of those who are chosen, so that they also may obtain the salvation which is in Christ Jesus and with it eternal glory" (2 Tim. 2:10).

While a childlike faith is sufficient to save, it is insufficient to ward off the deadly blows of confusion, doubt, discouragement, legalism, antinomianism, and other targeted deceptions that will inevitably come against the mind and heart of a believer engaged in the battle for truth. Immature saints who are content to sing, "Jesus loves me this I know, for the Bible tells me so" are at a far greater disadvantage than those who so revel in regenerating, redeeming, and reconciling grace that they cannot help but sing,

> Long my imprisoned spirit lay,
> Fast bound in sin and nature's night;
> Thine eye diffused a quick'ning ray—
> I woke, the dungeon flamed with light;
> My chains fell off, my heart was free,
> I rose, went forth, and followed Thee.[21]

The Sword of the Spirit

In addition to the apostolic exhortation to "take the helmet of salvation," Paul adds, "and the sword of the Spirit, which is the word of God" (Eph. 6:17). The imagery is derived from the eighteen-inch Roman dagger called a *machaira*. It was carried in a scabbard on a soldier's side and used in close-quarter combat. Without this weapon, a soldier would be defenseless and unable to attack the enemy. Likewise, this is a vital part of the warrior preacher's armament, a spiritual weapon to be used both outwardly and inwardly (Heb. 4:12). Pastors and church leaders who are poor swordsmen, unable to accurately exposit and apply the Word of God, will be easy prey for the deceptions and persecutions of the enemy. Worse yet, because they are ill-equipped to use the "sword of the Spirit," their congregations will be vulnerable to the attacks of the enemy, little children "tossed here and there by waves and carried about by every wind of doctrine, by the trickery of men, by craftiness in deceitful scheming" (Eph. 4:11). This topic will be addressed more fully in Chapter 3: *The Warrior's Weaponry*.

---

21 Charles Wesley, *And Can It Be?* 1738.

Challenge

The elite forces of the King of kings have been supernaturally out-fitted with all the necessary armaments to not only survive the assaults of Satan and his forces, but to gain victory over them. No matter how fierce the assault or how savage the hounds of hell, we are able to stand firm and resist in the strength of His might, for "in all these things we overwhelmingly conquer through Him who loved us" (Rom. 8:37). Only the most hardened heart would ignore this exhortation, "Put on the full armor of God, so that you will be able to stand firm against the schemes of the devil" (Eph. 6:11). What about you?

Chapter 2 Questions

1. As a pastor or church leader, do you see yourself as a high-value target of the enemy and therefore in desperate need of the spiritual armor God has provided, or do you have a cavalier attitude toward spiritual warfare?

2. In what ways are you standing firm against Satan's diabolical deceptions and subterfuge that can render you indifferent to those devices that produce disillusionment, frustration in ministry, and inflame your lusts to act wickedly?

3. Have pulpit attitudes of flippancy, comedy, and superficiality replaced the solemnity, reverence, and careful exposition of Scripture God requires in order for you to *stand firm* and *be strong* in the Lord?

4. Are you intentional in your thinking and do you put forth the necessary effort to discipline your thought life to make it ready for mortal spiritual combat?

5. Do you pursue personal integrity at all cost and abhor hypocrisy more in your own life than what you see in others?

6. Would others who know you best describe you as bold, forthright, and uncompromising in the pulpit, or timid, non-committal, and compromising?

7. Do you maintain a confident assurance in the character of God and in the body of doctrine He has revealed in His Word, or do you seek the wisdom of man?

8. Do you rejoice in the reality that salvation was ordained in eternity past according to God's uninfluenced will to bring glory to Himself, or do you believe God's will is subject to man's will?

3

The Warrior's Weaponry

And take . . . the sword of the Spirit, which is the word of God.
With all prayer and petition pray at all times in the Spirit, and
with this in view, be on the alert with all perseverance
and petition for all the saints.
(Ephesians 6:17–18)

The man, who was called Interpreter, said, "Come in; I will show you what will be profitable to you." So he had his servant turn on some lights and beckoned Christian to follow him. He led him into a private room and told his servant to open a door. When he had done so, Christian could see hanging on the wall a Picture of a very intense-looking man whose eyes were looking toward Heaven. He had the best of books in his hand, the law of truth written on his lips, and the world behind his back. He stood there as if pleading with men, and a golden crown rested upon his head.

JOHN BUNYAN[22]

22 John Bunyan, Translated by Cheryl V. Ford, *The Pilgrim's Progress in the Allegory of a Dream* (Wheaton, IL; Tyndale House Publishers, Inc., 1991), 26.

No reasonable soldier would enter a combat zone without proper protection and the necessary defensive and offensive weaponry. To do so would guarantee defeat. Yet this is exactly what we see happening on a routine basis with most evangelical pastors and church leaders. Oblivious to Satan's spiritual espionage and clever violence being perpetrated against them, they carry on their ministries in blissful ignorance, unprotected by the believer's armor and unskilled with the weaponry God has made available to them, namely, "the sword of the Spirit, which is the word of God" and "prayer . . . in the Spirit" (Eph. 6:17–18).

You might ask, "How can you say so dogmatically that most pastors are so ill-equipped and unskilled?" The answer is simple: I've heard them preach and I've seen the worldliness and apostasy in their churches. If you listen to the sermons of many prominent evangelical preachers around the country, especially pastors of megachurches, it is extremely rare to find one that accurately exposits and compellingly applies a specific text. And when they try, they butcher both so badly that what they say has nothing to do with the authorial intent and true meaning of the passage. Worse yet, their followers are too undiscerning to see it.

Most are topical preachers who use a particular passage as a launching pad to talk about whatever subject they believe their audience wants to hear, not what God has truly said. The motivation is to please the consumer, not to honor Christ; to sell a product, not make a disciple. The appeal is to the *emotions* rather than the *mind*, making the overall focus *man-centered*, not *God-centered*. Many preach on some variation of the love of God, loving our fellow man, being tolerant and non-judgmental, or God's desire to meet our felt needs. These rambling discourses are typically nothing more than a segue into addressing political, cultural, and social issues, depending upon the audience.

Twenty-Minute Sermons

Evidence of ill-equipped and unskilled swordsmen was well illustrated in a monthly ministerial association luncheon in my area that I was invited to attend. The expectation was that I would become a permanent member. Most all the pastors were older than me, so they welcomed me as their junior. I remember being introduced as "the new kid on the block with the little start-up, store-front church in Joelton." After the initial meet and greet was over and we settled down to eat, I noticed the conversation centered primarily on the number of baptisms, rededications, and new members that had joined their church over the last month. It was noticeably uncomfortable for those whose success rate was on the lower end of the scale. I was also uncomfortable because I knew the metrics they were using to evaluate their churches are never praiseworthy in the New Testament record. If they were, Jesus would have been a miserable failure. Even after His amazing authoritative teaching (Mark 1:27) and all the miracles He performed, it appears He only had a little over five hundred faithful followers (1 Cor. 15:6) by the time He ascended into heaven. Some of the men in the ministerial association had many more than that.

They all began comparing notes regarding the length of their sermons, each sharing funny anecdotes about people sleeping and snoring, babies screaming, and people who would leave at twelve o'clock sharp whether the sermon was over or not.

But it was really intriguing when the conversation shifted to the topic of preaching. They all began comparing notes regarding the length of their sermons, each sharing funny anecdotes about people sleeping and snoring, babies screaming, and people who would leave at twelve o'clock sharp whether the sermon was over or not. The overwhelming consensus was that the length of a sermon should never exceed twenty to thirty minutes. One elderly pastor who was clearly the respected patriarch of the group said, "Listen: if you can't say it in twenty minutes, you've lost them!" To which everyone (other than I) nodded in what appeared to be a choreographed group approval with the appropriate responses of "Hmmm . . . yes . . . amen!" added for emphasis.

What followed next had to have been a providential setup. Somehow, I knew what was coming. And sure enough, it did. My host turned to me and asked, "Brother Harrell, how long do you preach?" ("Brother" is a synonym for pastor in the South.) While I'm in no way proud of my response—in fact, it may have come more from my flesh than the Spirit—nevertheless, it was the truth. I said, "Well, I guess I'm the odd man out here. My introductions take about twenty minutes." They all laughed hilariously—most probably thought I was teasing. But then I went on to say, "As a Bible expositor, it takes me on average about fifty-five minutes to really unpack and apply a text." At that point the mood quickly shifted from joviality to incredulity. And I'll never forget the quick response of the patriarch; he leaned over toward me with a big grin, his eyebrows raised, and his head shaking from side to side as he said, "Brother, you better shorten up or you will never grow that church." We all had a good laugh—although it was tense—and, to my relief, the subject quickly went in another direction.

On the way home, my host turned to me and said, "Brother, I hope you weren't offended by what brother So-and-so said. He means well." To which I replied, "Oh no, I wasn't offended at all, but I was saddened." With a puzzled look he quickly replied, "Really? What do you mean?" What followed next was a very fruitful conversation that began with me saying (and this is a paraphrase of my best recollection), "In my humble opinion, if all you have to say only takes twenty minutes, you need to spend more time in your study. The Word of God is simply too vast and deep and marvelous to skim over the top. Plus, my people want more, not less."

Most Preachers Can't Preach

Honestly, most preachers can't preach. I struggle with it myself, although my flesh renders me hopelessly biased in my favor. By preaching, I mean *a clear and compelling exposition and application of the Word of God so convicting, edifying, and encouraging that all listeners know they have been in the presence of the Most High and are forever changed by what they heard.* This is truly a work of the Spirit, not the preacher; and every authentic Christian will crave more of it, never less.

But this kind of preaching is extremely rare. Most contemporary preaching is as shallow as frosting on a donut and as boring as watching paint dry. No wonder so many people insist on shorter sermons or look for better ways to spend their time on Sundays. Who can blame them? And most preachers who attract large audiences are nothing more than religious peddlers who know how to appeal to woke liberals, or showmen making promises of financial prosperity and physical health (as long as you have enough faith, positive thoughts, and money to donate to their ministry).

By preaching, I mean *a clear and compelling exposition and application of the Word of God so convicting, edifying, and encouraging that all listeners know they have been in the presence of the Most High and are forever changed by what they heard.*

Not surprisingly, it is extremely rare to hear the gospel plainly preached or Christ clearly exalted. Just ask the most prominent leaders in these churches to explain the gospel and you will quickly discover their lack of theological acumen and passion. Most are neophytes in the realm of soteriology and therefore unqualified to teach. No wonder their congregations are correspondingly illiterate concerning the most ineffably glorious blessing ever to be offered to sinful people: the gospel. Many pastors and teachers are unable to give clear explanations of the various soteriological concepts that define the biblical doctrine of salvation. These include concepts such as:

- The origin of sin
- The severity and scope of man's depravity
- The imputation of sin
- Grace
- Election
- Calling

- The significance and efficacy of the atonement
- Faith
- Repentance
- Conversion
- Union with Christ
- Justification
- Regeneration
- Sanctification
- Perseverance
- Glorification

Conversely, the warrior preacher will not only have a thorough grasp of these magnificent truths, but *these magnificent truths will have a thorough grasp on him as well*. He will be unable to restrain the doxologies of his heart, even when he is asked to give an academic explanation of these essential gospel concepts.

By the term *gospel* I'm referring to the true gospel of saving grace alone through faith in Christ alone as set forth in His Word alone; the pure gospel that offends sinners but saves those who have been humbled by regenerating grace and given the gift of repentant faith; the only gospel that can reconcile sinful men, women, and children to a holy God and deliver them from the bondage and eternal penalty of sin meted out by a holy and just God. If the unsearchable riches of Christ in the gospel do not animate your heart with breathless adoration and loosen your tongue with spontaneous outbursts of praise, there is something terribly wrong with your spiritual condition! Furthermore, you have no business standing behind a pulpit to put the glory of Christ on display and call sinners to repentance and saints to obedient faith, nor has God called and gifted you to do so. Instead, your life will be as pedestrian and powerless as your ministry.

Sadly, however, what I have just described has become the woeful norm among evangelical pastors and leaders. Far too many have become *men pleasers* rather than *God pleasers*, which will inevitably produce a distorted gospel presentation—an abominable sin that Paul condemned in the strongest of terms:

> As we have said before, so I say again now, if any man is preaching to you a gospel contrary to what you received, he is to be accursed! For am I now seeking the favor of men, or of God? Or am I striving to please men? If I were still trying to please men, I would not be a bond-servant of Christ. (Gal. 1:9–10)

To complicate these issues further, because religious *relativism* and *pluralism* are the only politically correct dogmas of our day, Bible doctrine is anathema! It is considered offensive to the vast majority of church attendees, most of whom are Christian in name only and have no capacity to understand and accept the things of the Spirit of God (1 Cor. 2:14). Given this, *expositional preaching* is virtually non-existent. By this I'm referring to a doctrinal proclamation of Scripture derived from an exegetical process that is concerned only with *the revelation of God, not the wisdom of man*. Therefore, such a process carefully and reverently conveys the God-intended meaning of a text, which will be linked to other great doctrines and theological truths. Then, when the text has been accurately explained, the preacher will passionately apply its meaning to the contemporary issues of life.

Satan has done a masterful job in convincing the world—including much of evangelicalism—that the Bible is not the inspired, inerrant, infallible, authoritative, and all-sufficient Word of the One true God.

Satan, however, has done a masterful job in convincing the world—including much of evangelicalism—that the Bible is not the inspired, inerrant, infallible, authoritative, and all-sufficient Word of the One true God. *Sola Scriptura* has been replaced by *sola cultura,* as Os Guinness once quipped. The very idea of a warrior preacher is therefore considered absurd, even offensive by most people—including many pastors who are little more than entrepreneurs with enough panache to appeal to the subjective whims of individualistic, tech-savvy, entertainment-addicted, truth-hating, self-absorbed audiences steeped in a godless culture. A true warrior preacher, however, will know how to defend against the enemy as well as engage him offensively. He will not only know what weapons to use, but he will be very skilled in using them.

Green Beret Weaponry

Once again, we would do well to learn from the elite warriors of our United States military. The effectiveness of pastoral leadership would be even greater if we were to give the same careful attention to our weaponry, training, and tactics as the Green Berets give to theirs. To this end, I wish to share the testimony of one such seasoned combat warrior, my retired Green Beret friend and fellow elder, Joel C., who responded to my inquiries concerning these matters. Here's what he said:

> For Direct Action missions, we carried SAWs, M4s and MP5s. MP5s were used by people in the stack because in close quarters you don't need a long barrel catching corners, walls, etc. We also carried sidearms. After a breach was made, either with a shotgun or demo, the guys in the stack with MP5s would enter a house, or building, etc. We don't always do simultaneous entries (roof and front; or front and back). Men in the vehicles are watching for possible reactionary forces coming to the aid of the target or watching for squirters (escapees from the target house).
>
> Needless to say, all of these weapons require skill and a knowledge of how to use them. They fire rounds very quickly and get jammed at times. You have to practice jammed weapons procedures all the time, so it's muscle memory in combat when this occurs so you can fix the jam and get back on target as quickly as possible. You must maintain all weapons daily—clean and lubricate them, so that when you need them most, they function as they should. You have to know each weapon intimately. We had drills assembling a stack of gun parts blindfolded so even in the dark you know every piece of your weapon by feel and can put it together.
>
> We (on a team) shot 3,000 to 4,000 rounds per week. Years later, I still have rough places on my fingers from shooting so much. We shoot left-handed, right-handed, standing,

kneeling, prone (strong and weak side) and even from up-side down. You also shoot while moving, running, walking, and in all directions. We do stress shoots also to simulate combat. Do ten pull-ups and then sprint to a covered position and fire at targets kneeling and then prone; all the while arti-sims[23] are exploding and there is the noise of flash bangs and automatic weapons. You run to another covered position and fire from both sides of a rock—strong and weak side. You may have someone screaming at you the entire time and kicking you or pushing you while you're shooting. It's all designed to make you lose focus and miss targets. If you can hit targets under this stress and these conditions, you'll probably do well in combat.

Bottom line: effective use of the weapons and application of the right weapon for the situation requires intimate knowledge and experience with all of them and much practice using them.[24]

Warrior Preacher Weaponry

While every true American patriot is deeply indebted to the brave sacrifice of our military personnel, we are also thankful for the defensive and offensive resources God has made available to them, not to mention the enormous amount of training they put into using them effectively. But every true Christian can also rejoice in what God has provided for us to effectively wage war against the enemy of our souls.

Having described the various pieces of armor the believer must wear in order to "be strong in the Lord" and "stand firm against the schemes of the devil" (Eph. 6:10, 11), the Spirit of God issues two more commands through His apostle, saying,

> And take up . . . the sword of the Spirit, which is the word of God. With all prayer and petition pray at all times in the Spirit, and with this in view, be on the alert with all perseverance and petition for all the saints, and pray on my

23   (artificial simulation of an explosive)

24   Joel C., from private correspondence.

behalf, that utterance may be given to me in the opening of my mouth, to make known with boldness the mystery of the gospel, for which I am an ambassador in chains; that in proclaiming it I may speak boldly, as I ought to speak. (Eph. 6:17–20)

Obedience to these inspired exhortations coming from a battle-scarred warrior like Paul is absolutely crucial, especially for those who stand in pulpits every week as pastor-teachers and who preach the Word to those whom God has brought to them.

First, notice his call to "take up . . . the sword of the Spirit, which is the word of God" (v. 17). Once again, Paul uses the familiar imagery of his day pertaining to the short-handled sword carried by a Roman soldier called a *machaira*. With a shield in one hand and a sword in the other, he was able to both defend and attack. In the same way, the Spirit of God has supplied us with a *defensive* and *offensive* weapon, "the word of God"—God's written revelation to man given to us by the Spirit (1 Cor. 2:7–14; 2 Peter 1:20–21), verbally inspired in every word and thus inerrant in the original documents. It is therefore "profitable for teaching, for reproof, for correction, for training in righteousness; so that the man of God may be adequate, equipped for every good work" (2 Tim. 3:16).

> With a shield in one hand and a sword in the other, he was able to both defend and attack. In the same way, the Spirit of God has supplied us with a *defensive* and *offensive* weapon, "the word of God."

Adding to this magnificent resource, the Spirit is also the resident instructor who gives us greater understanding of the Scriptures. For this reason Paul testified, "We impart this in words not taught by human wisdom but taught by the Spirit" (1 Cor. 2:13). This is also described in Paul's prayer for the Ephesians when he prayed that "the God of our Lord Jesus Christ, the Father of glory, may give you the spirit of wisdom and of revelation in the knowledge of him, having the eyes of your hearts enlightened, that you may know . . ." (Eph. 1:17–18; *cf.* 1 John 2:27; 1 Cor. 2:14–16).

The supernatural supremacy of Scripture, combined with the Spirit's enlightenment, underscores the sheer power of such a weapon and the authority it demands. In fact, *a man's effectiveness as a preacher is proportional to his commitment to this authority*—a devotion that has been largely abandoned these days in order to employ the unbiblical principles of evangelical pragmatism. The supremacy and authority of Scripture therefore demand our utmost care in interpretation and proclamation. This requires an unwavering commitment to sound hermeneutical principles, namely, a literal, grammatical-historical interpretation being applied to exegesis in order to determine the single, God-intended meaning of a text. Anything short of that is *speculation*, not *interpretation*.

> The supremacy and authority of Scripture therefore demand our utmost care in interpretation and proclamation.

We see this illustrated in 2 Peter 1:16–21. There Peter begins by testifying how he saw with his own eyes the effulgence of Christ's glory blaze forth from within Him on the Mount of Transfiguration (v. 16; *cf.* Matt. 17:1–8). Nevertheless he declared, "We have the prophetic word made more sure" (2 Peter 1:19)—more sure than what he was certain he had seen or experienced with all his senses. In other words, *the supremacy and authority of Scripture trump all we think we know or think we have experienced*. For this reason he went on to say, ". . . to which you do well to pay attention as to a lamp shining in a dark place, until the day dawns and the morning star arises in your hearts. But know this first of all, that no prophecy of Scripture is a matter of one's own interpretation, for no prophecy was ever made by an act of human will, but men moved by the Holy Spirit spoke from God" (vv. 19b–21).

Biblical preaching must therefore explain Scripture with utmost precision—carefully preserving the Spirit's work of inspiration by communicating to others the revelation of God without addition, subtraction, or modification. This requires far more than an academic knowledge of the Bible. It is one thing to know the contents of Scripture; but it is altogether another matter to know how to properly interpret and apply it. While rigorous training and study are crucial in this regard, they are not nearly enough. We must have the additional work of illumination that only the Spirit can provide. Moreover, we can rejoice knowing that He bears witness to every teachable Christian that Scripture is true and reliable (Acts 5:32; Heb. 10:15; 1 John 5:6).

In light of all this, the warrior preacher understands the serious nature of biblical preaching, for indeed, he is divinely called and gifted to wield the most powerful weapon every conceived—"the sword of the Spirit, which is the word of God."

Defensive Swordsmanship

It is important to consider how this divine sword can be used both *defensively* and *offensively*. First, let's examine its defensive capabilities inherent in Paul's exhortation: "Put on the full armor of God, so that you will be able to stand firm against the schemes of the devil" (Eph. 6:11). This is dramatically illustrated in Jesus' use of Scripture during His weakened state in the wilderness when He parried the blows of Satan who tempted Him to doubt His Father's perfect plan and to presume upon His grace. Refusing to transfer His allegiance to Satan, Jesus literally quoted Scripture to defend against the supernatural assaults of His archenemy (and ours). As a result, "When the devil had finished every temptation, he left Him until an opportune time" (Luke 4:13). James describes the same phenomenon when he says, "Submit therefore to God. Resist the devil and he will flee from you" (James 4:7).

> This is how we defend against the enemy, and, in a manner of speaking, how we rout the enemy at the same time. As the saying goes,
> "The best offense is a good defense."

Herein is the power of "the sword of the Spirit, which is the word of God" (v. 17). This is how we defend against the enemy, and, in a manner of speaking, how we rout the enemy at the same time. As the saying goes, "The best offense is a good defense." However, believers are never instructed in Scripture to initiate an attack on demonic forces by rebuking, binding, or exorcising them, as some erroneously teach and practice. That's not only unbiblical; it's dangerous!

In Acts 19, when the seven sons of Sceva tried to cast an evil spirit out of a man by the power of "Jesus whom Paul preaches, . . . the evil spirit answered and said to them, 'I recognize Jesus, and I know about Paul, but who are you?' And the man, in whom was the evil spirit, leaped on them and subdued all them and overpowered them, so that they fled out of that house naked and wounded" (Acts 19:13–16; *cf.* 2 Peter 2:11; Jude 9). What an amazing scenario! One demon overpowered all of them, stripped off their clothes, and caused them to run for their lives. Once again, as believers we don't engage demons in battle; we take up our spiritual sword and preach Christ. We don't *exorcise*; we *evangelize*. We unleash the gospel, cry out to God in prayer (Jude 9), and let the Spirit intervene as only He can do. He alone can drive away demonic spirits.

Of course, most pastors and church leaders are not defending against evil spirits *directly*. But they do so *indirectly* when they encounter false teachers that are influenced or even possessed by demons (2 Cor. 10:5). Paul described them as "deceitful spirits" that propagate "doctrines of demons" (1 Tim. 4:1). As a result, they exert enormous influence in Satan's kingdom of darkness where he presently rules the systems of this fallen world (1 John 5:19). Their influence can be manifested through the following actions:

1. Indwelling humans and animals (Mark 5:1–16)

2. Physically afflicting people (Mark 9:17, 22)

3. Terrorizing humans (1 Sam. 16:14–15; 18:10; 19:9; Acts 19:13–16; 2 Cor. 12:7)

4. Initiating false worship (1 Cor. 10:20–21)

5. Promoting false doctrines (1 Tim. 4:1)

6. Performing false signs and wonders (2 Thess. 2:9; Rev. 16:13–14)

7. Deceiving prophets (1 Kings 22:19–23)

8. Encouraging idolatry (Deut. 32:17; Ps. 106:37)

9. Engineering death (Judg. 9:23, 56–57)[25]

---

25 John MacArthur and Richard Mayhue: General Editors, *Biblical Doctrine: A Systematic Summary of Bible Truth* (Wheaton, IL: Crossway, 2017), 713.

The proper use of "the sword of the Spirit" is important in this particular discussion, as I hope to demonstrate. Satan loves to deceive Christian leaders with an errant understanding of spiritual warfare so they will be preoccupied with assaulting actual demons rather than the world systems they dominate. The proliferation of "deliverance" ministries exemplifies this error. Too many pastors are quick to blame life-dominating sins on demonic possession rather than evidence of a false profession of faith or a refusal to "walk by the Spirit" so they "will not carry out the deeds of the flesh" (Gal. 5:16). Their disobedience will typically be linked to bad doctrine as well (Eph. 4:14).

Skilled swordsmen will also understand that true believers cannot be indwelt by anyone other than the Holy Spirit (2 Cor. 6:14–18); He will not spatially co-habit a Christian with an unclean spirit. Believers have been delivered from Satan's domain of darkness and transferred to the kingdom of Christ (Col. 1:13; *cf.* 1 John 2:13–14; 4:4) and the Holy Spirit of promise has "sealed" us "for the day of redemption" (Eph. 4:30; *cf.* 2 Cor. 1:21–22). But demons do exert enormous influence in the world and in the church through false ideologies, what Paul calls "speculations and every lofty thing raised up against the knowledge of God" (2 Cor. 10:5).

Defending Against Critical Race Theory

We see this most vividly in evangelicalism's embrace of the satanically inspired neo-Marxist Critical Race Theory (CRT)—defined by Owen Strachan as "a deeply uncongenial point of view cynically weaponized for the deconstruction and dismantling of social structures."[26] This deceptive and demonstrably false ideology eschews data that undermines its claims of systemic racism; nevertheless, it remains prominent in liberal academia and progressive liberal politics. Worse yet, its manufactured outrage has given rise to the heretical Social Justice Gospel that elevates social inequities and ethnic injustices (whether real or perceived) over God's justice—a holy justice that can only be satisfied by the imputed righteousness of Christ, the ground of justification by faith which is at

---

26 Owen Strachan, *Christianity and Wokeness: How the Social Justice Movement Is Hijacking the Gospel—and the Way to Stop It* (Washington, D.C.: Salem Books, 2021), xix.

the heart of the true gospel. CRT also divides the world into two politically convenient groups: the *oppressed* and the *oppressors*— rather than the *saved* and the *unsaved*.[27] Of course, only the woke can see this. Owen Strachan assesses this accurately when he says,

> This is Marx's own tool, updated and revised. There is intellectual lineage here. CRT owes its major categories to Critical Theory, which owes its major categories to Marx. Yet this combative mentality of unfair victimization was whispered long before Marx. The ultimate source of this ideology does not sound like the voice of God, but like the slithery hiss of a serpent.[28]

These demonic deceptions have also given rise to the Black Lives Matter movement that is, according to Voddie Baucham, Jr., "an openly pagan, Marxist-Leninist organization . . . an openly feminist pro-LGBTQIA+ organization . . . (and) is openly anti-male and anti-family."[29]

The church is in desperate need of men who are bold and discerning—men who can also help believers obey Paul's exhortation recorded in Colossians 2:8.

The warrior preacher will be quick to identify these deceptions and skillfully wield his sword to defend against them, "for the weapons of our warfare are not of the flesh, but divinely powerful for the destruction of fortresses" (2 Cor. 10:4). The church is in desperate need of men who are bold and discerning—men who can also help believers obey Paul's exhortation recorded in Colossians 2:8: "See to it that no one takes you captive through philosophy and empty deception, according to the tradition of men, according to the elementary principles of the world, rather than according to Christ."

Needless to say, this kind of skilled biblical swordsmanship requires a firm grasp of the entirety of the Word of God—from

27 Ibid. 22.

28 Ibid.

29 Voddie T. Baucham Jr., *Fault Lines: The Social Justice Movement and Evangelicalism's Looming Catastrophe* (Washington, D.C.: Salem Books, 2021), 218-20.

Genesis to Revelation and everything in between—and not just pet passages. Like a Green Beret, the warrior preacher must be intimately acquainted with every aspect of the divine weaponry God has given him. He must train hard and be disciplined so he can know which verse (or verses) to use against the varied attacks that will come his way. He must "be able both to exhort in sound doctrine and to refute those who contradict" (Titus 1:9); he must be a diligent student of Scripture, capable of accurately handling the Word of truth (2 Tim. 2:15) and able to preach and teach the whole counsel of God (Acts 20:27). Far too many pastors are like many handgun owners I know. They possess a gun but they would be unable to use it effectively in a lethal situation. The same thing is true of many in church leadership: just because they have "the sword of the Spirit, which is the word of God" doesn't mean they know how to skillfully use it—especially in these days of mounting hostility.

Coming Alongside Defensively

It has always been a great joy to be able to defend against the common lies of the enemy that target pastors. Most of the men I have known and mentored have struggled primarily with conflict in their church brought about by factious, divisive, even slanderous people. For example, a large number of churches and denominations have split over the liberal social justice gospel and LGBTQIA+ abominations that have deceived many. But this is no surprise when we understand that God has ordained to allow divisions and factions to exist in a church, "in order that those who are approved may have become evident among you" (1 Cor. 11:19).

If you are a man who has become weary and worn, afraid and alone, discouraged and depressed, I wish to stand next to you with my sword drawn on your behalf and bring the following passages to bear upon your soul. I wish to encourage you in your defense against the enemy's assault and the attacks you must endure for speaking the truth in love—which may include your dismissal.

May I remind you of what the apostle Paul endured? To be sure, like all of us, Paul had his weaknesses. Evidently he was not a very impressive man to look at or to listen to. According to his critics, "his personal presence [was] unimpressive and his speech con-

temptible" (2 Cor. 10:10). How would you like to have that reputation spread all over social media? He even admitted that he was
"unskilled in speech" (2 Cor. 11:6). Add to this all the physical sufferings he endured over the course of his ministry (2 Cor. 11:23) and
you have to wonder how he could have ever survived, much less
thrived in his service to Christ. Yet still he said, "If I have to boast,
I will boast of what pertains to my weakness" (v. 29).

Then, as if all that wasn't enough to break him, to counterbal-
ance the gravity of his trip to the third heaven, God afflicted him
with "a thorn in the flesh" that he described as "a messenger of
Satan to buffet me. . . to keep me from exalting myself" (2 Cor.
12:7). As anyone would do, he petitioned three times for the Lord
to remove the thorn, but his request was denied. But instead of
moping around aimlessly in despair like Eeyore (the lugubrious,
pessimistic, depressed little donkey in Winnie-the-Pooh), he actually found strength in his weakness! Why? Because he knew Christ
would be a more glorious compensation! He knew Christ was able
to empower him in ways he could have never imagined as a result
of his affliction. In light of this, the Lord said to him, "My grace
is sufficient for you, for power is perfected in weakness," to which
Paul responded, "Most gladly, therefore I will rather boast about
my weaknesses, that the power of Christ may dwell in me. Therefore I am well content with weaknesses, with insults, with distress-
es, with persecutions, with difficulties, for Christ's sake; for when I
am weak, then I am strong." (See 2 Cor. 12:9–10)

Furthermore, think how Paul came alongside young Timothy, who was weak physically, spiritually, and emotionally, a timid young man who, according to the wise purposes of God, was
thrust into leadership at the church at Ephesus. But Paul's epistles
to him (1 and 2 Timothy) make it clear that he struggled with *personal problems, pastoral pressures,* and the *mounting persecution
of the world*. Even a cursory perusal of Paul's exhortations to him
demonstrates the severity and scope of his weaknesses, and how
Paul took up the sword of the Spirit on Timothy's behalf to help
him defend against all the devil was throwing his way (see 1 Tim.
4:7; 12–16; 6:11–14; 2 Tim. 1:6–8, 12–14; 2:1–4; 15–16; 4:1–2, 5).

Not one of us is able on our own to maintain the necessary
strength of character to be unwavering in our faith, uncompromis-

ing in our witness for Christ, and therefore able to joyfully and effectively serve Christ regardless of our circumstances. Recognizing this of himself, Paul declared, "Who is sufficient for these things?" (2 Cor. 2:16)—a question he had already answered in 1 Corinthians 15:10: "But by the grace of God I am what I am, and His grace toward me did not prove vain; but I labored even more than all of them, yet not I, but the grace of God with me." The mystery of divine empowerment for all who will humbly yield themselves to God's Word and Spirit was so overwhelming that it drove Paul to his knees in humility and supplication for the saints saying,

> For this reason I bow my knees before the Father, from whom every family in heaven and on earth derives its name, that He would grant you, according to the riches of His glory, to be strengthened with power through His Spirit in the inner man, so that Christ may dwell in your hearts through faith; and that you, being rooted and grounded in love, may be able to comprehend with all the saints what is the breadth and length and height and depth, and to know the love of Christ which surpasses knowledge, that you may be filled up to all the fullness of God. Now to Him who is able to do far more abundantly beyond all that we ask or think, according to the power that works within us, to Him be the glory in the church and in Christ Jesus to all generations forever and ever. Amen.
> (Eph. 3:14–19)

Offensive Swordsmanship

The supernatural offensive capability of "the sword of the Spirit, which is the word of God" (Eph. 6:17), can be seen most visibly when advancing upon enemy territory through the preaching of the gospel. It is truly "the power of God unto salvation" (Rom. 1:13). Although Satan, along with his demonic horde, continues to conduct guerilla warfare campaigns to deceive and enslave men and women in his kingdom of darkness, he is no match against the Ruler of heaven and earth who has promised to build His church (Matt. 16:18). Mankind's only hope is in God's redeeming grace set forth in Scripture, "For He rescued us from the domain of darkness, and transferred us to the kingdom of His beloved Son, in whom we have redemption, the forgiveness of sins" (Col. 1:13–14); causing us to turn "from darkness to light and from the dominion of Satan to God" (Acts 26:18). And it is up to the warrior preacher to make it clear that God justifies the ungodly and brings sinners into an eternal and living union with Him. He must plead for the Spirit to help him use his sword so effectively that lost men and women will understand clearly that "Christ also died for sins once for all, the just for the unjust, so that He might bring us to God, having been put to death in the flesh, but made alive in the spirit" (1 Peter 3:18).

> Today the church is under siege. Cultural Marxism, the gross immorality of the LGBTQIA+ movement, the insane ideologies of the transgender movement, the acceptance of the brutal murders of unborn and supposedly inconvenient children, the heretical Social Justice and Prosperity gospels, and the Christless Christianity that dominates evangelicalism are invading it.

Today the church is under siege. Cultural Marxism, the gross immorality of the LGBTQIA+ movement, the insane ideologies of the transgender movement, the acceptance of the brutal murders of unborn and supposedly inconvenient children, the heretical Social Justice and Prosperity gospels, and the Christless Christianity that dominates evangelicalism are invading it. This is all part of Satan's strategy to thwart the redemptive purposes of God. But thankfully we are not powerless in the battle, "For though we walk in the flesh, we do not war according to the flesh, for the weapons of our warfare are not of the flesh, but divinely powerful for the destruction of fortresses. We are destroying speculations and every lofty thing raised up against the knowledge of God, and we are taking every thought captive to the obedience of Christ" (2 Cor. 10:3–5).

What a marvel it is to see flawed logic and demonic fabrications yield to divine revelation and exhortation. By the power of the Spirit through His Word, we have the supernatural capability to blast through the most fortified prejudices and the most compelling deceptions. By His power, the most hardened sinners can understand and embrace the transforming gospel of God. So we must never underestimate the power of the Word of God.

In Psalm 19, David uses six names to describe God's Word along with six corresponding characteristics and benefits:

> The law of the LORD is perfect, restoring the soul;
> The testimony of the LORD is sure, making wise the simple.
> The precepts of the LORD are right, rejoicing the heart;
> The commandment of the LORD is pure, enlightening the eyes.
> The fear of the LORD is clean, enduring forever;
> The judgments of the LORD are true; they are righteous altogether.
> (vv. 7–9)

No wonder he would go on to describe the incomparable value of God's special revelation by saying, "They are more desirable than gold, yes, than much fine gold; sweeter also than honey and the drippings of the honeycomb. Moreover, by them Your servant is warned; In keeping them there is great reward" (vv. 10–11).

Coming Alongside Offensively

It is not at all uncommon for pastors to feel that their ministry is a failure. Shepherding is hard. Evangelism is harder. Sometimes we can feel like giving up. I often think about how Isaiah must have felt after he eagerly replied to the Lord's request for a missionary volunteer by saying, "Here am I! Send me" (Isa. 6:8). Instead of the Lord responding with, "Great! Your ministry will be fun and exciting," He told him that the vast majority of those who heard his preaching would reject God! Only a faithful remnant would hear and believe (vv. 9–13). In many ways, I can identify with this personally. Perhaps you can, too. If so, may I encourage you to press on, as Isaiah did, and as countless others have done throughout redemptive history. I must tell you what I have had to tell myself from time to time:

> Okay, it's time to cowboy up, buttercup! The pity party is over, and it is dishonoring to God! His plan is always perfect, and whatever He does is good and just. So get your thumb out of your mouth, stop your whining, get off the couch,

put on your big-boy pants along with your armor, pick up your sword, and get back in the fight. The church needs a warrior, not another wimp. After all, the victory has already been won! We are more than conquerors in Christ Jesus, and He has promised to build His church, come what may. As a steward I am to be found *faithful*, not *successful*. So get back to striving according to the power that works within me for I can do all things through Christ who strengthens me!

Like Timothy, we can all have our confidence shaken. And like Timothy, we need to heed Paul's strong exhortation to him: "I solemnly charge you. . . preach the word; be ready in season and out of season; reprove, rebuke, exhort, with great patience and instruction" (4:1–2). This is another way of saying, "[Take] up . . . the sword of the Spirit, which is the word of God" (Eph. 6:17). We must trust God to unleash His power through our ministry according to His plan and purpose. As counterintuitive as it may seem in our post-Christian culture that resents truth and craves subjective relativism, we must never retreat from preaching the gospel in all its fullness and power. We must be like Paul, who reminded the saints whom God had saved out of the exceedingly wicked culture of Corinth:

> For I determined to know nothing among you except Jesus Christ, and Him crucified. I was with you in weakness and in fear and in much trembling, and my message and my preaching were not in persuasive words of wisdom, but in demonstration of the Spirit and of power, so that your faith would not rest on the wisdom of men, but on the power of God.
> (1 Cor. 2:2–5)

Charles Spurgeon adds this helpful insight: "I have my own opinion that there is no such thing as preaching Christ and Him crucified, unless we preach what nowadays is called Calvinism. It is a nickname to call it Calvinism; Calvinism is the gospel, and nothing else."[30] I would wholeheartedly agree. A robust, Reformed soteriology that extols the doctrines of grace must never be compromised; to do so is to be ashamed of the gospel.

---

30 Charles Spurgeon, *The Essential Works of Charles Spurgeon* (Barbour Publishing, 2009), 64.

And when our preaching is based upon the authority of the Word, we can share Paul's testimony who, after giving thanks to God for the saints at Thessalonica (1 Thess. 1:2), said this: "Knowing, brethren beloved by God, His choice of you; for our gospel did not come to you in word only, but also in power and in the Holy Spirit and with full conviction" (vv. 4–5). He's saying, "We know you were chosen by God because our gospel did not come to you as some ordinary discourse; it had a supernatural force behind it that changed your very nature! It came 'in power and in the Holy Spirit and with full conviction.'" This is so fascinating, and certainly true! Those faithful missionaries could see the immediate effect of the Spirit's power and presence in *their* hearts—the ones who spoke the word (not a reference to the Thessalonians who heard it).

We must trust God to unleash His power through our ministry according to His plan and purpose.

This kind of Spirit-empowered gospel preaching is desperately lacking in churches today. We don't need men who are clever and cool, fashionable and funny, or who want to have a conversation to find common ground in order to be culturally acceptable. We need men who absolutely know ("with full conviction") that their message is, indeed, the Word of God that will either save and sanctify or judge and sentence. Men who can fully identify with what God told Jeremiah when He declared, "Is not My word like fire? . . . and like a hammer which shatters a rock?" (Jer. 23:29). These are the faithful warriors who will bear spiritual fruit in their ministry; their lives will match their message, and their churches will persevere in the faith.

While they may be few and often serve in obscurity, these are the Green Berets of the church militant—men of exceptional courage, dedication, and training who are well acquainted with the enemy and skilled in their use of "the sword of the Spirit." But they also, know that because "the god of this world has blinded the minds of the unbelieving so that they might not see the light of the gospel of the glory of Christ" (2 Cor. 4:4), God's Word alone is "divinely powerful for the destruction of fortresses . . . destroying speculations and every lofty thing raised up against the knowledge of God" (2 Cor. 10:4–5).

Without hesitation these men deploy the most powerful weapon on earth, the instrument God uses to cause a sinner to desire rescue from the bondage of sin and the kingdom of darkness—the only means by which God delivers men from Satan and brings them to God (2 Tim. 3:15).

Despite the worldly appetites of typical evangelicals and the marketing ethos of churches that cater to them, faithful pastors called and gifted by God will stand in stark contrast and heed the command to

> . . . preach the word; be ready in season and out of season; reprove, rebuke, exhort, with great patience and instruction. For the time will come when they will not endure sound doctrine; but wanting to have their ears tickled, they will accumulate for themselves teachers in accordance to their own desires, and will turn away their ears from the truth and will turn aside to myths. But you, be sober in all things, endure hardship, do the work of an evangelist, fulfill your ministry. (2 Tim. 4:2–5)

Unfortunately, most preachers falsely believe they are in compliance with this command when in truth they are not—which is exactly what the enemy would have them believe.

Prayer in the Spirit

Having exhorted the believer "to be strong in the Lord and in the strength of His might" (Eph. 6:10) through the use of the armor and the sword He has provided, the apostle closes this section with one final exhortation that is of utmost importance. If we expect God to aid us in our battle, we must "pray at all times in the Spirit" (v. 18). A man lax in prayer operates on his own strength and will inevitably suffer defeat. Being in constant communion with our divine General is foundational to combat effectiveness. Armor is useless on a wimpy warrior too weak to wield his sword and too proud to admit it. The powers of darkness will quickly overcome a man who sees no need to be dependent on God in prayer. D. Martyn Lloyd-Jones summarized this crucial priority this way:

The armour which is provided for us by God cannot be used except in fellowship and communion with God. The armour God provides for us must never be thought of mechanically, still less magically. The danger, the temptation, is to feel that as long as we put on this armour there is no more to be done; all is well, the armour will in and of itself protect us, and do so mechanically. So having put it on, we can relax, and put watching aside. But that is the exact opposite of the true position, says the Apostle; to think in that way means that you are already defeated. The armour, and the spiritual application of it must always be conceived of in a vital and in a living manner. Every single piece, excellent though it is in itself, will not suffice us, and will not avail us, unless always and at all times we are in a living relationship to God and receiving strength and power from Him.[31]

Paul is careful to offer clear details regarding the nature of our prayer life through the use of four "alls": "With *all* prayer and petition pray at *all* times in the Spirit, and with this in view, be on the alert with *all* perseverance and petition for *all* the saints" (Eph. 6:18; emphasis mine).

"WITH ALL PRAYER AND PETITION" refers to the warrior's continual communion with God; his perpetual and uninterrupted fellowship with God; his conscious awareness of God's soul-empowering presence; his humble dependency upon the Most High demonstrated by his passionate yearnings for help in specific areas of need. This is in keeping with Jesus' exhortation: "Keep on the alert at all times, praying in order that you may have strength to escape all these things that are about to take place" (Luke 21:36).

To "PRAY AT ALL TIMES IN THE SPIRIT" is to pray consistently with the Word and will of the Holy Spirit who guides us into all truth, puts the glory of Christ on display, and empowers us to serve Him faithfully. It is to be so "filled with the Spirit" (5:8) that our

---

31 D. Martyn Lloyd-Jones, *The Christian Soldier: An Exposition of Ephesians 6:10-20* (Grand Rapids, Michigan: Baker Books, 1977), 339.

prayers are in harmony with His. Greater yet, it is to pray with the astounding apprehension that the Holy Spirit actually prays *for* us and *with* us, for it is He who "helps our weakness; for we do not know how to pray as we should, but the Spirit Himself intercedes for us with groanings too deep for words; and He who searches the hearts knows what the mind of the Spirit is, because He intercedes for the saints according to the will of God" (Rom. 8:26–27).

To "BE ON THE ALERT WITH ALL PERSEVERANCE" is to pray for strength to endure in the hour of trial, as Jesus commanded His disciples in Gethsemane: "Keep watching and praying that you may not enter into temptation; the spirit is willing, but the flesh is weak" (Matt. 26:41). It is to plead for protection and discernment in our ongoing struggle against the forces of darkness so we will not succumb to discouragement and doubt, or, worse yet, surrender to the flesh's proclivity to spiritual lethargy and complacency.

To "PETITION FOR ALL THE SAINTS" is to pray for the spiritual welfare of other believers who are also under siege and are in great need of the Lord's strength and protection; that they also might wear the armor, take up the sword, and not yield ground to the enemy of their souls. For indeed, we are all members of the body of Christ, and when one suffers, we all suffer. We must be like Samuel who said, "Far be it from me that I should sin against the LORD by ceasing to pray for you" (1 Sam. 12:23).

Praying for Boldness in Battle

Despite the horrific conditions of being incarcerated in a Roman prison, Paul closes this section not by soliciting prayer for his physical needs, but for spiritual boldness and strength to fight on for the sake of the King and His kingdom. He said, "And pray on my behalf, that utterance may be given to me in the opening of my mouth, to make known with boldness the mystery of the gospel, for which I am an ambassador in chains; that in proclaiming it I may speak boldly, as I ought to speak" (Eph. 6:19–20). Can there be any greater illustration of a warrior preacher than this?

If it is our heart's desire to be faithful in ministry, we must be serious about praying "in the Spirit." Christ is our supreme example in this regard. He was reliant on the Spirit in all things, as Isaiah predicted (Isa. 11:2; 42:2; 61:1). He was dependent upon the Holy Spirit in His virgin conception and birth (Luke 1:35), His baptism (Luke 3:22), His temptation in the wilderness (Luke 4:1), His preaching (Luke 4:14), His crucifixion (Heb 9:14), and His resurrection (Rom 1:4); and it was the Holy Spirit who led Him in ministry (Acts 1:2).

In the humiliation of His incarnation until He went to the cross, our Lord Jesus Christ was in uninterrupted communion with the Father and the Spirit, utterly dependent upon Them to enable His human nature to be victorious over the temptations of sin and Satan, endure the cross, and be raised from the dead. Are we not even more dependent and in more need of divine enablement?

Paul closes this section not by soliciting prayer for his physical needs, but for spiritual boldness and strength to fight on for the sake of the King and His kingdom.

The warrior preacher knows that prayer calls forth the Spirit to help him understand and proclaim the unsearchable riches of Christ despite the world's fierce opposition. It is the Spirit who keeps him focused on Christ, as Christ Himself has promised: "When the Helper comes, whom I will send to you from the Father, that is the Spirit of truth who proceeds from the Father, He will testify about Me" (John 15:26). It is the illuminating power of the Spirit that helps the exegete bow before the authority of Scripture, interpret it with precision, and protect his heart from wandering off in clever but errant directions that fuel his pride and distort the truth; and it is the Spirit who will cause him to commit himself completely to what God has said in faithful obedience.

Only then will his preaching be done in the power of the Spirit. Only then will his feeble words become irresistible invitations to the called of God. Only then will the spiritually dead be raised to spiritual life. And only then will the great storehouse of divine truth be opened up and freely distributed. It is through disciplined, fervent, persistent prayer that the most cowardly and inept among us can become courageous, skilled, invincible warriors of Christ, zealous for His glory. This, my friend, is why we pray "in the Spirit," and why the Spirit helps us pray as we should.

The great Scottish warrior preacher and Reformed theologian, John Knox (1514–1572), put it this way:

> Without the Spirit of God supporting our infirmities (mightily making intercession for us with unceasing groans which can not be expressed with the tongue), there is no hope that we can desire anything according to God's will. I do not mean that the Holy Ghost mourns or prays, but that He stirs up our minds, giving unto us a desire or boldness to pray, and causes us to mourn when we are extracted or pulled from it. No strength of man suffices to conceive such things, nor is able to do so by itself. But in this matter it is plain that such as do not understand what they pray, or do not expound or declare the desire of their hearts clearly in God's presence—and in time of prayer do not expel vain cogitations from their minds as far as they can—profit nothing in prayer.[32]

Is it any wonder the vicious Roman Catholic, Mary, Queen of Scots (1542–1587), is reported to have said the following words? "I fear the prayers of John Knox more than all the assembled armies of Europe."

Challenge

I challenge every reader—especially pastors and church leaders—to prayerfully, honestly, and earnestly examine your life and ministry under the inescapable light of these biblical truths: "For the word of God is living and active and sharper than any two-edged sword, and piercing as far as the division of soul and spirit, of both joints and marrow, and able to judge the thoughts and intentions of the heart" (Heb. 4:12).

32   John Knox, *A Treatise on Prayer,* (© Reformation Press, 2004), http://www.reformationpress. co.uk/pdfs/knox_prayer.pdf

Chapter 3 Questions

1. Does your preaching focus primarily on man and his felt needs or God and His glory?

2. Are you more concerned about pleasing man in your preaching than you are in pleasing God?

3. Would unbiased listeners describe your preaching as a clear and compelling exposition and application of the Word of God that is so convicting, edifying, and encouraging that they knew they had been in the presence of the Most High and were forever changed by what they heard? If not, how would they describe your preaching?

4. Would you be able to extemporaneously explain the various soteriological concepts that define the biblical doctrine of salvation (listed in the chapter) and do they animate your heart to praise?

5. Are those you shepherd able to explain the biblical doctrines of salvation and do these things animate their hearts to praise?

6. Are you so committed to the authority and supremacy of Scripture that you have an unwavering commitment to sound hermeneutical principles in order to determine the single, God-intended meaning of a text?

7. Do you use Scripture to expose and destroy the satanically inspired woke ideologies of theological and political liberalism that are antithetical to the biblical gospel?

8. Are you a man devoted to disciplined, fervent, persistent prayer in your preparation and preaching of the Word, in such a way that you might be a bold, skilled, invincible warrior of Christ?

4

The Warrior's Mindset

Suffer hardship with me as a good soldier of Christ Jesus.
(2 Timothy 2:3)

A soldier of Jesus Christ acknowledges the divine Redeemer as his King, and confesses His sole and undivided sovereignty in the spiritual kingdom. He abhors Antichrist in all its forms, and every principle that opposes itself to the reign of the beloved Prince of Peace. Jesus is to him both Lord and God. The day when he enlisted, he did, as it were, put his finger *into the print of the nails,* and said with Thomas, "My Lord and my God." This was his enlistment declaration, and he remains true to it. "Christ is all," is his motto, and to win all men to obedience to Immanuel is his lifework! Till he sheathes his sword in the last victory, the crucified is sole monarch of his soul; for Him he lives, for Him he would even dare to die! He has entered into solemn league and covenant to maintain against all comers that Jesus Christ is Lord to the glory of God the Father.

CHARLES HADDON SPURGEON[33]

---

33 Charles Haddon Spurgeon, Sermon #938, "A Good Soldier of Jesus Christ," Metropolitan Tabernacle Pulpit 1, (www.spurgeon.org).

The idea of being a soldier engaged in conflict is foreign to most pastors and church leaders. It smacks of pugilism, the opposite of turning the other cheek. The act of aggressively resisting false teachers and exposing damning doctrine is considered unchristian in many evangelical circles—especially if you name names. The prized pastoral persona of our day can be summarized in a single word: *genteel*. The Cambridge Dictionary definition is: "very polite, graceful, calm and gentle, correct in manner, or trying to be polite and correct in order to appear to be of a high social class." While some of these characteristics are virtuous, appropriate, even biblical, as in the case of the apostle who "proved to be gentle among [the Thessalonians], as a nursing mother tenderly cares for her own children" (1 Thess. 2:7), there are times when, like Paul, we must "admonish the unruly" (5:14), name names (1 Tim. 1:20), oppose colleagues to the face (Gal. 2:20), publicly expose heresy (3:1–5), publicly rebuke bickering church members (Phil. 4:2), reject factious men (Titus 2:10–11), and boldly preach the Word to those who reject it (2 Tim. 4:1–5). Then, like Paul, we can say, "I have fought the good fight" (2 Tim. 4:7).

When the wolves come after the sheep, all gentility must be abandoned. It's time to go to war.

When the wolves come after the sheep, all gentility must be abandoned. It's time to go to war. It is often said there are three kinds of people in the world: *sheep, wolves,* and *sheepdogs.* We need more sheepdogs (shepherds) protecting the church, because the wolves are decimating the sheep! Worse yet, many shepherds are wolves in sheep's clothing that only appear to care for the sheep—and convincingly so. But in reality, they only care for themselves. Many are genteel, narcissistic cowards; others are vicious wolves that prey upon gullible and ignorant sheep for their own advantages. In both cases, those who follow them are vulnerable to the schemes of the devil that are so deceptive and so nefarious that they must be confronted with the same force a man would exert to protect his family against a violent aggressor. The enemy has entered our homes and churches, and is now carrying away our children. It's time to fight. And this requires a warrior's mindset— one of fearless devotion to the truth and the glory of Christ.

Before I address the necessary boldness of a warrior preacher, I wish to underscore the severity and scope of the clandestine attacks on society and the church that warrant such fortitude. Without a firm grasp of the specific strategies our enemy is using and the deadly effects they are having upon our families and evangelicalism at large, a man will see no need to adopt a warrior spirit. Gentility must give way to Spirit-empowered boldness (Eph. 6:19). Bottom line, I want to show church leaders what we are really up against in hopes that they will become "fighting mad" for the glory of Christ and the protection of all who are being duped by the enemy of our souls who operates in our culture.

The Marxist Invasion into the Church

"These are the times that try men's souls." This was the opening line of Thomas Paine's pamphlet, *The American Crisis* that George Washington ordered to be read aloud to embolden his demoralized troops on December 23, 1776, three days before they crossed the Delaware. Emboldened and inspired, they defeated the Hessian Army at Trenton and changed the course of the American Revolution. The times in which we live also "try men's souls." Like Washington and his desperate army who were one battle away from final defeat, the majority of the citizens of our great republic are equally demoralized and distressed, convinced our country is going in the wrong direction—and understandably so.

In countless casual encounters I have had with ordinary people during the course of my daily activities, the conversation almost inevitably turns to the moral and economic freefall we are witnessing in our country. This is a testimony to the fact that even the unregenerate "who do not have the Law do instinctively the things of the Law, these, not having the Law, are a law to themselves, in that they show the work of the Law written in their hearts, their conscience bearing witness and their thoughts alternately accusing or else defending them" (Rom. 2:14–15). A paraphrase of what I commonly hear is this: "I cannot believe what is happening in our country; we are losing our freedoms; and it's all happening so fast! It's insane. It's deliberate. It's frightening. It's infuriating. It's evil. Something has to be done!"

Sad to say, for most, hope is only found in political change rather than the gospel, which most do not understand or embrace. This is truly remarkable considering how politicians are the cause of our problems, not the solution; and to make matters worse, they have a stranglehold on the electoral process that a growing number of Americans no longer trust. The failed policies and corruption of progressive cultural Marxists and their allies in the media have deepened the ideological divide to a point where all civility is gone. *Ad hominem* attacks have replaced rational dialogue and reasoned discourse. Equally disturbing is how many conservatives focus on the material (economic) failures of socialism rather than their far more nefarious goal of eradicating all religion through militant atheism—the goal of *cultural* Marxism. Gullible Christians of all political stripes, especially within the clergy, are blissfully ignorant of Marx's goal of an atheist utopia that Satan continues to advance in various ways around the globe, including the United States of America.

> *Gullible Christians of all political stripes, especially within the clergy, are blissfully ignorant of Marx's goal of an atheist utopia that Satan continues to advance in various ways around the globe.*

In his internationally bestselling book, *The Madness of Crowds: Gender, Race and Identity*, Douglas Murray "investigates the great derangement of 'woke' culture and the rise of identity politics" especially as they relate to "the Marxist foundations of 'wokeness,' the impact of technology and how, in an increasingly online culture, we must relearn the ability to forgive."[34] In contrast to the famous 1911 socialist poster entitled "Industrial Workers of the World" supposedly depicting the "Pyramid of the Capitalist System," Murray rightfully argues that

---

34 Douglas Murray, *The Madness of Crowds: Gender, Race and Identity* (London: Bloomsbury Continuum, 2019), from the back cover.

111

. . . today a version of this old image has made its way to the centre of the social justice ideology. Just one of the things that suggest the Marxist foundations of this new system is the fact that capitalism is still at the top of the pyramid of oppression and exploitation. But the other top tiers of this hierarchy pyramid are inhabited by different types of people. At the top of the hierarchy are people who are white, male and heterosexual. They do not need to be rich, but matters are made worse if they are. Beneath these tyrannical male overlords are all the minorities: most noticeably the gays, anyone who isn't white, people who are women and also people who are trans. These individuals are kept down, oppressed, sidelined and otherwise made insignificant by the white, patriarchal, heterosexual, 'cis' system. Just as Marxism was meant to free the labourer and share the wealth around, so in this new version of an old claim, the power of the patriarchal white males must be taken away and shared around more fairly with the relevant minority groups.[35]

This satanic ideology is as ingenious as it is deadly. Its seduction is rooted in the almost universal social agreement that all people must be treated justly and loved for who they are or who they want to be. Anyone opposed to the axiomatic premise of social justice and the identity politics it fuels is automatically labeled a bigot, or worse. Biblical Christianity is therefore placed squarely in the crosshairs. Yet most Christians are oblivious to the danger. Like the proverbial frog in the kettle, they smile and whistle *Jesus Loves Me* while the water of persecution is heating up.

In Paul Kengor's classic work, *The Devil and Karl Marx*, he documents how "[Marx] envisioned a 'new morality' without God. The path to utopia was a classless albeit godless society. The 'classless society'—which would be a 'workers' paradise—would, said Marx, 'make its own history! It is a leap from slavery into freedom; from darkness into light.'"[36] Kengor goes on to say, "Belief in God stood

---

35 Ibid., 51-2.

36 Paul Kengor, *The Devil and Karl Marx: Communism's Long March of Death, Deception, and Infiltration* (Gastonia, NC: TAN Books, 2020), 28.

in the way of the totalitarian desire to transform human nature. God was a competitor to communist control of the body, mind, and spirit of man that Marx and Lenin wanted to redefine in their image."[37]

It should be no surprise that Marx—who was satanic to the very core—wanted to *fundamentally change human nature*! Naturally, Satan, the master counterfeiter, wants his own version of biblical *regeneration* (which makes man a new creature in Christ [2 Cor. 5:17]). Instead, Satan strives to make men in his image. That American citizens—especially evangelical Christians—cannot see the evils of Marxism invading our country is a testament to the supernatural forces behind it. The left's never-ending obsession with social justice and redeeming what they consider to be marginalized people groups—no matter how statistically rare they might be, like transgenders that make up less than one percent of the population—should be a clue that something nefarious is at play. Kengor explains the left's relentless search for victims—a baffling phenomenon that can only be explained by the invasion of *cultural* Marxism.

> That American citizens—especially evangelical Christians— cannot see the evils of Marxism invading our country is a testament to the supernatural forces behind it.

In a crucial respect, classical Marxism and cultural Marxism will always bear an essential, enduring commonality— one that explains a lot about today's modern left. Both classical Marxists and cultural Marxists see history as a series of struggles that divide the world into hostile/antagonistic groups of oppressors and the oppressed. Both seek out victim groups as the anointed group that will also serve as society's redeemer group. The victim group becomes the agent for emancipation in ushering in the new and better world. The Marxist must always, then, be on the search for the newest victim class which, in turn, must always be made aware of its victimization. Its "consciousness" must be raised.

---

37 Ibid., 108

In classical Marxism, this was simple: the victim group was identified by class/economics. It was the proletariat. It was the factory worker. In cultural Marxism, this has not been so simple, because the culture is always changing: the victim group is constantly being searched for anew by the cultural Marxist. The group one year might be women, the next year African Americans, the next year another group. Today, there's a hard push by cultural Marxists to tap the "LGBTQIA-plus" (People's World frequently uses that expansive label) movement as the championed victim group: lesbians, gays, bisexuals, transgenders, "queer" persons, "intersexuals," "asexuals," and on and on. Thus, a leading cultural Marxist like Angela Davis . . . could stand at the January 2017 Women's March in Washington, DC before a sea of oblivious girls wearing pink hats modeled after their genitalia and recite a litany of politically correct grievances. In her casting about for victim groups, the former Communist Bloc cheerleader hailed the transgendered Chelsea Manning, "trans women of color," "our flora and fauna," and "intersectional feminism," and denounced "white male hetero-patriarch," misogyny, Islamophobia, and capitalist exploitation. Victims, victims, victims.[38]

Even as God has His standard of righteousness, Satan has his standard of unrighteousness, and like God he will punish those who violate his godless law. But this is nothing new.

Again, Satan is the consummate counterfeiter. Even as God has His standard of *righteousness*, Satan has his standard of *unrighteousness*, and like God he will punish those who violate his godless law. But this is nothing new. The first-century Pharisees were much like the progressives of our day. They were the gatekeepers of religious Judaism, the politically elite know-it-alls of Israel, the religiously correct "fact checkers," a first-century version of cancel culture, and they saw Jesus as a threat to their po-

---

38 Ibid., 390

litical power. You might say they were the woke of Judaism that supposedly could see what others could not see.

The Pharisees' irrational antagonism toward Jesus knew no bounds. Despite His ability to read their minds (Mark 2:8; John 2:24) and perform miraculous public healings that amazed the crowds, even cast out demons and raise the dead, the Pharisees still insisted He was a fraud and a blasphemer worthy of death. They hounded Him like a pack of hyenas, trying "to catch Him in something He might say" (Luke 11:54; *cf.* John 12:37). They wanted to entrap and discredit Jesus; get Him to do or say something that violated either Jewish law or Roman law so they could indict Him for blasphemy or treason and get rid of Him once and for all (which they eventually did).

But this is the same strategy Satan uses today to eradicate authentic, biblical Christianity. The plan is simple: *legalize unrighteousness and criminalize righteousness, then prosecute those who refuse to obey.* This has been (and still is) the priority of cultural Marxism. And this is why warrior preachers must rise to the challenge. They must expose these diabolical tactics through the penetrating light of biblical truth that is "able to judge the thoughts and intentions of the heart. . . [for] there is no creature hidden from His sight, but all things are open and laid bare to the eyes of Him with whom we have to do" (Heb. 4:12–13). Whether it was the Pharisees in the first century, the Roman Catholic church during the sixteenth-century Protestant Reformation in Europe, or the progressive Democratic cultural Marxist in the twenty-first century, Satan employs a similar pattern to thwart the purposes of God. This can be summarized by eight sequential terms that naturally build upon each other:

1. CRITICIZE: find fault with the oppressor group and criticize its members relentlessly.

2. SCANDALIZE: falsely accuse the oppressor group to build a case against its members through the manufactured outrage of cancel culture.

3. DEHUMANIZE: demean the oppressor group members in terms so horrific they should no longer be considered human and thus deserving of inhumane treatment.

4. PROPAGANDIZE: silence the dissent of reasonable voices by indoctrinating the public with lies that appeal to their emotion.

5. ORGANIZE: mobilize disenfranchised individuals into a collective groupthink that are rabidly committed to fundamentally transforming the current social structure and eliminating natural moral principles held by the oppressor group.

6. LEGISLATE: enact laws the oppressor group will refuse to obey, then use coercive control to force its members to comply.

7. INCARCERATE: imprison those who violate the laws that were structured to entrap the oppressor group and free the oppressed group.

8. ERADICATE: kill them (e.g., Communist countries killed approximately 140 million people in the twentieth century[39]).

These are the driving forces behind the cultural Marxist mob mentality that continues to gain strength in our society, a terrifying Zeitgeist hidden from the average evangelical—a defining spirit that has already replaced moral (biblical) absolutes with the kind of moral relativism inherent in totalitarianism. These diabolical ideologies are so winsome to the naïve and ignorant that an increasing number of Millennials actually prefer communism and socialism over capitalism. Kengor writes,

> In retrospect, a turning point came in 2011, when a major study by Pew Research Center found that 49 percent of Americans aged eighteen to twenty-nine have a positive view of socialism, exceeding the 43 percent with a positive view of capitalism. Three years later, in 2014, a survey by *Reason Magazine* and the Rupe Foundation did a deeper dive. It found that 53 percent of those aged eighteen to twenty-nine view socialism favorably. Not long after that survey, Gallup turned up a gem, learning that 69 percent of Millennials said they would be willing to vote for a social-

---

39 Paul Kengor, *The Devil and Karl Marx: Communism's Long March of Death, Deception, and Infiltration* (Gastonia, NC: TAN Books, 2020), xviii.

ist as president of the United States of America—a country founded on the antithesis of socialist principles. They did just that in 2016, contributing mightily to Bernie Sanders' twelve million votes in the Democratic Primary. . . the latest survey by Victims of Communism Memorial Foundation (conducted by YouGov), released in November 2019, shows that 36 percent of Millennials say they approve of communism, and 22 percent believe "society would be better if all private property was abolished."[40]

With such alarming trends, you would think every pastor and church leader in America would be sounding the alarm. Instead, *the sound of silence is deafening.* We are moving toward a totalitarian state that cannot co-exist with biblical Christianity. But like the protestant churches in Germany that tried to stay neutral toward Hitler's National Socialism in the 1930s, evangelicals—including many clergymen—are ashamed of the gospel and refuse to fight lies with truth. Many today are no different than most of the German Protestants who believed the Nazi propaganda poster from 1933 with Luther's picture superimposed over a swastika that read: "Hitler's fight and Luther's teaching are the best defense for the German people."[41] Nothing could have been further from the truth.

Mass Formation

The social and psychological dynamics for any kind of totalitarian movement (like cultural Marxism) to form and advance upon its manufactured enemy requires what secularists call *mass formation.* In his book *The Psychology of Totalitarianism*, Mattias Desmet defines *mass formation* as "a kind of group hypnosis that destroys individuals' ethical self-awareness and robs them of their ability to think critically. This process is insidious in nature; populations fall prey to it unsuspectingly."[42] He argues that this destructive social phenomenon is now the hallmark of the global pan-

40   Ibid., 447.

41   https://www.facinghistory.org/holocaust-and-human-behavior/chapter-5/protestant-church-es-and-nazi-state

42   Mattias Desmet, *The Psychology of Totalitarianism* (London: Chelsea Green Publishing, 2022), 2.

demic where "humanity is being forcibly, unconsciously led into a reality of technocratic totalitarianism, which aggressively excludes alternative views and relies on destructive groupthink, vilifying non-conformist thought as 'dissident.'"[43] According to Desmet, *mass formation* explains the

> psychological characteristics of a totalitarian population: the willingness of the individuals to blindly sacrifice their personal interests in favor of the collective, radical intolerance of dissident voices, a paranoid informant mentality that allow government to penetrate the very heart of private life, the curious susceptibility to absurd pseudo-scientific indoctrination and propaganda, the blind following of narrow logic that transcends all ethical boundaries (making totalitarianism incompatible with religion), the loss of diversity and creativity (making totalitarianism the enemy of art and culture), and intrinsic self-destructiveness (which ensures that totalitarian systems invariably annihilate themselves in the end).[44]

Desmet argues that historically four conditions in society have been present when mass formation has given rise to totalitarian regimes (like Nazism and Stalinism); and he makes a compelling case that these same conditions are present now in our society. He states, "The first condition is generalized loneliness, social isolation, and lack of social bonds among the population." This leads to the second condition: "a lack of meaning in life"; which produces a third condition: "a widespread presence of free-floating anxiety and psychological unease within a population." Together these dynamics result in a final condition: "frustration and aggression."[45] He explains how these conditions lead to mass formation:

> The catalyst for mass formation is a suggestion in the public sphere. If, under the aforementioned circumstances, a suggestive story is spread through the mass media that indicates an object of anxiety—for example, the aristocracy

---

43 Ibid., jacket.

44 Ibid., 90-91.

45 Ibid., 94-96.

under Stalinism, the Jews under Nazism, the virus, and, later, the anti-vaxxers during the coronavirus crisis—and at the same time offers a strategy to deal with that object of anxiety, there is a real chance that all the free-flowing anxiety will attach itself to that object and there will be broad social support for the implementation of the strategy to control that object of anxiety. . . . Through this process, an individual pivots from a highly aversive and painful psychological state of social isolation to the maximum interconnectedness that exists among the masses. This creates a kind of intoxication, which is the actual impetus to go along with the mass-forming narrative. . . . The masses believe in the story not because it's accurate but because it creates a new social bond."[46]

Certainly these observations have merit, especially as we witness the destructive phenomena of *mass formation* in the coronavirus groupthink and the various expressions of the Marxist woke cult of progressive Democrats (and an increasing number of Republicans and Independents). For example, in the current coronavirus narrative (driven primarily by leftists in the government and the pharmaceutical industry), so-called "experts" have been so hypnotized by their ideology that some have been forced to openly admit to deliberately misleading the population. This is no surprise to fair-minded people who have studied the mounting evidence of prejudicial disregard for objective data and the subjective conclusions and assumptions relating to the crisis.[47] So indeed, the sociological and psychological construct of *mass formation* is helpful in explaining this phenomenon, but it fails to address these dynamics from a biblical perspective.

What the secularists call *mass formation* is what the Bibles describes as *mass depravity—a manifestation of the wrath of divine abandonment where God has lifted His restraining grace on a mass of depraved human beings who reject Him, allowing them to collectively voice their deceptions in the echo chamber of their rage and ultimately experience the damning consequences of their*

---

46 Ibid., 96.

47 Ibid., 53-58.

iniquities. Individually they have sown the wind, now collectively they reap the whirlwind. Beyond the coronavirus groupthink, the unspeakably vile nature of gay pride parades, the looting and arson of the Black Lives Matter racists, and the ANTIFA anarchist protests are all graphic examples of this kind of unrestrained mob depravity.

Man's arrogant rejection of God leads to God's righteous rejection of man, as Paul declares in Romans 1:28. "And just as they did not see fit to acknowledge God any longer, God gave them over to a depraved mind, to those things which are not proper." This is a state of godless corruption so severe that it renders individuals incapable of rational thought. Nevertheless, because they act as part of a collective whole, they find strength in numbers and are therefore convinced their actions are justified—the result of judicial hardening where God allows the wicked to be consumed and destroyed by the myths they embrace (2 Tim. 4:4). This is similarly stated in Titus 1:15–16: "to those who are defiled and unbelieving, nothing is pure, but both their mind and their conscience are defiled. They profess to know God, but by their deeds they deny Him, being detestable and disobedient and worthless for any good deed."

> What our culture refuses to believe is that man's problem is *spiritual*, not *psychological* or *sociolological*. Jesus made this clear when He said, "Out of the heart come evil thoughts, murders, adulteries, fornications, thefts, false witness, slanders" (Matt. 15:19).

To be sure, a secular worldview derived from the wisdom of man rather than God fails to take into consideration the diabolical schemes of the kingdom of darkness and its ability to appeal to the innate depravity of man, for indeed, "The hearts of the sons of men are full of evil, and insanity is in their hearts throughout their lives" (Eccl. 9:3). What our culture refuses to believe is that man's problem is *spiritual*, not *psychological* or *sociolological*. Jesus made this clear when He said, "Out of the heart come evil thoughts, murders, adulteries, fornications, thefts, false witness, slanders" (Matt. 15:19). Humankind is hopelessly prone to evil. Nevertheless, because of our depraved nature, we believe just the opposite. It is axiomatic for man to perceive himself as being innately *selfless*, not *selfish*, and *good*, not *evil*.

However, an honest evaluation of our own character and conduct will betray the corrupting presence and power of indwelling sin, which is proportional to our willingness to see the holiness of God. When God is small, sin is insignificant. But when we see God as He really is—the thrice-holy Lord of hosts whose glory fills the earth (Isa. 6:3)—we will respond like Isaiah and cry out, "Woe is me, for I am ruined! Because I am a man of unclean lips, and I live among a people of unclean lips; for my eyes have seen the King, the LORD of hosts" (v. 5). This is the kind of vision every man needs—a vision of God's soul-terrifying purity that contrasts the staggering ugliness of sin. This must be the bold message of the warrior preacher—a message that is tragically missing in most pulpits.

The two corresponding evils of *human depravity* and *satanic deception* are threatening the Constitutional Republic of the United States. With an irrepressible malignity, they are wreaking havoc on every institution in America and around the world, including the destruction of the nuclear family, the bedrock of society. Moreover, these two evils find friendship in groupthink where they gain strength and momentum in the echo chamber of their own deceptions and ultimately find their fullest expression in totalitarianism. This is where we are headed in America. This is what the warrior preacher is up against.

Public School Indoctrination

The dynamics of *mass formation* can also be seen in our progressive public school systems that indoctrinate children with cultural Marxist propaganda—a pernicious threat that most Christians are completely unaware of because their pastors and church leaders refuse to warn them. As Pete Hegseth states in his book, *Battle for the American Mind*, public school educators and local school boards are essentially telling parents,

> *Get with the program! White people are inherently oppressive. Gender is completely fluid. Climate change will destroy the world. And America is the ultimate source of evil in the world.* Up is down, left is right, good and evil are subjec-

tive—until an educator tells you who or what is good and evil, and then you must comply.[48]

Lenin was an economic Marxist. American Progressives are cultural Marxists. Underneath our noses, Progressives in America quietly labored to gain control over an even more powerful set of "commanding heights"—those that steer the hearts and minds of America's children. With American conservatives mostly preoccupied with defending economic freedom and military might, American Progressives knew that social control was far more powerful than economic control. As such, they set out to gain direct national control of the "commanding heights" of America's schools. A project set in motion more than one hundred years ago is today leveraged through 16,000 hours of government instruction.[49]

"Diversity, equity, and inclusion" are the centerpiece of their curriculum. Teachers demand conformity to the woke lexicon, lest the student grades take a hit. As such, it becomes their woke language. They are indoctrinated.

The goal of that indoctrination? It's not about racism, or equality, or even gender. It's about deconstructing anything and everything that reflects not just the founding principles of America, but the foundations of our families and our faith. It's about control—of thought, and behavior. To the Left, our Western Judeo-Christian roots are the problem—they must be dismantled, one theory, one word, one classroom, and one mind at a time.[50]

These are the kinds of satanic deceptions that now hold America hostage, including many in evangelicalism who have abandoned their children to the godless indoctrination of government-subsidized public schools, colleges, and universities. But this lack of

---

48   Pete Hegseth with David Goodwin, *Battle for the American Mind: Uprooting a Century of Miseducation* (New York, NY: Broadside Books, HarperCollins Publishers, 2022), 6.

49   Ibid., 27.

50   Ibid., 31.

biblical discernment in many churches should be no surprise given the popularity of evangelical pragmatism that cannot exist apart from *a rejection of biblical authority*. By appealing to the carnal whims of spiritual cadavers alienated from God, these churches primarily attract those who are Christian in name only and have no desire to exalt Christ in holiness (Rom. 12:1) and have no aptitude to understand spiritual truth (1 Cor. 2:14). As a result, they join the collective woke groupthink. Anyone in Christian leadership who refuses to confront these issues head-on has no business being in ministry.

Faithful pastors and church leaders, however, will help their people understand the cultural and political chicanery the enemy is using to destroy them, despite the shrill vilifications of those who try to drown them out. They will not only help them think *critically*, but they will also help them to think *biblically*. For this reason we are warned, "See to it that no one takes you captive through philosophy and empty deception, according to the tradition of men, according to the elementary principles of the world, rather than according to Christ" (Col. 2:8).

> Faithful pastors and church leaders, however, will help their people understand the cultural and political chicanery the enemy is using to destroy them, despite the shrill vilifications of those who try to drown them out.

Evidence that this warning has gone unheeded can be seen, for example, in the growing number of evangelicals that have now embraced the depraved immorality of the LGBTQIA+ culture, especially the transgender ideology. This is appalling! What would possess anyone who claims to follow Christ to believe children should be encouraged to explore gender options because their biological gender doesn't match their perceived identity? Jesus made it clear that those who believe such absurdities have no basis to claim genuine saving faith (Luke 6:45–46; 1 Cor. 6:9–10). *Those who struggle with identity need the gospel where they can find their identity in the soul-satisfying joy of being united with Christ, the Lover of their soul.* Irreversible physical mutilation and chemical castration to pretend to be what one can never be—the opposite gender—is child abuse, plain and simple!

"Trans kids" (as they are often called) are primarily young adolescents who struggle to fit in with their peers, who are uncomfortable with their biological gender, who are depressed, confused, and often abused. Because of their innate depravity and the deceptive voices around them, they are misled into believing they could find happiness and acceptance if they were the opposite sex. As a result, they create their own subjective identity regardless of biology, their own subjective sense of self that others must celebrate. Defying objective science and reality itself, they even choose their own pronouns and demand others either join their delusion or incur the wrath of cancel culture for inflicting emotional violence upon them. Any attempt to dialogue with the so-called experts in the gender ideology movement is futile. Circular reasoning and a frightening refusal to embrace reality demonstrate the satanic power that fuels this insanity. Despite the horrific evidence of the physical and psychological damage caused by experimental hormone blockers and surgical and chemical castrations, those who try to discuss these issues from a logical, scientific, moral, and reasonable perspective are immediately dismissed as ignorant transphobic bigots. End of discussion!

Unable and Unwilling

In biblical terms, these ideologies are satanic in nature, "schemes of the devil" (Eph. 6:11) that require every believer to "to take up the full armor of God, so that you will be able to resist in the evil day, and having done everything, to stand firm" (v. 13). Yet sadly, many pastors and church leaders are unable and unwilling to have a warrior's mindset and bring truth to bear in the kingdom of darkness. Some will say, "I don't want to talk about politics in the pulpit; it's too divisive." To which I respond, "Then you should resign; you are part of the problem, not the solution. The church doesn't need another man-pleaser; it needs pastor-teachers committed to equipping, edifying, and maturing the saints in Christ (Eph. 4:11–1)."

Because of this kind of spiritual cowardice, most Christians are completely ignorant of Satan's devices being thrust upon them, their family, and their church through the political machinations in culture. In their utter lack of biblical knowledge and discernment, they even elect politicians dedicated to advancing agendas that are an abomination to God—an evil so severe that it calls into question the genuineness of the faith of those who vote for these people. "The fear of the LORD is the beginning of wisdom and the knowledge of the Holy One is understanding" (Prov. 9:10); they do not have the latter because they lack the former. And without faithful, godly, and bold warrior preachers, they simply cannot see how the enemy uses politics to eradicate biblical theology and damn the souls of men and women to the eternal torments of hell. As a result, countless professing evangelicals along with unbelievers are hopelessly adrift in a bewildering sea of deception, like "children, tossed here and there by waves and carried about by every wind of doctrine, by the trickery of men, by craftiness in deceitful scheming" (Eph. 4:14).

Because of this kind of spiritual cowardice, most Christians are completely ignorant of Satan's devices being thrust upon them, their family, and their church through the political machinations in culture.

More specifically, because of the scarcity of faithful pastors and church leaders, many Christians fail to see how liberal political ideologies are a part of the socialist scheme to not only divide the country between the *oppressed* and the *oppressor*, but also condition its citizens to believe the most absurd ideologies and thus become mindless automatons of the state—the transgender ideology being a case in point. This kind of social engineering and indoctrination, combined with the deconstruction of all societal norms and values—especially biblical Christianity—is foundational to totalitarianism. Sexual perverts of all stripes, especially trans activists, are the useful idiots being used by liberal elites to help them achieve their tyrannical utopia. Astonishing as it is, they are so powerful in our culture today that even politicians and corporate CEOs are afraid to challenge them. Worse yet, Christians who oppose the LGBTQIA+ agenda on the basis of God's righteous standard of morality are hated more than all others combined—with the most severe vitriol reserved for those who were once held captive by the LGBTQIA+ deceptions but have since been given new life in Christ and warn others to pursue the same.

Unquestionably, the level of frustration over the demise of our culture is even more pronounced among those who follow Christ and long for His return. Having the mind of Christ causes authentic Christians to see the world clearly (1 Cor. 2:16) because of the illuminating power of the indwelling Holy Spirit. As new creatures in Christ, we are exceedingly more offended by every evil for which our Savior suffered and died. Biblical discernment causes us to be even more appalled by what we are witnessing in our neo-Marxist, deceptive woke culture that uses every means available to force everyone to embrace their racist agendas, moral perversions, and biological absurdities. Truly, "these are the times that try men's souls." These are the times that cry out for bold men and women of God to take a stand and say, "Thus says the Lord!" Those who wander in darkness are in desperate need of the light of truth to deliver them from the blinding smog of evil enveloping our land.

I often hear believers say, "I just can't believe the Lord will allow this to continue much longer!" Although we understand the metastasizing corruption of sin in our world is satanic by design and proof that God has given our country over to the wrath of His abandonment that we might destroy ourselves (Rom. 1:18–32), we nevertheless "groan within ourselves, waiting eagerly for our adoption as sons, the redemption of our body" (8:23). Though we fear and grieve, we do so in confident hope of our King's return. With Paul we say, "For I consider that the sufferings of this present time are not worthy to be compared with the glory that is to be revealed to us. For the anxious longing of the creation waits eagerly for the revealing of the sons of God" (vv. 18–19).

Parallels of Wickedness and Judgment

What we are witnessing in America today parallels the hopelessly corrupt Canaanites God instructed His chosen people to "conquer . . . and utterly destroy" (Deut. 7:2). Their idolatry and sexual deviancy knew no bounds, from ritual prostitution as part of their fertility cult observances, to what God called the "abomination" of homosexuality and "perversion" of bestiality (Lev. 18:22–23). Their depraved polytheistic worship included

> the sacrifice of human adults and children, temple prostitution, mutilation of the human body, and sorcery or divination. Among some of the surrounding nations there was official religious sanction for the practice of bestiality, which was punishable by death among the Hebrews (Ex. 22:19). The NIV translation of Deuteronomy 23:17, 18, makes the Hebrew reaction to temple prostitution very clear: "No Israelite man or woman is to become a temple prostitute. You must not bring the earnings of a female prostitute or of a male prostitute into the house of the LORD your God to pay any vow, because the LORD your God detests them both." Human sacrifice, divination, and sorcery were prohibited among the Hebrews: "Let no one be found among you who sacrifices his son or daughter in the fire, who practices divination or sorcery, interprets omens, engages in witchcraft, or casts spells, or who is a medium or spiritist or who consults the dead. Anyone who does these things is detestable to the Lord" (Dt. 18:10–12, NIV).[51]

Like the antediluvian civilization God judged through a worldwide flood (Gen. 6:11–13; 7:23; *cf.* 2 Peter 3:6) because their "wickedness" was so great "that every intent of the thoughts of his heart was only evil continually" (Gen. 6:5), the Canaanites also deserved to be exterminated. For this reason, God commanded His covenant people Israel to, ". . . utterly destroy them, the Hittite and the Amorite, the Canaanite and the Perizzite, the Hivite and the Jebusite, as the LORD your God has commanded you, so that they may not teach you to do according to all their detestable things which they have done for their gods, so that you would sin against the LORD your God" (Deut. 20:17–18).

Yet today we see all these forms of wickedness flourishing in our culture and around the world: the gross abominations of LGBTQIA+ community, the unspeakable perversion of bestiality, the growing

---

51   Entry: "Canaanite Deities and Religion," W.A. Elwell & B.J. Beitzel, *Baker Encyclopedia of the Bible Vol. 1* (Grand Rapids, MI: Baker Book House: 1988), 413–414.

acceptance of pedophilia, the multi-billion-dollar pornography industry, the sacrifice of unborn children on the altar of personal convenience, Satan worship, divination, fortune telling, necromancy—you name it, we do it. Like the unspeakable evils of the ancient Canaanites that resulted in divine judgment, these demonic practices are equally offensive to our holy God, and equally deadly in their ability to influence those who have rejected divine revelation. Like the Canaanites, Americans have been given over to a depraved mind to pursue the vilest forms of wickedness and delight in those who join them (Rom. 1:28–32), for indeed, "to those who are defiled and unbelieving, nothing is pure, but both their mind and their conscience are defiled" (Titus 1:15). Yet in His grace, God continues to stay His inevitable hand of judgment, "not wishing for any to perish but for all to come to repentance" (2 Peter 3:9).

> Like the Canaanites, Americans have been given over to
> a depraved mind to pursue the vilest forms of wickedness
> and delight in those who join them (Rom. 1:28–32).

While this is exceptionally good news for Christians who long to see their friends and loved ones come to faith in Christ and be saved from the wrath to come, it also animates within us a solemn sense of divine urgency, for indeed, the world is moving inexorably toward a day of divine reckoning—not from the hands of Christians, but from God Himself in what the Old Testament prophets and New Testament writers refer to as "the day of the LORD" (Isa. 2:12; 13:6, 9; Zeph. 1:7, 14; Ezek. 13:5; 30:3; Zech. 14:1; Mal. 4:5; Acts 2:20; 1 Thess. 5:2: 2 Thess. 2:2: and 2 Peter 3:10). The apostle Paul describes this most vividly:

> . . . the Lord Jesus will be revealed from heaven with His mighty angels in flaming fire, dealing out retribution to those who do not know God and to those who do not obey the gospel of our Lord Jesus. These will pay the penalty of eternal destruction, away from the presence of the Lord and from the glory of His power, when He comes to be glorified in His saints on that day, and to be marveled at among all who have believed.
> (2 Thess. 1:7–8)

Be Strong and Courageous

Our culture has now sunk to the very lowest point of wickedness. Because of America's rejection of the gospel, in addition to other depraved abominations she celebrates, we have now exceeded the evils of Sodom and Gomorrah and will one day experience a similar judgment. Given the seriousness of the times in which we live, and the deadly influence Satan's world systems are having upon the church, many pastors and church leaders feel overwhelmed, frightened, powerless, and defeated. If this is you, I wish to encourage and challenge you.

We must remember that none of this catches God by surprise. In His sovereignty, He maintains absolute rule and authority over all things; He is the One who, "[declares] the end from the beginning, and from ancient times things which have not been done, saying, 'My purpose will be established, and I will accomplish all My good pleasure'" (Isa. 46:10). Knowing God is fully *aware of* and *in charge of* all that happens instantly delegitimizes thoughts of abandonment, indifference, or randomness (though in our humanness, we are bound to *feel* otherwise). Indeed, He is a *sovereign*, not a *contingent*, God. There is therefore nothing in our life He has not *ordained to accomplish, allow,* or *understand completely*, including the sufferings, tragedies, and atrocities we experience.

We can find great comfort knowing there is nothing that can thwart His sovereign purposes to build His church and bring glory to Himself, despite even our fears and failures. *What He expects of us is to be faithful and obedient warriors who rely solely on His power to accomplish only what He can do in and through us.* We see this most dramatically in God's instructions to Joshua when the mantle of leadership was given to him after the death of Moses, and he received his military commission for the bloody conquest of Canaan. His marching orders must be ours as well. Here's what God commanded Joshua:

> Be strong and courageous, for you shall give this people possession of the land which I swore to their fathers to give them. Only be strong and very courageous; be careful to do according to all the law which Moses My servant com-

manded you; do not turn from it to the right or to the left, so that you may have success wherever you go. This book of the law shall not depart from your mouth, but you shall meditate on it day and night, so that you may be careful to do according to all that is written in it; for then you will make your way prosperous, and then you will have success. Have I not commanded you? Be strong and courageous! Do not tremble or be dismayed, for the LORD your God is with you wherever you go.
(Josh. 1:6–9)

While we are not commissioned to exterminate the wicked militarily or in any way take revenge upon them (Rom. 12:19), we are commissioned to make disciples through the preaching of the gospel (Matt. 29:19–20). To accomplish such an arduous mission in Satan's kingdom of darkness requires our utmost exertions in faith and godliness. But fortitude alone is insufficient. Our strength and courage is only found in the Lord who has promised, ". . . and lo, I am with you always, even to the end of the age" (v. 20)—the same promise He made to Joshua, "for the LORD your God is with you wherever you go" (Josh. 1:9). And like the Lord's instruction to Joshua, the key to being "strong and courageous" is to be saturated with the Word of God and obedient to it. We must be careful to obey "all the law" and avoid any deviation from it; neither "to the right or to the left." This is what informs our conscience, instructs our mind, animates our will, and generates our emotions.

This is what it means to "walk by the Spirit" so we "will not carry out the desire of the flesh" and bear the "the fruit of the Spirit" (Gal. 5:16, 22). To this end, the wise French theologian, pastor, and reformer in Geneva during the Protestant Reformation, John Calvin offers this insight:

As many exert their strength to no purpose in making erroneous or desultory attempts, it is added as a true source of fortitude that Joshua shall make it his constant study to observe the Law. By this we are taught that the only way in which we can become truly invincible is by striving to yield a faithful obedience to God. Otherwise it were better to lie indolent and effeminate than to be hurried on by headlong audacity.[52]

Moreover, like Joshua, we are commanded to "meditate on it day and night, so that you may be careful to do according to all that is written in it" (Josh. 1:8). The importance of meditating upon the Word of God cannot be overestimated, though it is foreign to most Christian leaders by their own admission. *To meditate on the law of God is to pensively reflect upon the realities of divine revelation so intently that they bring conviction, repentance, encouragement, courage, and soul-satisfying joy in Christ.* The man that desires God above all else will fill his mind with holy musings of Christ's infinite perfections, love, and promises. Grace and glory will dominate his heart; his life will be ruled by the Word of God, the unfailing love of Christ will be the constant topic of his conversations, for indeed, "the book of the law [will] not depart from [his] mouth" (v. 8). The inferior pleasures of this world, as enticing as they can be, will increasingly lose their appeal, and with the hymn writer he will sing:

> *Turn your eyes upon Jesus,*
> *look full in His wonderful face,*
> *and the things of earth will grow strangely dim,*
> *in the light of His glory and grace.*

This is the "blessed . . . man whose delight is in the law of the LORD, and in His law he meditates day and night. He will be like a tree firmly planted by streams of water, which yields its fruit in its season and its leaf does not wither; and in whatever he does, he prospers" (Ps. 1:2–3). We must never forget that success is conditioned upon courage through obedience, and these virtues grow strong in the rich soil of meditation. The godly Puritan warrior of the faith, Thomas Manton, described it this way:

> Meditation is when we exercise ourselves in the doctrines of the word, and consider how truths known may be useful to us . . . an act of knowledge reiterated, or a return of the

---

52   John Calvin, *Calvin's Commentaries, Vol. IV* (Grand Rapids: MI; Baker Books, 1998), 31.

mind to that point to which it arrived before; it is the inculcation or whetting of a known truth, the pause of reason
on something already conceived and known, or a calling
to remembrance what we know before . . . the end of study
is information, but the end of meditation is practice, or a
work upon the affections . . . the fruit of study is to hoard
up truth, but the fruit of meditation is to practise it.[53]

The Fruit of Meditation in Combat

The warrior preacher will find his greatest joy in relationship with
Christ, an intimacy that will nourish his soul and strengthen his
resolve to carry on the fight. Only then will he be "strong and courageous"; only then will he "not tremble or be dismayed, for the
LORD your God is with you wherever you go" (Josh. 1:6–9). Perhaps the testimony of our Green Beret brother, Joel C., will once
again provide some helpful parallels between physical and spiritual combat as they relate to the warrior's mindset.

> The first time I was in a combat zone was at the peak of the
> insurgency in Iraq and US forces were sustaining about 150
> attacks each day, just in Anbar province where I was located
> in Ramadi. I didn't know what to expect and neither did I
> know how I'd respond. I had my iPod which contained the
> music and sermons I listened to on deployment, and on
> the back was inscribed "The battle is the Lord's." One of my
> favorite quotes and scenes in the Old Testament is where
> David ran toward Goliath because he knew that the battle
> IS the Lord's and he totally trusted Him.
>
> Rockets and mortars were raining down on our little
> Firebase in the middle of Ramadi regularly. Rounds were
> launched at us at a minimum five times per day. Some
> men on the compound were afraid and didn't want to be
> caught out in the open—especially after prayers. The at-
> tacks seemed to fall just after each call to prayer (which
> could be heard over multiple loudspeakers from multiple
> mosques around the city). I remember lying in bed one

---

53 Thomas Manton, *The Works of Thomas Manton, Vol. XVII* (Edinburgh: The Banner of Truth
Trust, 2020), 268-9.

night listening to a sermon on my iPod. I heard the call to prayer begin and knew it was just a matter of time before our enemies would start the indirect fire toward our little base. I just turned up my headphones and ignored it. Suddenly, I felt the ground shake and felt and heard the explosion of the first of probably four or five rockets, and I thought, "Wow that was really close." I thought to myself that they would probably walk the next round in closer. I prayed and the only thought I had was "Lord, You trace the path for the lightning bolts and these rockets are not out of Your control. . .I trust YOU." I felt total peace and didn't even move from where I was, lying on my cot in my tent. It was NOT like in *Band of Brothers* where one of the brave officers said to a cowardly soldier, "You know what your problem is. . .you have hope that you're going to live. You have to just know you're already dead and then you can be at peace and operate as a soldier like you should."

Maybe that's how an unbeliever thinks, but not a child of God. It wasn't just being resolved to die; it was a living trust that I served a sovereign God who controlled ALL things, even the seemingly random rockets and mortars of our enemies. That was the settled peace and contentment that carried me through every close call or mission thereafter. I was abiding in the Lord and reliant on Him, my God, and not anything else. I was walking with my Savior and knew the worst-case scenario was that He would call me home. I trusted Him with that as well, and knew that if He did take me, no training or self-conjured courage would help. I was in His hands. On the other hand, if it was not my time to go, I would be invincible to my enemies. That was the sole basis of my courage during all my deployments. Because of that abiding belief, I volunteered for things that *had* to be done, but others didn't want to do because they were so risky. I wasn't careless; I just knew I could trust my God and Savior with my life or with my death.

Real courage comes only from a full knowledge of who God is and a total resting in Him. It's not reckless or indifferent. It is based solely in Him! I am not brave, or courageous, but I know the Lord and trust Him completely, and I know Him through His Word alone.[54]

This is the mindset of every believer willing to take a stand for Christ, especially faithful pastors willing to boldly confront the culture rather than capitulate to it. Men like Joshua, whose mind was saturated with the Law of God and who therefore submitted to the "captain of the LORD's host" (Josh. 5:15) in all that he did; a soldier-servant (a concept discussed in the next chapter, *The Warrior's Character*) who humbly served his Master as a willing slave, but who also served those his Master had placed in his care. This is what the church desperately needs in these dark days of deception and apostasy.

Warrior Field-Preachers of Scotland

Redemptive history records many such men, including the young "Field-Preachers" who, under the "threat of fine and imprisonment, of torture or death"[55] preached the gospel in Scotland during the dreadful years of persecution between 1663 and 1688. Because of the edicts of King Charles II of England, they were forbidden to proclaim a decidedly Calvinistic soteriology that extolled the doctrines of grace. Though thoroughly biblical, their teachings were considered to be hostile to the "doctrines of Pelagianism and Arminianism" that "ultimately developed into deism and indifferentism"[56]—doctrinal errors that dominate American evangelicalism today. During that dreadful season of persecution (which may also be our fate in the coming years of American tyranny), the nineteenth-century historian and theologian, William Blaikie (1820–99), wrote this in his monumental work: *The Preachers of Scotland from the Sixth to the Nineteenth Century*:

> The wildest efforts were made by the bishops and their friends to put down conventicles; grievous fines were imposed on men of property who might attend them . . . to harbour a preacher, or to help him in any way, exposed one

---

54 Joel C., from a private conversation.

55 William Garden Blaikie, *The Preachers of Scotland from the Sixth to the Nineteenth Century* (Edinburgh: T. & T. Clark, 1888; reproduced by BiblioLife, LLC), 150.

56 Ibid., 150.

either to a heavy fine, or to imprisonment, perchance with the boot and thumbkins [instruments of torture], possibly even to death; the preacher, with a great price on his head, had no certain dwelling-place, and where there was no friendly cottage to shelter him, had to wander about in wild lonely places sleeping in woods and caves, often cold and wet and hungry; racked by rheumatism or prostrated by dysentery, glad if he could succeed in keeping his pocket-Bible dry, and not so much as dreaming of the luxury of books, or of a quiet room for study.[57]

These were considered the "warrior-preachers" of Scotland,[58] men like James Renwick who was captured, tortured, and hanged at the Grassmarket of Edinburgh on 17 February 1688. He was a man like many who refused to bow to the demonic edicts of a Stuart king and the apostate Christianity he forced upon his subjects through his own tyranny and that of the phony religionists that served him. In his timeless work, *Fair Sunshine: Character Studies of the Scottish Covenanters*, Jock Purves (1901–1988) records the final minutes of this warrior-preacher who was strong and courageous to the end:

By the side of the scaffold, a curate said, "Own our king and we shall pray for you." He answered, "I will have none of your prayers; I am come to bear my testimony against you, and such as you are." The curate persisted, "Own our king and pray for him, whatever you say against us." And Renwick replied, "I will discourse no more with you. I am within a little to appear before Him who is King of kings, and Lord of lords, who shall pour shame, contempt and confusion upon all the kings of the earth who have not ruled for Him.". . . While the drums beat out their wild disharmony, he magnified and blessed the Lord in singing from the 103rd Psalm, and in reading his last chapter, Revelation 19. Amid all the din, his manly voice thrilled with rapturous faith as he read the words, "He hath on his vesture and on his thigh

57 Ibid., 156-7

58 Ibid., 7

a name written, King of kings and Lord of lords." To prayer he went again while the drums continued their deafening earthborn, earthbound thunder, and was heard of him in Heaven, his dwelling place . . . The harsh order was given to him to go up the death ladder. He climbed up and prayed again, being heard to say, "Lord, I die in the faith that Thou wilt not leave Scotland, but that Thou wilt make the blood of Thy witness the seed of Thy church, and return again and be glorious in our land. And now, Lord I am ready; the Bride the Lamb's wife, hath made herself ready."

The blinding napkin was tied about his face, and he spoke to his friend, close by his side, "Farewell; be diligent in duty, make your peace with God through Christ. There is a great trial coming. As to the remnant I leave, I have committed them to God. Tell them from me not to weary nor be discouraged in maintaining the testimony, and the Lord will provide you teachers and ministers; and when He comes, He will make these despised truths glorious in the earth." With his last words in his mouth, "Lord, into Thy hands I commend my spirit, for Thou has redeemed me, Lord God of truth," the hangman turned him over.[59]

Challenge

Herein is the mindset of warrior preachers—soldiers of the cross who are unwilling to bow to tyrannical deceptions or entangle themselves with the affairs of life (2 Tim. 2:4). Instead, they are men devoted exclusively to the bold proclamation of the only truth that can save sinners and sanctify saints, the gospel of Jesus Christ. May we all have the fortitude to do the same—that in all things Christ might have the preeminence. Then at the end of our life we can say with that great warrior of the faith, the apostle Paul, "I have fought the good fight, I have finished the course, I have kept the faith" (2 Tim. 4:7).

---

59 Jock Purves, *Fair Sunshine: Character Studies of the Scottish Covenanters* (Edinburgh: The Banner of Truth Trust, reprinted 2015), 104-5.

Chapter 4 Questions

1. Do you have a warrior's mindset—one of fearless devotion to the truth and the glory of Christ, come what may?

2. In what ways are you protecting your sheep from the specific strategies of the enemy who targets them?

3. Are you able to identify the Marxist invasion into the church, especially as it relates to the woke culture, identity politics, and the heretical social justice gospel?

4. Are you warning people of the dangers of *groupthink* (e.g., *mass formation*) which is really *mass depravity*—a manifestation of the wrath of divine abandonment where God has lifted His restraining grace on a mass of depraved human beings who reject Him, allowing them to collectively voice their deceptions in the echo chamber of their rage and ultimately experience the damning consequences of their iniquities?

5. Are you warning people about the threats posed by our progressive public school systems that indoctrinate children with cultural Marxist propaganda—ideologies such as the brutal murder of the unborn, systemic racism, the depraved immorality of the LGBTQIA+ culture, and the biological absurdities of transgender ideology?

6. Do you meditate on the law of God, as Joshua was ordered to do, that you might reflect upon the realities of divine revelation so intently that they bring conviction, repentance, encouragement, courage, and soul-satisfying joy in Christ?

7. Can you identify with the great warrior preachers of the Bible and history—soldiers of the cross who were unwilling to bow to tyrannical deceptions or entangle themselves with the affairs of life so they could be devoted exclusively to the bold proclamation of the gospel of Jesus Christ?

8. At the end of your life will you be able to say with the apostle Paul, "I have fought the good fight, I have finished the course, I have kept the faith." (2 Tim. 4:7)?

5

The Warrior's Character

Pursue righteousness, godliness, faith, love, perseverance and gentleness. Fight the good fight of faith; take hold of the eternal life to which you were called, and you made the good confession in the presence of many witnesses.
(1 Timothy 6:11–12)

Do not forget the culture of the inner man—I mean of the heart. How diligently the cavalry officer keeps his saber clean and sharp; every stain he rubs off with the greatest care. Remember you are God's sword, his instrument—I trust, a chosen vessel unto him to bear his name. In great measure, according to the purity and perfection of the instrument, will be the success. It is not great talents God blesses so much as likeness to Jesus. A holy minister is an awful weapon in the hand of God.

ROBERT MURRAY M'CHEYNE[60]

---

60 Robert Murray M'Cheyne quoted in C.H. Spurgeon, *Lectures To My Students* (Peabody, MA; Hendrickson Publishers Marketing, LLC., 2012), 8.

Down through redemptive history, God has raised up many great warrior preachers who proclaimed the unsearchable riches of Christ with holy boldness—sober-minded men with a fervent zeal for the glory of God, an unyielding commitment to the authority of Scripture, and a deep burden for the salvation of souls. With a longing for heaven and contempt for this world, they only speak the oracles of God and devote their life to meditating upon sacred realities for the purpose of knowing Christ and shepherding the sheep of His pasture. Although each has a distinct calling and differing gifts and opportunities for ministry, certain spiritual character traits are evident in all of them.

The purpose of this chapter is to examine what may be considered the most foundational qualities of their lives and apply them to our lives and ministries. Whether you are a pastor or serve in some other realm of ministry, the divinely prescribed marks of a godly shepherd apply to you, and, apart from them, your service will be of little use for the cause of Christ and His kingdom.

Biblical Qualifications

Sadly, there have been (and always will be) scandals among pastors and church leaders due to a lack of spiritual and moral character. Their conduct is a stain upon the church, the gospel, and Christ Himself. However, sin is a metastasizing corruption in all of us that must be dealt with aggressively. For this reason, the apostle Paul said, "I discipline my body and make it my slave, so that, after I have preached to others, I myself will not be disqualified" (1 Cor. 9:27). Spiritual and moral integrity is paramount in pastoral ministry. For this reason, the first and foremost qualification of an elder that Paul lists in 1 Timothy 3:1–7 and Titus 1:1–6 is that he must be "above reproach," meaning his life in general is not open to attack or criticism, particularly as at it relates to the specific lists of qualifications that follow.[61]

---

61 G.W. Knight, *The Pastoral Epistles: A Commentary on the Greek Text* (Grand Rapids, MI: W.B. Eerdmans; Carlisle, England: Paternoster Press, 1992), 156.

An overseer, then, must be above reproach, the husband of one wife, temperate, prudent, respectable, hospitable, able to teach, not addicted to wine or pugnacious, but gentle, peaceable, free from the love of money. He must be one who manages his own household well, keeping his children under control with all dignity (but if a man does not know how to manage his own household, how will he take care of the church of God?), and not a new convert, so that he will not become conceited and fall into the condemnation incurred by the devil. And he must have a good reputation with those outside the church, so that he will not fall into reproach and the snare of the devil.
(1 Tim. 3:2–7; *cf.* Titus 1:1–6)

When these character traits are missing, a man's marriage, family, ministry, and church will suffer. I have personally experienced the frustration and embarrassment of knowing and even co-laboring with men who are unqualified to lead and preach. Often a man's true character is concealed under a cloak of hypocrisy, although in time his true nature will show. Paul put it this way: "The sins of some men are quite evident, going before them to judgment; for others, their sins follow after" (1 Tim. 5:24). It is therefore crucial that every man who aspires to pastoral ministry not only examine his own heart with brutal honesty, but also be examined carefully by other discerning individuals in the church.

Integrity and Character in the Green Beret

In order to illustrate the importance of integrity and proper vetting, I wish to draw your attention once again to U.S. Army Green Berets and the extremely high value they place on integrity and character in the Special Forces. I asked my fellow elder and retired Green Beret combat veteran, Joel C., to comment on this issue. His experience and observations were fascinating. The parallels in pastoral ministry will be obvious. Here's what he had to say:

Integrity and character are very important in the special-operations community. During training, one of the fastest ways to be disqualified is to commit integrity violations. During land navigation training, it is not unusual to travel alone for 40–50 kilometers per day. (Land Nav is one training week out of all of "selection" and one week out of the eighteen months of the Qualification Course.) The goal each day is to reach all five points you are given using a map and compass. The problem is that you are moving with a 45 lb rucksack with a specific packing list that makes your ruck weigh around 75–80 lbs. They take a group out into the middle of nowhere and leave you with a cadre member. At roughly 11 pm, they give each person grid coordinates for your first point. You are not allowed to speak with any trainees. You hurriedly plot your present position and then your coordinates are given. Each member has a different direction, and the event usually starts in the middle of a thick draw[62] that looks like Jurassic Park. You're in the dark and cannot use roads or any light, flashlight, or headlamp. If you do have to look at your map, you must put your poncho over your body and use a red lens on your headlamp. This is all to simulate light discipline used in combat.

When you are super tired and are not certain where you are, since you have had no sleep, your sinful nature wants to break the rules, such as speaking with another student you may run into to try to figure out where you are; or going to a trail that's on the map and use that as opposed to the nearly impossibly thick brush, marshes, swamps, or creeks you have to traverse otherwise; or dumping weight out of your rucksack to reduce the weight you're carrying, etc. They impose all these rules to test one's integrity. Land Nav is the middle of selection and people's feet are already very sore and everyone is already worn down. The chances of cheating are high. Oh yeah, you are not allowed to stop and take a nap either—and you haven't slept in a while. All of these rules and difficulties are a part of the many tests for perseverance and character.

The last point brings the students back to a rallying point where you must stand in formation until the last candidate makes it back. While there, I heard many talking about get-

---

62 A large ravine, smaller than a canyon.

ting a red card for breaking a rule. Some men walked on one of the trails and got "road killed" (red carded for being on a road/trail). Some got too close to a road and got road killed because you're not allowed to stop within fifty meters of a road. You can only cross each road you come to perpendicularly (straight across and away); there are to be no angles or walking along at all. Some got caught talking with other students. Some got caught eating, using a white light, sleeping, etc. The bottom line is this: all those who got red cards for any violation were NOT SELECTED at the end of the course for integrity violations.

By the end of training, you had a good idea of everyone's integrity and character. Sometimes people slip through the cracks and someone with shaky character makes it through and gets on a team. Trust me, everyone knows your character by the way you do things, behave, apply yourself, work, etc. We had a couple of slackers and shady characters in my battalion. We had names (not nice ones) for those people, and they never went on deployments with a team. They were relegated to a C Team—that's the team with the headquarters element so they couldn't get anyone hurt and could be watched closely; or they were left home to run the office and process orders for incoming and outgoing personnel.

You have to be able to trust your teammates and know they have your back. You can only rely on someone if they have a quality character.[63]

While the rigors of pastoral ministry are not nearly as physically demanding, the temptation to "cheat" and violate God's rules are the same. Character matters. Neither fellow elders nor the church at large will be able to function biblically if even one of the elders— especially the pastor-teacher—lacks personal integrity. Their lives will grieve and quench the Holy Spirit and, as they operate in the flesh rather than the Spirit, their preaching, praying, and shepherding will betray the absence of God's presence and power in their heart. Oh, what a great need there is for true men of God!

---

63   Joel C., from private correspondence.

Man of God

In Scripture, God identifies His choice servants with the phrase "man of God." It is first used to describe Moses (Deut. 33:1; *cf.* Josh. 14:6), the man God chose, gifted, and empowered to be His prophet and theocratic leader of Israel. Other Old Testament prophets received the same appellation (*cf.* 1 Sam. 9:6, 10; 1 Kings 13:1, 8; 17:18; 2 Kings 4:7, 9, 16, etc.). These were all Spirit-empowered preachers called by God to be His spokesmen. For this reason, the apostle Paul called his young protégé, Timothy, "you man of God," then exhorted him to "pursue righteousness, godliness, faith, love, perseverance and gentleness. Fight the good fight of faith; take hold of the eternal life to which you were called, and you made the good confession in the presence of many witnesses" (1 Tim. 6:11–12).

These are men who so feared the just wrath of God they deserved that they cried out for mercy, and, upon receiving grace, they forsook all to follow Christ.

These, and many others, were *God's men*—the chosen champions of His glorious cause. And they still exist today—though I fear they are few. These are men who so feared the just wrath of God they deserved that they cried out for mercy, and, upon receiving grace, they forsook all to follow Christ. They are men who so abhor the law of sin in their own heart that they preach first to themselves before preaching to others; men who have learned to hate hypocrisy in themselves more than in others. These are holy men, set apart to God by God Himself. These are men called and gifted by God—men whose lives reflect the glory, power, authority, and holiness of the thrice-holy God the seraphs praise as they hover around His throne, ever ready to do His bidding (Isa. 6:2–3).

These are men whose Christlike character emanates a divine luster that others can readily see. A "man of God" is God-fearing in his heart, God-centered in his thoughts, and God-honoring in his life, both privately and publicly. The steel of his character has been forged in the furnace of affliction, shaped on the anvil of adversity, and sharpened on the wheel of the Word. The driving priority of his life is to know and love Christ above all else, to serve Christ as

His appointed man, and to be a faithful steward of the mysteries of God. His life is devoted to mining the inexhaustible treasures of the Word of God and fearlessly proclaiming the wondrous perfections of Christ and His love for sinners. Habitual, fervent, persistent prayer is the Spirit-empowered bore used to drill deep into the depths of divine revelation, lifelong study the means to bring the riches of grace to the surface, and expository preaching the divinely appointed method to disperse the precious jewels of grace to those who have been chosen to treasure them.

God's man places no value in gimmicks and theatrics. He has no desire to draw attention to himself through the cultural accoutrements of wardrobe, hairstyles, or any other trendy look the godless world applauds. His pulpit demeanor is one of solemnity, profundity, and dignity, a natural manifestation of the unrestricted rule of the Spirit of God in his heart. He has a godly presence about him, a noticeable aura of humility and love that draws others to him—and through him to Christ. This is a man who exudes spiritual strength, confidence, boldness, wisdom, and a noticeable fervency that marks him as a man of God; that rare man whose authority enters a room with him and commands respect without ever seeking it.

*God's man places no value in gimmicks and theatrics.
He has no desire to draw attention to himself through
the cultural accoutrements of wardrobe, hairstyles, or
any other trendy look the godless world applauds.*

His prayers and sermons are the natural expression of his godly character, and those who follow Him know that he is a man who lives in the presence of the Most High and has heard Him speak through His Word. His hearers are forever changed by his message, because they know that it is the Word of God, not the word of man. This man fights for doctrinal purity and yields no ground to the enemy. Those who observe his life can see and experience the love of Christ and are therefore drawn to him as unto Christ, because his godly character yields the irresistible fruit of Christ Himself. To be God's man! Can there be any greater privilege in the world? This is the character of a warrior preacher. Is it yours?

Encomium of John Owen, a Man of God

Apart from the spiritual giants revealed in Scripture, there are few men whose character towers in mature holiness and passionate fortitude as the godly Puritan theologian, John Owen—one of the men whom God has used most profoundly in my life. I was deeply moved by the Latin encomium engraved on the monument of his tomb in Bunhill Fields, a Nonconformist burial ground in London dating from the 1660s where approximately 123,000 saints are buried. In J.I. Packer's classic work, *A Quest for Godliness: The Puritan Vision of the Christian Life*, he records that moving tribute to John Owen. Packer writes this:

> The epitaph engraved on the monument that adorns Owen's tomb in Bunhill Fields reflects the respect in which he was held by his contemporaries, and indicates something of his quality as a man of God and a teacher of godliness. Here is a translation:
>
> John Owen, born in Oxfordshire, son of a distinguished theologian, was himself a more distinguished one, who must be counted among the most distinguished of this age. Furnished with the recognized resources of humane learning in uncommon measure, he put them all, as a well-ordered array of handmaids, at the service of theology, which he served himself. His theology was polemical, practical, and what is called casuistical, and it cannot be said that any one of these was peculiarly his rather than another.
>
> In polemical theology, with more than herculean strength, he strangled three poisonous serpents, the Arminian, the Socinian, and the Roman.
>
> In practical theology, he laid out before others the whole of the activity of the Holy Spirit, which he had first experienced in his own heart, according to the rule of the Word. And, leaving other things aside, he cultivated, and realized in practice, the blissful communion with God of which he wrote; a traveler on earth who grasped God like one in heaven.
>
> In casuistry, he was valued as an oracle to be consulted on every complex matter.

A scribe instructed in every way for the kingdom of God, this pure lamp of gospel truth shone forth on many in private, on more from the pulpit, and in all in his printed works, pointing everyone to the same goal. And in this shining forth he gradually, as he and others recognized, squandered his strength till it was gone. His holy soul, longing to enjoy God more, left the shattered ruins of his once-handsome body, full of permanent weaknesses, attacked by frequent diseases, worn out most of all by hard work, and no longer a fit instrument for serving God, on a day rendered dreadful for many by earthly powers but now made happy for him through the power of God, August 25, 1683. He was 67.[64]

Here is another in a long line of warrior preachers. Like a mighty oak, the towering character of men like John Owen provide a stark contrast to the shrub-sized character of many pastors and church leaders in our age where superficial evangelical collectivism now marches proudly to the drumbeat of country-club Christianity and outright apostasy. Laodicean compromise has so seared the conscience of modern evangelicalism that it has no capacity to evaluate its own self-deception.

The Character of a Warrior Preacher

Every serious Christian must examine the nature of his or her own character, especially men God has called to be pastor-teachers. By character, I'm referring to *the Spirit-empowered disposition of the inner man to pursue holiness for the glory and enjoyment of God.* This will have a unique quality for a *warrior preacher*—which as I have stated before is simply a title used to describe a *biblical preacher*, a true *"man of God"* who, unlike many today, fearlessly expounds the whole of Scripture without compromise, despite the culture's militant antipathy toward him and the message he proclaims. Without a godly character wholly yielded to the indwelling Spirit, his flesh will rule both his life and ministry and also his congregation's. Like naïve and foolish children, together the

---

64   J.I. Packer, *A Quest for Godliness: The Puritan Vision of the Christian Life* (Wheaton, IL; Crossway Books, 1990), 192.

pastor and his flock will be "tossed here and there by waves and carried about by every wind of doctrine, by the trickery of men, by craftiness in deceitful scheming" (Eph. 4:14), and like so many others who have been seduced by the vanities and allurements of the world, he will preach the endless inventions of man instead of the oracles of God. Consequently, he will do further damage to the church and forfeit blessing in his life.

In light of this, I wish to examine the rare and distinct character of a warrior preacher—how it is *formed*, *strengthened*, and *deployed*. I trust these considerations will be helpful to you.

First, the character of a warrior preacher is formed in the fires of suffering and persecution.

We see this, for example, in God's commissioning of the apostle Paul, perhaps the greatest of all warrior preachers—a man whose sufferings first began when the Spirit tormented his conscience with the convicting guilt of his sin and called him to repentant faith. But that was just a foretaste of the character-building difficulties to come. Immediately on the heels of his conversion, the Lord sent his messenger, Ananias, to commission His soon-to-be apostle, and, "the Lord said to him, 'Go, for he is a chosen instrument of Mine, to bear My name before the Gentiles and kings and the sons of Israel; *for I will show him how much he must suffer for My name's sake*'" (Acts 9:15; emphasis mine). Paul would later recount that momentous event in Galatians 1:15–16 where he spoke of "God who had set me apart even from my mother's womb and called me through His grace, was pleased to reveal His Son in me so that I might preach Him among the Gentiles."

Men who have suffered little for the cause of Christ are like soldiers who have only marched but never fought.

The violent persecutor of the church would himself be persecuted. Like Peter and the other apostles who, after being beaten and commanded not to speak in the name of Jesus again, "went on their way from the presence of the Council, rejoicing that they had been considered worthy to suffer shame for His name. And every day, in the temple and from house to house, they kept right on teaching and preaching Jesus as the Christ" (Acts 5:42–42).

Men who have suffered little for the cause of Christ are like soldiers who have only marched but never fought. Their character will be underdeveloped and their service of little value. Being a faithful witness for Christ is a costly task—sometimes brutally so—one that requires a supernatural infusion of divine grace in the inner man. "Indeed, all who desire to live godly in Christ Jesus will be persecuted" (2 Tim. 3:12). Notice the very *desire* to honor Christ incites the hatred of the world—a satanic system that despises those who care nothing for its approval and mocks Christians who refuse to run with them in the same excess of dissipation. Jesus said He had not come to bring peace to earth, but a sword (Matt. 10:34), and the warrior preacher is the *tip of the spear*. Moreover, because the world hates Christ, it will also hate and persecute all who follow Him (John 15:18, 20), especially those who preach the marvels of His person and work of redemption.

> *God has commissioned and gifted him to be his spokesman, a "man of God." This is the highest and most sacred calling, one that requires an extra measure of Spirit empowerment to boldly speak with divine authority and undying love.*

To persevere in such an environment requires a special work in the heart of a man that only God can accomplish. Like all the redeemed, the character of every faithful preacher first comes to life at the moment of *regeneration: that supernatural, instantaneous impartation of spiritual life to the spiritually dead characterized by both washing and renewal.* Paul used the term in Titus 3:5–7: "He saved us, not on the basis of deeds which we have done in righteousness, but according to His mercy, by *the washing of regeneration and renewing by the Holy Spirit*, whom He poured out upon us richly through Jesus Christ our Savior, so that being justified by His grace we would be made heirs according to the hope of eternal life" (emphasis mine).

But because there is a special calling upon God's chosen messenger, a special character is required to fulfill that calling—one that God alone must form in him. God has commissioned and gifted him to be his spokesman, a "man of God." This is the highest and most sacred calling, one that requires an extra measure of Spirit empowerment to boldly speak with divine authority and undying love. Because God has uniquely gifted him, he is commanded to "[speak] the utterances of God" (1 Peter 4:11)—referring to the words God has spoken out of His own mouth and recorded in Scripture (*cf.* Acts 7:38; Rom. 3:2; Heb. 5:12). Indeed, "All Scripture is inspired by God and profitable for teaching, for reproof, for correction, for training in righteousness; so that the man of God may be adequate, equipped for every good work" (2 Tim. 3:16, 17).

For this reason, Timothy, whom Paul called a "man of God" (1 Tim. 6:11), was "solemnly [charged] in the presence of God and of Christ Jesus" to

> . . . preach the word; be ready in season and out of season; reprove, rebuke, exhort, with great patience and instruction. For the time will come when they will not endure sound doctrine; but wanting to have their ears tickled, they will accumulate for themselves teachers in accordance to their own desires, and will turn away their ears from the truth and will turn aside to myths. But you, be sober in all things, endure hardship, do the work of an evangelist, fulfill your ministry. (2 Tim. 4:2–5)

Obviously, this would be no easy task, especially for a young man who struggled with fear and youthful lusts. So straightaway Paul continued with a strong exhortation and warning that pours forth from the heart of one about to die. His words seem to come from quivering lips as he pensively reflects upon the intense battle in which he has been engaged—a testimony that speaks to the unique nature of his character and how it was formed. He says,

> For I am already being poured out as a drink offering, and the time of my departure has come. I have fought the good fight, I have finished the course, I have kept the faith; in the future there is laid up for me the crown of righteousness, which the Lord, the righteous Judge, will award to me on that day; and not only to me, but also to all who have loved His appearing. (2 Tim. 4:6–8)

Paul's Character-Building Suffering

It is impossible for any of us to identify with the level of persecution the apostle Paul experienced over the course of his ministry. Most people hated him. His Jewish countrymen hated him because they hated the Christ he preached. They even made fun of his personal appearance and his speech (2 Cor. 10:10; 11:6). His gnarled skin on his back must have looked like spaghetti from all the beatings. Every limb and every joint must have been tender from the arthritis that invaded areas of traumatic injury. When considering all the physical sufferings he endured over the course of his ministry (2 Cor. 11:23), it's a wonder he ever survived, much less thrived in his service to Christ. Yet still he said, "If I have to boast, I will boast of what pertains to my weakness" (v. 30).

Paul went on to say in 2 Corinthians 12:7, "Because of the surpassing greatness of the revelations, for this reason, to keep me from exalting myself, there was given me a thorn in the flesh, a messenger of Satan to torment me—to keep me from exalting myself!" Like all of us, Paul struggled with pride and overconfidence in his own resources. This is just the kind of man Satan loves to inflate with an exaggerated sense of self-importance and over-confidence—the kinds of attitudes God abhors and will not bless. So, God gave his choice servant a gift of suffering to keep him humble and therefore dependent upon God's resources and not his own. The term "thorn" (Greek: *skolops*) refers to something pointed that produces pain. In this case, the vexing torment was "a messenger of Satan" (v. 7). The term "messenger" (Greek: *angelos*) is used 186 times in the New Testament and in every case it refers to a person, either human or angelic. Given the context of 2 Corinthians where Paul defends his apostleship against the self-styled false apostles that were seeking to destroy him, it is reasonable to believe that this "messenger of Satan" refers to the leader of this pack of wolves.

Like every believer, the sufferings Paul endured extended beyond the opprobrium of the world's persecution, to include things like chronic illness, disease, poverty, bereavement, broken relationships, and many other difficulties God used to mold his character (see James 1:2–4). He also carried with him the heavy burden of shepherding those he loved, protecting them from the savage wolves (predatory preachers) seeking to devour them. We can feel the weight of his burden when he said, "Apart from such external things, there is the daily pressure on me of concern for all the churches" (2 Cor. 11:28). No wonder he would say, "Who is adequate for these things?" (2 Cor. 2:16).

But all faithful ministers of the gospel will testify that God did His greatest work in their hearts amidst some crucible of grace that He ordained to allow in their lives. As in the furnace with Shadrach, Meshach, and Abednego, it is in the refining fires of adversity that we most experience the soul-exhilarating presence of God. It is in our weakness that He proves Himself powerful on our behalf. It is through sorrow and suffering that He refines the character of his champions, and thus ignites within them the holy fire of gospel preaching. The great evangelist, George Whitefield described it this way:

> Ministers never write or preach so well as when under the cross; the Spirit of Christ and of glory then rests upon them. It was this, no doubt, that made the Puritans . . . such burning and shining lights. When cast out by the black Bartholomew-act [the 1662 Act of Uniformity] and driven from their respective charges to preach in barns and fields, in the highways and hedges, they in an especial manner wrote and preached as men having authority. Though dead, by their writings they yet speak; a peculiar unction attends them to this very hour.[65]

Though the providential workings of divine grace in the lives of His servants will inevitably include all manner of difficulties—especially when the authority of the Word is upheld with a holy boldness in preaching—we must never forget that God is in it for our good and His glory. With this as the bedrock of a godly character, the warrior preacher is able to stand firm, come what may, and rejoice with Paul, saying, "I am content . . . for when I am weak, then I am strong" (2 Cor. 12:10). Knowing this is how character is *formed*; we can then understand how it must be *strengthened*.

---

65   George Whitefield, *Works Vol. IV* (London, 1771), 306.

Second, the character of a warrior preacher is strengthened through a personal pursuit of holiness.

We see the evidence if this in Paul's exhortation to Timothy, when, in contrast to the plague of false teachers that were fleecing and corrupting the church, he emphatically declared,

> But flee from theses things, you man of God, and pursue righteousness, godliness, faith, love, perseverance and gentleness. Fight the good fight of faith; take hold of the eternal life to which you were called, and you made the good confession in the presence of many witnesses.
> (1 Tim. 6:11–12)

I will never forget a sermon John MacArthur preached on this text at the Shepherds' Conference on March 22, 1987, when I was a young man. His outline remains with me to this very day. Here's a direct quote from his exposition:

> In verse 11 it begins, "But thou, O man of God." "But thou" is set in contrast to the false teachers. The false teachers are into everything mentioned from verse 3 through 10, "But you," he says in contrast, "You are God's man." They are money's man; they are materialism's man; they are the world's man; they are their own man; they are sin's man, Satan's man, hell's man. "But you, O man of God." Contrast. The word "O" is a personal appeal. It's an emotional appeal. It's very rare, by the way, in personal greetings in the Greek that word would be used, and it shows the pleading in the heart of Paul. "But you, O man of God," remember your spiritual beginnings, your spiritual calling. Don't lose sight of your identity. As a man of God, you have a unique calling. As a man of God, you are to be uniquely identifiable. As a man of God, you are to have characteristics that can be seen and measured.
>
> How is a man of God known? What is Paul going to say to Timothy as to the character of a man of God? Four things: Timothy, you man of God, here are four things that

should mark you. One, a man of God is marked by what he flees from. Two, a man of God is marked by what he follows after. Three, a man of God is marked by what he fights for. And four, a man of God is marked by what he is faithful to. A tremendous practical outline for every man of God who stands to speak in the place of divine truth.[66]

It is impossible to improve upon MacArthur's outline or exposition. The overall theme of this passage is to exhort Timothy (and, by extension, all believers—especially pastors) in a way that will *strengthen his character through a personal pursuit of holiness.* This is a call to *piety*—to resurrect an old English term. This is a call to discipline, consistent with Paul's earlier exhortation to Timothy where he said, "Discipline yourself for the purpose of godliness" (1 Tim. 4:7). Every regenerate heart that has been thoroughly broken over its innate estrangement and antipathy toward God and has experienced the wonders of His presence amidst great trials will readily, yes, gladly *flee from evil and pursue righteousness.* The natural desire of a godly character is to strengthen it with a secret devotion to God in prayer and Bible study so it might grow in Christlikeness still more. Herein is the source of lasting joy and powerful preaching. If such a disposition is absent in a pastor, if such a decisive determination is seldom to be found, there is something amiss in the inner man. A fruitless vine must therefore be pruned by the Father's loving discipline, which can be quite painful. This is affirmed in the testimony of the psalmist: "It is good for me that I was afflicted that I may learn Your statutes" (Ps. 119:73).

> *The natural desire of a godly character is to strengthen it with a secret devotion to God in prayer and Bible study so it might grow in Christlikeness still more.*

When a passion to feel the presence of God in the inner man through communion with Him is missing, so, too, will be the prominence of Christ in preaching. How can we speak of the love of Christ if we experience so little of it? How can we extol the glories of being united to the One who satisfies the longings of our

---

66 https://www.gty.org/library/sermons-library/54-47/the-man-of-god

heart if we have so little desire to enjoy it? We must understand that fellowship with Christ unleashes the power of Christ in our preaching, and only a Spirit-empowered zeal for the glory of Christ will cause sinners to tremble and saints to rejoice in tears of worship. It is our personal pursuit of holiness that produces *unction* in preaching—to resurrect another term from bygone days that is seldom used or manifested in pulpits today. This kind of preaching is the natural and irrepressible overflow of the doxologies of a man's heart, like those first-century preachers described in Acts 4:31: "And when they had prayed, the place where they had gathered together was shaken, and they were all filled with the Holy Spirit and began to speak the word of God with boldness."

This is noticeably lacking in the church today. As one writer put it, "We need men of God who bring the atmosphere of heaven with them into the pulpit and speak from the borders of another world."[67] Without the proper strengthening of the inner man through private worship, a preacher's character will quickly atrophy like an unused muscle. He will gradually lapse into a state of worldliness and unwittingly be shaped into the mold of the godless culture in which he lives (Rom. 12:2). Woke evangelicalism—an oxymoron—is a classic example of this progressive spiritual deterioration.

A Command to Flee and Pursue

The valiant apostle Paul was acutely aware of the deceitfulness and power of indwelling sin, causing him to lament over its tormenting presence (Rom. 7:15–25)—a proclivity in the inner man that is easily seduced by the lusts of the flesh and the temptations of the world. All the more reason for him to warn Timothy to "flee from these things, you man of God" (1 Tim. 6:11), which not only includes "the love of money" in the immediate context, but the many other forms of wickedness associated with worldly lusts. Instead, he is exhorted to "pursue" six virtues:

RIGHTEOUSNESS: uprightness; personal integrity; living in harmony with the Word of God; walking by the Spirit; outwardly mani-

---

67   Iain H. Murray, *Seven Leaders: Preachers and Pastors* (Edinburgh: The Banner of Truth Trust, 2017), 151.

festing an inward righteousness; being so yielded to God that we "present [our] bodies a living sacrifice, holy, acceptable to God" (Rom. 12:1) and thereby manifest our love for God and our neighbor. Paul reiterates this same concept in 2 Timothy 2:22: "Now flee from youthful lusts and pursue righteousness, faith, love and peace, with those who call on the Lord from a pure heart."

GODLINESS: piety; a personal pursuit of holiness and secret devotion to God; holy living that flows from an intimate communion with God and a conscious seeking after His presence through prayer and the Word. Paul exhorted Timothy to "lead a tranquil and quiet life in all godliness and dignity" (1 Tim. 2:2); and in Titus 2:11 he reminds us that Christ's saving grace instructs "all men . . . to deny ungodliness and worldly desires and to live sensibly, righteously and godly in the present age" (Titus 2:11).

FAITH: an unwavering confidence in the perfections and promises of God; We are reminded to "continue in the faith firmly established and steadfast, and not moved away from the hope of the gospel that you have heard, which was proclaimed in all creation under heaven, and of which I, Paul, was made a minister" (Col. 1:23).

LOVE: the self-sacrificing love of choice, like the love that impelled Christ's self-sacrifice on the cross for undeserving sinners; love being foundational to ministry, "For the love of Christ controls us, having concluded this, that one died for all, therefore all died; and He died for all, so that they who live might no longer live for themselves, but for Him who died and rose again on their behalf" (2 Cor. 5:14–15).

PERSEVERANCE: having a Spirit-empowered inner fortitude rooted in Scripture that is capable of withstanding adversity and stress: "For whatever was written in earlier times was written for our instruction, so that through perseverance and the encouragement of the Scriptures we might have hope. Now may the God who gives perseverance and encouragement grant you to be of the same mind with one another according to Christ Jesus, so that with one accord you may with one voice glorify the God and Father of our Lord Jesus Christ" (Rom. 15:4–6).

GENTLENESS: a mild, tender temperament and an even-tempered demeanor as Paul described in 2 Timothy 2:24–25: "The Lord's bond-servant must not be quarrelsome, but be kind to all, able to teach, patient when wronged, with gentleness correcting those who are in opposition, if perhaps God may grant them repentance leading to the knowledge of the truth."

The "man of God" who pursues these virtues of personal holiness will fortify his godly character even further. As a result, he will be increasingly amazed at his sin and thereby increasingly amazed at God's grace. He will gladly, like Paul, "discipline [his] body and make it his slave" (1 Cor. 9:27); his life's priority will be to give himself completely to the service of his King, for indeed, "No soldier in active service entangles himself in the affairs of everyday life, so that he may please the one who enlisted him as a soldier" (2 Tim. 2:4). His vision of the infinite perfections and majesty of God combined with his intimate communion with Him will invigorate his joyful obedience all the more and thus enable him to follow the apostle's next admonition to Timothy: "Fight the good fight of faith; take hold of the eternal life to which you were called, and you made the good confession in the presence of many witnesses."

Because the marks of habitual Christlikeness were first evident in the apostle's character, they served as a model for all young warrior preachers. We see this in Paul's reminder to Timothy:

Now you followed my teaching, conduct, purpose, faith, patience, love, perseverance, persecutions, and sufferings, such as happened to me at Antioch, at Iconium and at Lystra; what persecutions I endured, and out of them all the Lord rescued me! Indeed, all who desire to live godly in Christ Jesus will be persecuted.
(2 Tim. 3:10–12)

The Example of the Puritans

It is quite rare to witness this depth of godly character in modern evangelicalism, although this paucity is nothing new. With the "pervasive God-centeredness" of Puritans as his example, J.I. Packer exposes the pervasive man-centeredness and shallowness of character that typifies most pulpits and churches today—an indictment that is well deserved in my life as well. He says,

> It seems undeniable that the Puritans' passion for spiritual integrity and moral honesty before God, their fear of hypocrisy in themselves as well as in others, and the humble self-distrust that led them constantly to check whether they had not lapsed into religious play-acting before men with hearts that had gone cold towards God, *has no counterpart in the modern-day evangelical ethos*. They were characteristically cautious, serious, realistic, steady, patient, persistent in well-doing and avid for holiness of heart; we, by contrast, too often show ourselves to be characteristically brash, euphoric, frivolous, superficial, naïve, hollow and shallow.[68]

Packer continued: "Owen's advice to 'my fellow-laborers and students in divinity' about the way to approach the task of upholding the faith against falsehood and folly climaxes with a call to 'diligent endeavor to have the power of truths professed and contended for abiding upon our hearts.'[69] When considering the need for warrior preachers to *strengthen their character through a personal pursuit of holiness*, Owen's words are worth quoting:

> When the heart is cast indeed into the mould of the doctrine that the mind embraceth; . . . when not the sense of the words only is in our heads, but the sense of the things abides in our hearts; when we have communion with God in the doctrine we contend for, then shall we be garrisoned, by the grace of God, against all the assaults of men. And with-

---

68 J.I. Packer, *A Quest for Godliness: The Puritan Vision of the Christian Life* (Wheaton, IL: Crossway Books, 1990), 217.

69 Ibid., 217.

out this all our contending is, as to ourselves, of no value. What am I the better if I can dispute that Christ is God, but have no sense of sweetness in my heart from hence that he is a God in covenant with my soul? What will it avail me to evince, by testimonies and arguments, that he hath made satisfaction for sin, if, through my unbelief, the wrath of God abideth on me, and I have no experience of my own being made the righteousness of God in him? . . . Will it be any advantage to me, in the issue, to profess and dispute that God worketh the conversion of a sinner by the irresistible grace of his Spirit, if I was never acquainted experimentally with the deadness and utter impotency to good, that opposition to the law of God, which is in my own soul by nature, [and] with the efficacy of the exceeding greatness of the power of God in quickening, enlightening, and bring for the fruits of obedience in me? . . . Let us, then, not think that we are any thing the better for our conviction of the truths of the great doctrines of the gospel . . . unless we find the power of the truths abiding in our own hearts and have a continual experience of their necessity and excellency in our standing before God and our communion with him"[70]

Needless to say, the sin-cursed world in which we live violently opposes these efforts and will stop at nothing to prevent them. Piety is considered by many in evangelical circles to be an insult to grace, a form of legalism. Few preachers and church leaders strive to these ends, banishing congregations to an island of spiritual infancy and carnality.

Cyber World Make-Believe

Worse yet, very few Christians see the dangers associated with the comforts of our modern world combined with its endless opportunities for pleasure that can stifle character development. Think how easily the Internet seduces worldly Christians into living in a parallel universe detached from reality. The cyber world with its social media platforms offers a numbing utopia where people

70   John Owen, *Works, Vol. XII*: 52

can be whoever they want to be and say whatever they want to say with little if any consequence. Thoughts of God, judgment, and eternal life are easily displaced by the more satisfying pleasures of visual and audio stimulation with their uncanny ability to shape a subjective and false sense of self. Godly character simply cannot develop in a world of make-believe. The result is devastating. Spiritual dwarfs are leading most churches today—men who bear no resemblance to the "man of God" described in Scripture, and their congregations love them for it. God addressed this through His prophet Jeremiah in the days of Judah's deceptions and apostasy:

> The prophets prophesy falsely,
> And the priests rule on their own authority;
> And My people love it so!
> (Jer. 5:31)

Bereft of genuine piety, doctrinal discernment, sobriety, and fortitude, far too many pastors are self-indulgent and success-oriented entrepreneurs entertaining crowds rather than evangelizing the lost and equipping the saints. Much of what passes for preaching and worship today is alien to Scripture.

How different were the great men and women of faith in the Bible, and others down through redemptive history who have gone on before us—mature saints devoted to godliness and shepherded by true men of God, warrior preachers of the highest order. For most in days gone by, life was *hard* and *short*. Debilitating disease or injury was inevitable. Every aspect of life was therefore devoted to the glory of God because those who loved Him knew they could enter into His presence at any moment. Millions in underdeveloped countries today experience this, too.

This certainly characterized the Puritans of the seventeenth century where over half of all children died in infancy and the average life expectancy was around thirty-five years. They lived in light of eternity because their character was formed in that same light. While we can and should rejoice in the blessings of common grace (what would we do without modern medicine?), we must never forget that the wages of sin is death (Rom. 6:23). Indeed, as with the Puritans, death is also our constant companion—though we don't experience as much of it in terms of its seeming untimeliness—and we would do well to consider its arrival, "inasmuch as it is appointed for men to die once and after this comes judgment" (Heb. 9:27).

To be sure, when facing our own mortality, we tend to ask the right questions about life and eternity, and it is here that God does some of His greatest work in building our character. For this reason, some of the most helpful truths pertaining to the character of a warrior preacher can be gleaned from the priorities of men who were on the very brink of eternity, as we have seen in the life of the apostle Paul. In fact, during his final imprisonment just before his death, he revealed the unfailing priority of his heart, namely, *to be nourished by the Word*. For this reason, he asked Timothy to bring him a copy of the Scriptures (2 Tim. 4:13).

> What were the burdens of his heart that were so important to pass on? The answer is found in the content of his epistle, namely, the absolute trustworthiness of Scripture (1:16–21); the danger of false doctrine and how to spot false teachers (2:1–22); and the certainty of God's judgment despite the dangerous deceptions of false teachers that deny it (3:1–18).

We see this dynamic in the final days of Peter's life as well. In similar fashion, while he awaited his crucifixion, "knowing that the laying aside of my earthly dwelling is imminent, as also our Lord Jesus Christ has made clear to me," Peter penned his final epistle. Why? So the saints "will be able to call these things to mind" (2 Peter 1:14). And what were those things? What were the burdens of his heart that were so important to pass on? The answer is found in the content of his epistle, namely, the absolute trustworthiness of Scripture (1:16–21); the danger of false doctrine and how to spot false teachers (2:1–22); and the certainty of God's judgment despite the dangerous deceptions of false teachers that deny it (3:1–18). Without question, the crisis in the first-century church has not changed. Yet the last words of a dying apostle (that should be the rallying cry for every faithful preacher) are sorely neglected today.

You will be hard-pressed to find preachers who are willing to expound upon Peter's inspired words recorded in his second epistle. Only a true warrior of the cross will take up such a grand and glorious cause.

When the character of a warrior preacher is *formed in the fires of suffering and persecution*, then *strengthened through a personal pursuit of holiness*, it will produce a valiant warrior that God will certainly use to glorify the King and advance His kingdom purposes.

Third, the character of a warrior preacher will be deployed in evangelism and discipleship.

Even as God chose and gifted men of God in the Old and New Testaments to speak on His behalf, He continues to do so today. Christ possesses the authority and sovereignty to assign spiritual gifts to those He has called to serve Him in the building of His church (Eph. 4:7–8)—godly leaders divinely enabled to lead His people (1 Thess. 5:12–13; Heb. 13:7, 17). The church was "built on the foundation of the apostles and prophets, Christ Jesus Himself being the cornerstone" (Eph. 2:20). Together they declared the revelation of God's Word (Eph. 3:5; *cf.* Acts 11:28; 21:10–11) and confirmed their message with miraculous signs (2 Cor. 12. 12:12; *cf.* Acts 8:6–7; Heb. 2:3–4).[71] Once the foundation was completed, the offices of *apostle* and *prophet* ceased, and in their place God called and gifted *evangelists* (missionaries and church planters) and *pastor-teachers* to build upon that foundation through the faithful proclamation of the Word in keeping with the Great Commission (Matt. 28:18–20). Paul describes these offices in the order of their unique calling and role in Ephesians 4.

> And He gave some as apostles, and some *as* prophets, and some *as* evangelists, and some *as* pastors and teachers, for the equipping of the saints for the work of service, to the building up of the body of Christ; until we all attain to the

---

71   John MacArthur and Richard Mayhue, General Editors, *Biblical Doctrine: A Systematic Summary of Bible Truth* (Wheaton, IL: Crossway, 2017), 755.

unity of the faith, and of the knowledge of the Son of God, to a mature man, to the measure of the stature which belongs to the fullness of Christ.
(Eph. 4:11–13)

The warrior preachers of the church today are gifted *evangelists* dedicated to reaching lost sinners with the saving truths of the gospel, along with *pastor-teachers* who are to be the under-shepherds of the great Shepherd (Heb. 12:20–21; 1 Peter 2:25; 5:2). Their primary function is to feed the sheep (*cf.* John 21:15–17), a responsibility they accomplish through teaching the Word (*cf.* 2 Tim. 3:16–19; 1 Peter 2:2–3). Although teaching can be identified as its own ministry (1 Cor. 12:28), it is best to regard "shepherds and teachers" in Ephesians 4:11 as describing two facets of a single office of pastoral leadership. Other New Testament texts indicate that pastors are expected to be both shepherds (Acts 20:28; 1 Peter 5:2) and teachers (1 Tim. 3:2: 5:17).[72]

The Character of a Pastor-Teacher

My chief concern in this book concerns the office of pastor-teacher. Pastor-teachers are men whose character has first been *formed in the fires of suffering and persecution, strengthened through a personal pursuit of holiness*, and thus prepared them to be good soldiers of Jesus Christ, ready to be *deployed in evangelism and discipleship*. These men are both *soldiers* and *shepherds* (Eph. 6:10–20; Matt. 20:25–28; 23:11)—brave soldiers submissive to "the captain of the LORD's host" (Josh. 5:15; a reference to the pre-incarnate Christ), ready to fight the enemies of the gospel, as well as humble shepherds, dedicated to caring for the sheep of the Lord's pasture as He has commanded them to do, saying:

> . . . shepherd the flock of God among you, exercising oversight not under compulsion, but voluntarily, according to the will of God; and not for sordid gain, but with eagerness; nor yet as lording it over those allotted to your charge, but proving to be examples to the flock.

72 Ibid., 757.

And when the Chief Shepherd appears, you will receive the unfading crown of glory.
(1 Peter 5:2–4)

These are men who stand behind pulpits every Sunday in faithful obedience to Christ's Great Commission to "make disciples of all nations" (Matt. 28:19); *cf.* Luke 24:47) and to "preach the gospel to every creature" (Mark 16:15 NKJV). Theirs is the responsibility to proclaim the true gospel, which Jesus described as the proclamation of "repentance for the forgiveness of sins" in His name (Luke 24:47). Committed to the preaching of the Word in all its purity and power, these men understand this to be the God-ordained method for teaching, reproof, correction, and training in righteousness (2 Tim. 3:16–17).

This is the kind of bold preaching that upset the ancient world (Acts 17:6). In fact, *if preaching is not upsetting to the vast majority of those who hear it, it is not authentic biblical preaching.* It is "wide gate . . . broad way" preaching "that leads to destruction, and there are many who enter through it" (Matt. 7:13). This is the glib, superficial, theatrical, conversational preaching the world craves and Christ abhors.

In his timely book, *Called to Preach: Fulfilling the High Calling of Expository Preaching*, Steven J. Lawson warns against this kind of preaching, rightly referring to it as, "The Pulpit of the Broad Path."[73] He describes the broad path this way:

> It is the way most traveled in the ministry. It is easily accessed and requires no sense of calling to enter. It allows very little study to advance on it. In fact, many who enter here rely on others, whether through plagiarism or a "preaching team." The way is so wide that it allows any theology to be taught. It is far and away the most popular and appealing road in ministry. Larger crowds may attend it. It is light on Bible content but heavy on personality and charisma. This route is more about style than substance. It is a wide-open thoroughfare that attracts many preachers.
>
> This pulpit avoids the controversial subjects taught in

73 Steven J. Lawson, *Called to Preach: Fulfilling the High Calling of Expository Preaching* (Grand Rapids, MI: Baker Books, 2022), 193.

the Bible. It preaches only those truths that people want to hear. It gives plenty of illustrations and applications but no doctrine or admonition. It makes no demands upon those who sit under it.

This is the pulpit of the broad path. Tragically, it leads its listeners down the broad road. It panders to the fleshly appetites of its many travelers. It amuses them to death. It fills the building with people but leaves the pulpit devoid of truth. This is the ear tickling about which Paul warns (2 Tim. 4:3). In the end, this kind of preaching leads to destruction of many.[74]

Rest assured that the character of churchmen who fall into this category of preaching have not been *formed in the fires of suffering and persecution*, nor have they been *strengthened through a personal pursuit of holiness*. Therefore, they are ill prepared to be good soldiers of Jesus Christ, unfit for *deployment in evangelism and discipleship*. Moreover, they have never been called or gifted by God to assume the role of pastor-teacher. They will have no desire to be a student of the Word; no commitment to unearth the unlimited riches of truth found in Scripture; and no understanding of how to practically apply them to their own life and to those they pretend to shepherd.

The Divine Calling

This is in stark contrast to those whom God has truly called and gifted. As I have written elsewhere, a man whom God has graciously called into vocational ministry will manifest five characteristics:

A longing to know and serve Christ;
A sense of urgency to preach the gospel;
A pervasive feeling of inadequacy;
A burden to shepherd the flock;
A public confirmation of spiritual gifts, character, and abilities.[75]

---

74   Ibid., 193-4.

75   David A. Harrell, *Seven Key Principles for Effective Ministry: Nurturing Thriving Churches in a Postmodern Culture* (Wapwallopen, PA: Shepherd Press, 2019), 70.

Without an unshakeable conviction of being called by God into pastoral ministry, a man will never be able to withstand the inevitable struggles and sorrows associated with it. When a man is uncertain of his calling, that lack of assurance will haunt him. Doubt and discouragement will be his ruin. Down deep he will know he is in a position for which he is not suited. Others will eventually concur. I have witnessed this many times over the course of my life in ministry. If that is you, there is no shame in changing course and serving Christ in a capacity for which you are suited.

Without an unshakeable conviction of being called by God into pastoral ministry, a man will never be able to withstand the inevitable struggles and sorrows associated with it.

However, that man whom God has truly set apart to pastoral ministry—by His grace alone—will echo the confident assurance of Paul and say, "Of this church I was made a minister according to the stewardship from God bestowed on me for your benefit, so that I might fully carry out the preaching of the word of God" (Col. 1:25). Like the prophet Jeremiah, even when ridicule and rejection seem to be more than he can bear, when he feels as though he is drowning in depression and tempted to stop speaking altogether, the powerful presence of the indwelling Christ will animate his soul with a renewed zeal to keep preaching the Word, and with the prophet he will say, "Then in my heart it becomes like a burning fire shut up in my bones; and I am weary of holding it in, and I cannot endure it" (Jer. 20:9). Every faithful steward of the mysteries of God knows this feeling and rejoices because of it. Nothing can silence the warrior preacher. Like the prophet Amos, he will declare, "A lion has roared! Who will not fear? The Lord GOD has spoken! Who can but prophesy?" (Amos 3:8); and with Paul he will say, "For if I preach the gospel, I have nothing to boast of, for I am under compulsion; for woe is me if I do not preach the gospel" (1 Cor. 9:16).

Final Charge

It is my great burden to see God raise up faithful young men who will take the fight to the enemy for the glory of Christ and His kingdom. What a joy it is to see sinners rescued from the domain of darkness and brought into the kingdom of God's beloved Son (Col. 1:13).

In his book, *Seven Leaders: Preachers and Pastors,* Iain Murray records the words of the great twentieth-century American Presbyterian New Testament scholar at Princeton Seminary, J. Gresham Machen—a man who shared my passion. To this end, that great warrior preacher gave a solemn charge to his students that is as contemporary today as it was then. I offer this quote as a summarizing challenge of this chapter, praying it will stir every minister of the gospel to a new level of dedication and bold determination, especially in the realm of godly character development. As the leader of a conservative revolt against theological liberalism, Machen's words are part of a sermon he preached in 1925 on "The Separateness of the Church." Here's his powerful observation and charge:

> Gradually the church is being permeated by the spirit of the world; it is become what the Auburn Affirmationists call an "inclusive" church; it is become salt that has lost its savour and is henceforth good for nothing but to be cast out and trodden under foot of men.
>
> What are you going to do, my brothers, in this great time of crisis? What a time it is to be sure! What a time of glorious opportunity! Will you stand with the world, will you shrink from controversy, will you witness for Christ only where witnessing costs nothing, will you pass through these stirring days without coming to any real decision? Or will you learn the lesson of Christian history; will you penetrate, by your study and your meditation, beneath the surface; will you recognise in that which prides itself on being modern, an enemy that is as old as the hills; will you hope and pray, not for a mere continuance for what is now, but for a recovery of the gospel that can make all things new? God grant that some of you may do that![76]

---

[76] J. Gresham Machen, *God Transcendent* (Edinburgh: Banner of Truth Trust, 1982), 115.

Chapter 5 Questions

1. Is it your passionate desire to be God-fearing in your heart, God-centered in your thoughts, and God-honoring in your life, both privately and publicly?

2. Are you wholeheartedly devoted to mining the inexhaustible treasures of Scripture and fearlessly proclaiming the perfections of Christ and His love for sinners?

3. Is your pulpit demeanor one of solemnity, profundity, and dignity—a natural manifestation of the unrestricted rule of the Spirit of God in your heart? If not, how would you describe your pulpit demeanor?

4. Are others drawn to you because of your Christlike character or because of your similarity with the world?

5. Would others describe you as a man who fights for doctrinal purity and yields no ground to the enemy, or a man who promotes tolerance and avoids controversial issues and doctrines?

6. Do you flee from evil and pursue righteousness in your inner man for the glory and enjoyment of God, or is this a foreign concept to you?

7. Are you confident that God has called and gifted you to be in vocational ministry based upon the five characteristics described in this chapter and the qualifications set forth in 1 Timothy 3:1–7 and Titus 1:1–6?

8. When ridicule and rejection seem more than you can bear and you are tempted to give up, does the powerful presence of the indwelling Christ animate your soul with a renewed zeal to keep preaching the Word?

6

The Warrior's Rewards

I have fought the good fight, I have finished the course, I have kept the faith; in the future there is laid up for me the crown of righteousness, which the Lord, the righteous Judge, will award to me on that day; and not only to me, but also to all who have loved His appearing.
(2 Timothy 4:7–8)

We mortify sin by cherishing the principle of holiness and sanctification in our souls, labouring to increase and strengthen it by growing in grace, and by a constancy and frequency in acting of it in all duties, on all occasions, abounding in the fruits of it. Growing, thriving, and improving in universal holiness, is the great way of the mortification of sin. The more vigorous the principle of holiness is in us, the more weak, infirm, and dying will be that of sin. The more frequent and lively are the actings of grace, the feebler and seldomer will be the actings of sin. The more we abound in the "fruits of the Spirit," the less shall we be concerned in the "works of the flesh." And we do but deceive ourselves if we think sin will be mortified on any other terms.

JOHN OWEN[77]

77 John Owen, *The Works of John Owen, Vol. 3.* (Edinburgh: W.H. Goold, Edition, T&T Clark, n.d.), 552.

The vast majority of pastors and missionaries will spend their life serving Christ in obscurity. Most will struggle with limited finances their entire life. Some will be imprisoned or killed for their faith, or both, and many will be buried in unmarked graves. Most preachers will never preach to more than a handful of people. Very few will pastor a church over one hundred people. I have had the privilege of counseling and mentoring many like this, and without fail I can see fatigue on their faces. The subdued tone of their voice is often in the minor key and their eyes will quickly fill with tears as they describe the great difficulties they happily endure out of love for their Savior and King. I always have a large supply of tissues on hand, and often I weep with them.

The vast majority of pastors and missionaries will spend their life serving Christ in obscurity. Most will struggle with limited finances their entire life.

There is a noticeable familial love that exists when we encounter fellow believers. It's as though every child of God has a spiritual radar system within him that can immediately detect other brothers and sisters in Christ, even when they have never met before. Then, after a short conversation, it becomes manifestly obvious that we are part of the same family of God—His adopted children and joint heirs with Jesus. But there exists a special bond between fellow pastors, one that has been forged in the fires of adversity for the glory of Christ. Often a man's very presence betrays the combat he has endured and the love of Christ that emboldens him. Casual encounters quickly become intense interactions as we discover our shared calling, sufferings, and passionate longings to see Christ exalted. I have carried many wounded men off the battlefield, as others have carried me.

It is little wonder we can finish each other's sentences. What a comfort to know that the One who never slumbers nor sleeps (Ps. 121:4) takes into account all our wanderings and captures all our tears in His bottle of remembrance (Ps. 56:8). Better yet, to know that a day is promised when "[our] grief will be turned into joy" (John 16:20); that day in glory when "He will wipe away every tear from their eyes; and there will no longer be any death; there will no longer be any mourning, or crying, or pain; the first things have passed away" (Rev. 21:4).

Green Beret Brotherhood

Having served together in spiritual combat many years ago where we had to protect the sheep from some ravenous wolves that had infiltrated our church, my Green Beret brother in Christ and fellow elder, Joel C., commented on the parallels of warrior brotherhood that exists among Special Forces soldiers and that of fellow believers who are seriously engaged in kingdom warfare. Here's what he said:

> It is the same for Special Operations warriors. Anytime I've run into a Special Forces guy, we connect immediately due to the shared suffering. We know each of us has had the same Special Forces Assessment and Selection (SFAS), also known as "School for Advanced Suffering," and the same Qualification Course. The entire pipeline is full of suffering, so when you meet someone who suffered the same as you, you bond on some level. I can almost spot a Special Forces guy before we talk, just by how he carries himself and behaves. The bond is even deeper with soldiers who suffered *with* you. I'll never forget the guys in my team during team week in SFAS and even more the guys who suffered for eighteen months with me in the Qualifications Course. There is something meaningful about shared suffering, especially in combat. Accomplishing a great task while enduring tremendous hardship forges incredible bonds where you wouldn't think twice about dying for that person.[78]

The sacred ties of combat brotherhood I have for fellow pastors and missionaries also includes a special burden for every man and

---

78   Joel C., from private correspondence.

woman who has been divinely deployed into combating the wickedness of this world through some form of gospel ministry. This includes many single women, along with many wives who sacrifice themselves alongside their husbands as together they battle on as good soldiers of the cross. To this day I have the joy of mentoring and fellowshipping with other faithful pastors and missionaries—including their wives and families—from other countries around the world where I have taught and served. Many of them have suffered for their faith in significant ways, and many still do.

The world hates us because it hates Christ, and because we are not of this world. Slander and ridicule are to be expected. Persecution is inevitable. Far more people will reject the gospel than embrace it.

It is manifest that serving Christ on the front line of battle is very difficult. The world hates us because it hates Christ, and because we are not of this world. Slander and ridicule are to be expected. Persecution is inevitable. Far more people will reject the gospel than embrace it. Often feelings of discouragement and futility are so overwhelming that seemingly the only way to find relief is to abandon the ministry altogether. This is when the subject of *eternal rewards* is so needed and so welcomed. This is when every faithful soldier of Christ needs to hear the encouraging reminder, "Your labor is not in vain" (1 Cor. 15:58). This is when hope must be bolstered by the words of the Master we all long to hear, "Well done, good and faithful slave" (Matt. 25:23). This is when this subject is most refreshing and motivating, as Jesus makes clear, "Be glad in that day and leap for joy, for behold, your reward is great in heaven" (Luke 6:23).

Eulogizing the Godly Warrior

Memorial tributes are perhaps the best summary of a man's life. Together, what is said and left unsaid distills the very essence of who a man truly was, where he abides for eternity, and the likelihood of the rewards he may receive. Eulogies of the ungodly are noticeably silent about a life lived for the glory of God. They make much of the man and say nothing of his love and service for Christ because it did not exist. They typically include superficial sentiments like, "He was a good man who loved his family, had a great sense of humor, never met a stranger, loved to hunt and fish, and was always ready to help someone in need." In stark contrast, the tributes of a godly man—especially a warrior preacher—will have the sacred elements of the one I quote below written by Susie Spurgeon, the wife of the "Prince of Preachers," Charles Spurgeon. He whispered to his precious wife as death approached and said, "Susie. . . . Oh, wifie, I have had such a blessed time with my Lord!"[79]

Knowing her husband of thirty-six years better than anyone else on earth, she wrote this moving tribute upon his death that occurred at 11 p.m. on the Lord's Day, January 31, 1892:

> His "abundant entrance," the "Well done, good and faithful servant!" of the Master, the great throng of white robed spirits, who welcomed him as the one who first led them to the Savior, the admiring wondering angels, the radiant glory, the *surprise* of that midnight journey which ended at the throne of God; all this, and much more of blessed reality for him, has lifted our bowed heads, and enabled us to bless the Lord, even though he has taken from us so incomparable a friend and pastor. All that was choice, and generous, and Christ-like, seemed gathered together in his character, and lived out in his life. He was pre-eminently "the servant of"; yet he served with such humility and wisdom, that, with him, to *serve* was to *reign*. All feeling now the power he wielded over men's hearts; and because a prince of God, and a leader of men, has passed away, "our houses are left unto us desolate." I must not attempt to speak of his worth; words would utterly fail me; but the tears of multitudes, all over the world, testify to the irreparable loss they have sustained.[80]

When it is my turn to meet the Lord, I can truly say to my precious wife, Nancy, "I have had such a blessed time with my Lord!"

79 Ray Rhodes Jr., *Yours, till Heaven: The Untold Love Story of Charles and Susie Spurgeon* (Chicago, IL: Moody Publishers, 2021), 176.

80 Ibid., 176–7.

The rewards for serving Christ in this life are wonderful indeed, despite the trials associated with Christian ministry. Every faithful pastor, missionary, and church leader can affirm this reality. The refrain of the old hymn I sang as a boy resonates within my heart more strongly every day:

> There is joy, joy,
> Joy in serving Jesus,
> Joy that throbs within my heart;
> Ev'ry moment, ev'ry hour,
> As I draw upon His power,
> There is joy, joy,
> Joy that never shall depart.[81]

Despite the "chains and tribulations" that awaited him, Paul told the elders in Ephesus, ". . . none of these things move me; nor do I count my life dear to myself, so that I may finish my race with *joy*, and the ministry which I received from the Lord Jesus, to testify to the gospel of the grace of God (Acts 20:24, NKJV; emphasis mine). Indeed, soul-thrilling joy and the confidence of eternal reward will be the faithful companions of every man of God who gives his life for the gospel. For this reason, Paul could say this at the very close of his life:

> I have fought the good fight, I have finished the course, I have kept the faith; in the future there is laid up for me the crown of righteousness, which the Lord, the righteous Judge, will award to me on that day; and not only to me, but also to all who have loved His appearing.
> (2 Tim. 4:7–8)

You most likely share the passion of every warrior preacher and therefore have an experiential understanding of both *temporal blessings* and *eternal rewards*. Knowing this, I'm sure in many ways I'm "preaching to the choir," as the saying goes. Nevertheless, the magnificent blessings God lavishes upon His under-shepherds are worth repeating over and over again. Therefore, the purpose of

---

81 Oswald J. Smith, *There is Joy in Serving Jesus*.

this chapter is to encourage every faithful minister of the gospel by reviewing some of the *temporal blessings* he receives in this life for his service to his King, as well as the *eternal rewards* he will enjoy in the eternal state, where at His "right hand there are pleasures forever" (Ps. 16:11).

The Temporal Blessings of a Warrior Preacher

By temporal blessings, I'm referring to the gratifying favors God bestows upon those who wholeheartedly worship and serve Him. We get a sense of this in Jesus' promise in John 12:26 where He says, "If anyone serves Me, he must follow Me; and where I am, there My servant will be also; if anyone serves Me, the Father will honor him" (*cf.* 1 Sam. 2:30). While the fullness of the Father's esteem will not be completely realized until eternal glory (2 Tim. 2:10), the experience of it begins in this life. For example, faithful servants can also attest to the gift of God's protection and can echo the testimony of the psalmist: "I will say to the LORD, 'My refuge and my fortress, my God, in whom I trust!'" (Ps. 91:2). Who among us can deny the "peace of God, which surpasses all comprehension" that guards our hearts and minds in Christ Jesus (Phil. 4:6); or the indescribable reality of divine fellowship Jesus promised: "If anyone loves Me, he will keep My word; and My Father will love him, and We will come to him and make Our abode with him." (John 14:23)?

> *The blessings God grants us this side of glory*
> *are mere samplings of the eternal bliss we will*
> *experience when we "stand in the presence of His*
> *glory blameless with great joy" (Jude 24).*

To be sure, whatever form they take, God's temporal blessings enrich our soul, fortify our faith, and animate our will to press on with joy regardless the cost, a foretaste of the *eternal rewards* we will receive at the judgment seat of Christ (2 Cor. 5:10). The blessings God grants us this side of glory are mere samplings of the eternal bliss we will experience when we "stand in the presence of His glory blameless with great joy" (Jude 24). They are grace gifts that cause us to delight ourselves more fully in the Most High, for "He is a rewarder of those who seek Him" (Heb. 11:6). Although the ultimate reward is God Himself, we experience His goodness and grace even now. As the psalmist says, "For it is You who blesses the righteous man, O LORD, You surround him with favor as with a shield" (Ps. 5:12).

This is a profound motivator for the combat-weary soldier of the cross. The battle for truth is fierce and the sufferings can be severe throughout the life and ministry of every warrior preacher. But the blessings God lavishes upon His faithful servants are always *precious, motivating, empowering,* and *praiseworthy.* We must never forget that the penetrating eye of divine omniscience "understand[s] [our] thoughts from afar" and is "intimately acquainted with all [our] ways" (Ps. 139:3). Nothing is hidden from His sight, and He rewards accordingly; therefore, ". . . let us not lose heart in doing good, for in due time we will reap if we do not grow weary. So then, while we have opportunity, let us do good to all people, and especially to those who are of the household of faith" (Gal. 6:7). The Lord is always perfectly aware of the strength and encouragement we need and gives it just when we need it. And we can be assured that when "the Lord comes [He] will both bring to light the things hidden in the darkness and disclose the motives of men's hearts; and then each man's praise will come to him from God" (1 Cor. 4:5).

> The battle for truth is fierce and the sufferings can be severe throughout the life and ministry of every warrior preacher. But the blessings God lavishes upon His faithful servants are always *precious, motivating, empowering,* and *praiseworthy.*

May I challenge every reader engaged in spiritual warfare to contemplate three (out of many) categories of *temporal blessings* that you might be encouraged, strengthened, and perhaps convicted, and thus enjoy all that is available to you in Christ this side of heaven.

1. The blessing of fellowship with God through the study of Scripture

When considering temporal blessings, it is perhaps best to first consider the astounding reality of *enjoying fellowship with God through the study of His Word.* This is especially powerful for the warrior preacher. He treasures this gift of grace because he knows that apart from Christ, he can do nothing (John 15:5). He knows he must "be filled with the Spirit" (Eph. 5:18), which means he must "let the word of Christ dwell in [him] richly" (Col. 3:16). He will therefore spend his life immersed in study, not out of *duty*, but out of *desire*; and not merely as an academic exercise to gain knowledge, but *as an act of worship to know and enjoy the Triune God he loves and serves.*

One of the most prized realities of salvation is to know that God has redeemed us that He might dwell within us and thereby conform us to the likeness of Christ. But during our journey of sanctification, *He also allows us to enjoy sweet communion with Him* through various means of grace, which primarily include *God's Word, baptism, the Lord's Table, prayer, worship,* and *fellowship.* While they are all important, it is beyond the purview of my discussion to address each of them. Instead, I will focus primarily on the relationship between the believer's sanctification and Scripture, especially as it relates to the warrior preacher who longs to know more of Christ and experience more of His presence and power. This is what brings lasting joy to his heart.

The Westminster Shorter Catechism says it best: "Man's chief end is to glorify God, and to enjoy him for ever."[82] And this enjoyment begins in this life! Perhaps you can remember when it began in your life, when the Holy Spirit softened your heart and opened your mind to the truths of divine self-disclosure in the Scriptures, then brought those truths to bear upon your mind, caused you to see the horror of your sin and the glory of the cross, and raised you from spiritual death to spiritual life in the miracle of regeneration.

---

82 *Westminster Shorter Catechism*, Answer to Question 1.

As believers, we can all attest to the fact that through the agency of the Spirit and the instrument of His Word, He has shone "the Light of the knowledge of the glory of God in the face of Christ" (2 Cor. 4:6) in our hearts. As such, our primary responsibility is to worship the Lord our God. But this cannot be acceptable unless we worship Him in "spirit and in truth" (John 4:23), that is, to have a proper heart attitude that results in worship consistent with Scripture and centered on the person and work of Christ. Furthermore, Jesus made it clear that our sanctification is dependent upon the truth revealed in Scripture, and He actually prayed that His Father would help us to that end (John 17:17). Obviously, this means we must study and meditate upon it, gleaning from it all that God would have us understand and apply to our lives, *and in that process we enjoy rich fellowship with Him*. As His Word dwells within us richly, so too does Christ (Col. 3:16). In light of this, Paul declared, "I count all things to be loss in view of the surpassing value of knowing Christ Jesus my Lord" (Phil. 3:5); and this is accomplished by feeding upon God's written revelation.

> *Jesus made it clear that our sanctification is dependent upon the truth revealed in Scripture, and He actually prayed that His Father would help us to that end (John 17:17).*

For this reason, every warrior preacher cherishes the many hours he spends every week in prayer and Bible study—which must be inseparable disciplines. Because he knows that when he devotes himself to communing with God in this way, two realities transpire: first, a spiritual metamorphosis occurs as he is "transformed by the renewing of the mind, that [he] may prove what the will of God is, that which is good and acceptable and perfect" (Rom. 12:2); and second, he enjoys rich communion that comes *from* God as He reveals Himself to His servant—a divine gift of His grace. This is beautifully illustrated in the favor God affords the "blessed man" described in Psalm 1.

His delight is in the law of the LORD,
And in His law he meditates day and night.
He will be like a tree firmly planted by streams of water,

Which yields its fruit in its season
And its leaf does not wither;
And in whatever he does, he prospers.
(Ps. 1:2–3)

The rich treasures found in Scripture are truly staggering, be-yond our ability to fully grasp, although we witness their effects upon our life and those we shepherd. But as we search for them, something amazing happens: *we commune with the Most High God as He reveals Himself to us and we thereby experience the soul-de-lighting joy of His company*. We get a sense of this in the psalmist's descriptions of the supernatural benefits of God's special revela-tion in Scripture and their impact on those who reverence them:

The law of the LORD is perfect, restoring the soul;
The testimony of the LORD is sure, making wise the simple.
The precepts of the LORD are right, rejoicing the heart;
The commandment of the LORD is pure, enlightening the eyes.
The fear of the LORD is clean, enduring forever;
The judgments of the LORD are true; they are righteous al-together.
They are more desirable than gold, yes, than much fine gold;
Sweeter also than honey and the drippings of the honey-comb.
Moreover, by them Your servant is warned;
In keeping them there is great reward.
Who can discern his errors? Acquit me of hidden faults.
Also keep back Your servant from presumptuous sins;
Let them not rule over me;
Then I will be blameless,
And I shall be acquitted of great transgression.
Let the words of my mouth and the meditation of my heart
Be acceptable in Your sight,
O LORD, my rock and my Redeemer.
(Ps. 19:7–14)

The Forfeiture of Divine Blessing

The plethora of shallow and often unbiblical sermons these days betrays the forfeiture of divine blessing that exists among pastors who are lax in study—many of whom are completely unaware of their condition. We have all heard men preach about things they obviously know so little about and enjoy even less. Equally disturbing are congregations that are too undiscerning to hold these men accountable or refute the casuistry and heresy they hear on a routine basis. Far too many preachers skim across texts, making the obvious even more obvious; or they ignore passages they don't understand or ones that may be controversial; or they make a text say what they want it to say rather than what it actually says; or they purchase sermon outlines others have written, and some even plagiarize sermons others have preached. Consequently, by not "[working] hard at preaching and teaching" (1 Tim. 5:17), *they rob themselves of the joy of communing with God as He discloses the infinite perfections of His character, the marvels of His grace, and the glory of His redemptive purposes.*

> *We have all heard men preach about things they obviously know so little about and enjoy even less. Equally disturbing are congregations that are too undiscerning to hold these men accountable or refute the casuistry and heresy they hear on a routine basis.*

Unlike the apostles who were wholly devoted to "prayer, and to the ministry of the word" (Acts 6:4), far too many pastors today are wholly devoted to everything but that. Many show a total disregard to the command found in 2 Timothy 2:14–16 where Paul exhorted young pastor Timothy: "Be diligent to present yourself approved to God as a workman who does not need to be ashamed, accurately handling the word of truth. But avoid worldly and empty chatter, for it will lead to further ungodliness." By not "longing for the pure milk of the word, so that by it you may grow in respect to salvation" (1 Peter 2:2), many are spiritually malnourished and therefore unable to provide their congregations with the doctrinal nutrition they need to grow in holiness and in effectiveness in their gospel witness. Consequently, most evangelicals are indistinguishable from the godless culture in which they live, and as such have no gospel impact on it.

Moreover, with respect to preachers, *without a reverence for revealed truth they will not only forfeit fellowship with Christ but their preaching will proclaim little of Him!* The true gospel will therefore be distorted and replaced by a false gospel that will fit the Zeitgeist of the day, and people will perish in their sin.

The Vine, the Branches, and the Word

But the blessing of fellowship with God through the study of Scripture will be the valued prize of the warrior preacher who is obedient to Jesus' command to abide in Him (John 15)—a magnificent picture of our union with Christ. The imagery our Lord provides in the analogy of the *Vine and the Branches* is a powerful reminder of the mutual indwelling of Christ and His own and the fruitful harvest such an intimate union will produce. Every genuine disciple of Christ is a branch attached to the Vine that is Christ, and each branch is a conduit through which the fruit-producing spiritual molecules will flow to produce these magnificent clusters of God-honoring fruit. Fruit bearing is the essence of genuine discipleship, the result of abiding in Christ through faithful obedience to His self-disclosure in Scripture.

While it is the Spirit who imparts the principle of holiness within us at regeneration and perfects that good work that He began in us, our new nature cannot operate on its own power. It requires a continued work of sanctification through the inculcation of the Word of truth (John 17:17; *cf.* 1 Peter 2:2). This produces a constant sustaining and continuous renewing, ". . . for apart from Me you can do nothing" (v. 5). And it is our Lord's great desire for us to "bear much fruit" so God may receive great glory. Paul stated it this way: ". . . so that you may approve the things that are excellent, in order to be sincere and blameless until the day of Christ; having been filled with the fruit of righteousness which comes through Jesus Christ, to the glory and praise of God" (Phil. 1:10–11).

As we glorify Christ through our obedience—empowered and

directed as a result of our living union and communion with Him—we also glorify the Father as He does. The spiritual fruit that adorns the true disciple will reflect the character of Christ to whom we are united, especially when it is bountiful. Like Christ, we glorify the Father through our loving and joyful desire to do His will as it is revealed in Scripture. As others watch our lives manifest the character of God, they get a small glimpse of who He is, and in this He is glorified and our faith is validated as we show ourselves to be His disciples.

> *While it is the Spirit who imparts the principle of holiness within us at regeneration and perfects that good work that He began in us, our new nature cannot operate on its own power.*

As a result, we *will experience the love and joy of intimate fellowship with God.* Herein is God's gracious favor toward those who commune with Him. This would have been so encouraging to the disciples of the nascent church, as it is to all believers, when Jesus said, "Just as the Father has loved Me, I have also loved you; abide in My love. If you keep My commandments, you will abide in My love; just as I have kept My Father's commandments and abide in His love. These things I have spoken to you so that My joy may be in you, and that your joy may be made full" (vv. 9–11). *This is the soul-satisfying, Spirit-generated, subjective joy of Christ in the consciousness of the abiding believer who is saturated with the Word of God.* This is what animates a "hope [that] does not disappoint, because the love of God has been poured out within our hearts through the Holy Spirit who was given to us" (Rom. 5:5). Peter described this as "joy inexpressible and full of glory" (1 Peter 1:8), the kind of joy that permeates and controls the life of every obedient believer. Knowing this, Jesus prayed to His Father: "But now I come to You; and these things I speak in the world so that they may have My joy made full in themselves" (John 17:13). What a magnificent temporal reward! As the hymnist exclaimed, "Oh, what a foretaste of glory divine."[83]

---

83 Fanny Crosby, *Blessed Assurance*, 1873.

This will be the passionate longing of the warrior preacher. Would that every branch be a live branch that is truly attached *to* the Vine and abides *in* the Vine. Only then can a believer experience and manifest these God-glorifying characteristics that stand in stark contrast to the characteristics of those branches that have never been attached to the Vine through genuine saving faith.

Bible Study and Prayer—Acts of Worship

But again, the reward of fellowship with God through our study of Scripture is only realized experientially when *our study is an act of worship done in the atmosphere of prayer*. It must never be an academic exercise; if so, we miss the whole point of *God's desire to reveal Himself to us that we might know and enjoy Him now and forevermore*. I find David Martyn Lloyd-Jones' insight to be helpful in this regard:

> What foolish creatures we are! Many of us are not interested in doctrine at all; we are lazy Christians who do not read, do not think, and do not try to delve into the mysteries. We have had a certain experience and we desire no more. Others of us, deploring such an attitude, say that, because the Bible is full of doctrine, we must study it and grapple with it and possess it. So we become absorbed in our interest in doctrine and stop at that. The result is that, as regards this question of the love of Christ, we are no further on than the others because we have made doctrine an end and a terminus. In this way the devil trips and traps us and robs us of our heritage. If your knowledge of the Scriptures and of the doctrines of the gospel of the Lord Jesus Christ has not brought you to this knowledge of the love of Christ, you should be profoundly dissatisfied and disturbed. All biblical doctrine is about this blessed Person; and there is no greater snare in the Christian life than to forget the Person Himself and to live simply on truths concerning Him.
>
> It is for this reason that some of us have always had a feeling that it is dangerous to have examinations on scriptural knowledge . . . because it tends to encourage this tendency to stop at truths and to miss the Person. We

should never study the Bible or anything concerning biblical truth without realizing that we are in His presence, and that it is truth about Him. And it should always be done in an atmosphere of worship. Biblical truth is not one subject among others; it is not something that belongs to a syllabus. It is living truth about a living Person. That is why a theological college should be different from every other kind of college; and that is why a religious service is essentially different from every kind of meeting the world can organize. It is always a matter of worship; we are in the presence of a Person.[84]

I trust this is the passion of every reader that together we might know and enjoy the One who deserves our utmost. When this is true, our enjoyment of the temporal blessing of fellowship with God through the study of Scripture will produce a second, and certainly overlapping blessing—that of *seeing sinners saved and sanctified.*

2. The blessing of seeing sinners saved and sanctified

This second blessing experienced by the warrior preacher overlaps the first, for indeed, *as we enjoy rich fellowship through the prayerful study of Scripture we experience an increased burden for the lost.* Our desire to fulfill the great commission grows stronger, fueling the fires of evangelism and discipleship. And the Lord rewards our efforts by allowing us to celebrate the salvation of sinners with Him—a foretaste of future reward. We see this expressed in Paul's words to the new believers at Thessalonica: "For who is our hope or joy or crown of exultation? Is it not even you, in the presence of our Lord Jesus at His coming? For you are our glory and joy" (1 Thess. 2:19–20).

As a pastor, I can attest to *the exhilarating joy of seeing sinners saved and sanctified*—yet another gracious gift from the hand of

---

84   David Martyn Lloyd-Jones, *The Unsearchable Riches of Christ—Studies in Ephesians, Chapter 3;* https://graceonlinelibrary.org/doctrine-theology/d-martyn-lloyd-jones-attituted-toward-the-study-of-doctrine/

God where He fills our heart with praise and thus animates our will to stay in the fight, knowing the battle has already been won at the cross where Christ defeated sin, Satan, and death. It is important to remember, however, that God's saving work is always according to His saving plan. The manifestation of His sovereign grace in saving and sanctifying sinners is therefore a testimony to His infinite love and power that animates within us a heightened sense of breathless adoration and awe, which only enhances our joy. This has practical implications for the ministry of faithful preachers and their congregations.

Fully aware that fallen human beings are spiritually dead (Eph. 2:1), having no capacity to accept or understand the things of the Spirit of God (1 Cor. 2:14), therefore totally unable to repent and believe in Christ apart from renewing grace (Rom. 9:16), *the warrior preacher trusts solely in the sovereignty of God to save those He has elected by His uninfluenced grace alone.* Rejecting the Pelagian heresy that man is wholly able on his own to surrender to God in saving faith and the preacher's responsibility is to merely persuade him to do so, the warrior preacher rests in the *effectual call* of God to use His Word to convert sinners according to His sovereign decree and power (Rom. 8:30; 2 Thess. 2:14; 2 Tim. 1:9).

> *I've seen the Spirit bring the most hardened reprobates to saving faith. I've seen ungodly men and women melt under the heat of gospel truth during the course of an exposition and begin to sob with conviction.*

Over the years, I have seen many conversions, often among those we might think would be the least likely to believe. With no altar calls and no emotional pleadings pitting my will against that of the sinner to overcome his resistance (methods notorious for producing false conversions), I've seen the Spirit bring the most hardened reprobates to saving faith. I've seen ungodly men and women melt under the heat of gospel truth during the course of an exposition and begin to sob with conviction. I remember one man who was so overcome by guilt that he began to sob during a communion service and was saved that very day. I've witnessed God break the heart of fornicators, homosexuals, prostitutes, and hardened criminals. I've seen people from all walks of life come to saving faith in the most unlikely ways and places—mostly in the privacy of their own homes or some other quiet place God providentially arranged. But in every case, God used His Word to accomplish His saving purposes.

The Amazing Power of Providence in Salvation

I'm always humbled to see the unique ways God draws sinners to Himself. The testimony of John Bunyan in his book *Grace Abounding to the Chief of Sinners* (originally published in 1666) is a great example. There he described how God used the Christ-exalting conversation of women he did not know as His method to call Bunyan to saving faith. He described it as follows:

> I thought no man in England could please God better than I. But poor wretch as I was! I was all this while ignorant of Jesus Christ; and going about to establish my own righteousness; and had perished therein, had not God in mercy showed me more of my state by nature.
>
> But upon a day, the good providence of God called me to *Bedford*, to work on my calling; and in one of the streets of that town, I came where there were three or four poor women sitting at a door, in the sun, talking about the things of God; and being now willing to hear them discourse, I drew near to hear what they said, for I was now a brisk talker also myself, in the matters of religion; but I may say, *I heard but understood not*; for they were far above, out of my reach. Their talk was about a new birth, the work of God on their hearts, also how they were convinced of their miserable state by nature; they talked how God had visited their souls with His love in the Lord Jesus, and with what words and promises they had been refreshed, comforted, and supported, against the temptations of the devil: moreover, they reasoned of the suggestions and temptations of Satan in particular; and told to each other, by which they had been afflicted and how they were borne up under his assaults. They also discoursed of their own wretchedness of heart, and of their unbelief; and did contemn, slight and

abhor their own righteousness, as filthy, and insufficient to do them any good.

And, methought, they spake as if joy did make them speak; they spake with such pleasantness of scripture language, and with such appearance of grace in all they said, that they were to me, as if they had found a new world; as if they were people that dwelt alone, and were not to be reckoned among their neighbours. Numb. xxiii. 9.

At this I felt my own heart began to shake, and mistrust my condition to be naught; for I saw that in all my thoughts about religion and salvation, the new-birth did never enter into my mind; neither knew I the comfort of the word and promise, nor the deceitfulness and treachery of my own wicked heart. . . . Thus, therefore, when I had heard and considered what they said, I left them . . . but their talk and discourse went with me; also my heart would tarry with them, for I was greatly affected with their words.[85]

What a powerful reminder that salvation is all of grace, and the means by which the Lord might bring His Word to bear upon the souls of sinners is multifaceted indeed. But it is always His Word, whether read or heard, that He uses; for "faith comes from hearing, and hearing by the Word of Christ" (Rom. 10:17).

My mind is flooded with examples as I write this testimony. And every time I behold the saving power of God, I am overwhelmed with joy—like the rejoicing over the recovery of the lost sheep in Jesus' parable in Luke 15:1–7, symbolic of Christ searching for and recovering one lost sinner. In light of this, Jesus says, "I tell you that in the same way, there will be more joy in heaven over one sinner who repents than over ninety-nine righteous persons who need no repentance" (v. 7). In like manner we rejoice, *not only over the extent by which the Lord exerts Himself to seek and to save the lost, but also over the one who has been rescued.* And this celebratory joy is yet another temporal reward from God, a small sampling of the ultimate joy when we celebrate with all the redeemed!

My precious wife, Nancy, and I never stop thanking the Lord

---

85   John Bunyan, *Abounding Grace to the Chief of Sinners* (London: The Religious Tract society, 1905), 35–40.

for the magnificent gift of allowing us to see Him save our children and grandchildren—a most glorious answer to our prayers. What a grace-granted gift from God to be able to weep with them in sacred joy and embrace them in the waters of baptism. And to know this is all the gracious work of our sovereign God who effectually called them—this according to the love set upon them before the foundations of the earth.

The Amazing Power of Effectual Calling

I give credit to J.I. Packer for calling my attention to *The Westminster Confession X:i* in this regard, in that it paraphrases Romans 8:30 and thereby provides a succinct theological summary of the miracle of God's effectual calling upon sinners:

> All those whom God hath predestinated unto life, and those only he is pleased, in his appointed and accepted time, effectually to call, by his Word and Spirit, out of that state of sin and death in which they are by nature, to grace and salvation by Jesus Christ.[86]

Packer further stated, "*The Westminster Shorter Catechism*, answer 31, gives this analysis":

> Effectual calling is the work of God's Spirit whereby, convincing us of our sin and misery, enlightening our minds in the knowledge of Christ, and renewing our wills, he doth persuade and enable us to embrace Jesus Christ, freely offered to us in the gospel.[87]

But beyond the reward of seeing a sinner delivered from the kingdom of darkness by saving grace, we are also blessed with the gift of seeing such individuals grow in the grace and knowledge of Christ. Remember, we are not only commanded to make disciples, but also to teach them to observe all that our Lord Jesus has commanded us (Matt. 28:20). Every pastor is therefore called to "proclaim Him,

---

86 J.I. Packer, *A Quest for Godliness: The Puritan Vision of the Christian Life* (Wheaton, IL: Crossway Books, 1990), 294.

87 Ibid., 295

admonishing every man and teaching every man with all wisdom, so that we may present every man complete in Christ" (Col. 1:28).

Like Paul, a dedicated pastor will be so passionate about shepherding he will say, "I am again in labor until Christ is formed in you" (Gal. 4:19). And what a wonderful gift it is to be some small part of that spiritual birth process, to be able to witness with our own eyes God raising the spiritually dead to spiritual life, and then to see people of all ages and backgrounds grow in Christ and serve Him faithfully. Like the apostle John, we can say, "I have no greater joy than to hear that my children walk in truth" (3 John 1:4)—a joy that will one day explode into its ultimate fullness in the splendors of heaven.

When the first two categories of temporal blessings are realized in the life of a warrior preacher—*enjoyment of fellowship with God through the study of Scripture* and *seeing sinners saved and sanctified*—a third category I wish to underscore will naturally emerge, namely, *the blessing of a clear conscience before God.*

3. The blessing of a clear conscience before God

Together, the immense joy of fellowship with God through the study of Scripture and the marvelous gift of seeing sinners saved and sanctified yield the pleasant fruit of *a clear conscience before God.* To be sure, we must all "[hold] to the mystery of the faith with a clear conscience" (1 Tim. 3:9; *cf.* 2 Tim. 1:3). This is yet another gift bestowed upon those who walk with integrity before the Lord. It is to the warrior preacher what oxygen is to life. Without it, he will operate in the flesh rather than the Spirit, and the deeds of the flesh will corrupt all that he does (Gal. 5:17). In contrast, the apostle Paul rejoiced in this unique blessing, saying, ". . . our proud confidence is this: the testimony of our conscience, that in holiness and godly sincerity, not in fleshly wisdom but in the grace of God, we have conducted ourselves in the world, and especially toward you" (2 Cor. 1:12).

Our conscience is that innate moral faculty God has given us to bring His Word to bear upon our soul, a moral sense of right and wrong that holds us to the highest standard of righteousness to which it has been informed. For this reason, it must be instructed, purged, and purified on a regular basis by the objective truths of Scripture and the convicting work of the indwelling Spirit. It is an inward monitor that either accuses or excuses our thoughts and actions, as the case demands. It is that inner witness that indicts, testifies, convicts, judges, and sentences—an internal tribunal that exists in both the *believing* and *unbelieving* heart:

> For when Gentiles who do not have the Law do instinctively the things of the Law, these, not having the Law, are a law to themselves, in that they show the work of the Law written in their hearts, their conscience bearing witness and their thoughts alternately accusing or else defending them, on the day when, according to my gospel, God will judge the secrets of men through Christ Jesus.
> (Rom. 2:12–16)

Having a clear conscience concerning our walk with God and service to Him (2 Tim. 1:3) is a magnificent blessing from the Lord, a Spirit-wrought confidence affirming the integrity of our heart that, in turn, produces the manifold gifts associated with Christian joy. This is a blessed reward for every warrior preacher that will cause him to testify with Paul, ". . . the goal of our instruction is love from a pure heart and a good conscience and a sincere faith" (1 Tim. 1:5). While God alone can accurately discern our motives (1 Cor. 4:1–5), no minister of the gospel can function effectively apart from a pure conscience. Hypocrisy will eventually be his undoing. Moreover, a clear conscience serves as a buttress against malicious slander and ridicule (1 Cor. 4:3–4). Better yet, it provides a tiny foretaste of our Master's affirmation when He says, "Well done, good and faithful slave" (Matt. 25:21); for indeed, ". . .godliness is profitable for all things, since it holds promise for the present life and also for the life to come" (1 Tim. 4:8).

*Having a clear conscience concerning our walk with
God and service to Him (2 Tim. 1:3) is a magnificent
blessing from the Lord.*

When the Spirit affirms godly sincerity in the inner man, we can confidently testify as Paul did before Felix and say, "I . . . do my best to maintain always a blameless conscience both before God and before men" (Acts 24:16). We must be men who can say with utmost conviction, ". . . we are not like many, peddling the word of God, but as from sincerity, but as from God, we speak in Christ in the sight of God" (2 Cor. 2:17). Living our life in His presence (*coram Deo*) according to the enlightenment and empowerment of the Holy Spirit is the soil in which the fruit of the Spirit flourishes: "Love, joy, peace, patience, kindness, goodness, faithfulness, gentleness, self-control" (Gal. 5:19). It is the exercise of conscience that energizes the discipline of self-examination and protects against doctrinal drift and worldly compromise. It is that Spirit-empowered certainty that enables the warrior preacher to say with Luther, "My conscience is captive to the Word of God. I cannot and will not recant anything, for to go against conscience is neither right nor safe. God help me. Amen."

Watchman on the Wall

Every faithful pastor has been tormented by a guilty conscience that brings misery to the body and soul. We can all identify with David's confession when he said, "When I kept silent about my sin, my body wasted away through my groaning all day long" (Ps. 32:3). But oh, the sacred bliss of a clear conscience—one that has been awakened by divine truth and has thereby produced genuine repentance! Only then can a preacher be bold in his proclamation of the Scriptures to others. The great Puritan divine, John Owen, said it best: "If the word doth not dwell with power in us, it will not pass with power from us."[88] When the conscience is at peace, all is well within us, but when it arouses accusing guilt, all comfort is gone; the Spirit is quenched, and the clouds of divine chastening threaten a storm of loving discipline.

Regrettably, the church knows little of this today. The collective conscience of evangelicalism is ill-informed and neglected. Worldly men and women whose consciences are "seared" (1 Tim. 4:2) and

---

88   John Owen, *The True Nature of a Gospel Church and Its Government*, ed. John Huxtable (London: James Clarke, 1947), 66.

"defiled" (Titus 1:15) have silenced their divine warning system for so long that it no longer functions. This indictment holds true for many who fill pulpits every week. As a result, they heartily affirm that good is evil and evil is good (Isa. 5:20–21). They have been given over to a depraved mind that is spiritually and morally corrupt (Rom. 1:28–32). Such is the curse of an "evil conscience" (Heb. 10:22) upon the "natural man [who] does not accept the things of the Spirit of God, for they are foolishness to him; and he cannot understand them, because they are spiritually appraised" (1 Cor. 2:14). Their followers are therefore like them, men and women who are

> . . . darkened in their understanding, excluded from the life of God because of the ignorance that is in them, because of the hardness of their heart; and they, having become callous, have given themselves over to sensuality for the practice of every kind of impurity with greediness.
> (Eph. 4:18–19)

Knowing the power of sin and the greater power of the gospel to conquer it, the warrior preacher will cherish the gift of a "clear conscience" (2 Tim. 1:1); he will not be able to function in or out of the pulpit without it. This is especially true as it relates to fulfilling the divine mandates of his calling regarding *evangelism, discipleship, preaching the Word, and shepherding the flock of God*. For example, he will be able to discern the spiritual and moral anarchy in our woke culture that foreshadows a dystopian world of unrestrained wickedness and misery. He will see how its satanic tentacles are reaching into the lives of his people and in his church, and, with his heart breaking over the infiltration of evil, he will take up his sword and go to war. He will take seriously his responsibility to be a watchman on the wall (Ezek. 33), one who sounds the alarm and warns the people of coming judgment so that they may repent. He will be like Jeremiah and Ezekiel (*cf.* Ezek. 3:16–21), a man of God who is able to see the approaching enemy when others cannot, who sounds the trumpet of an imminent invasion, and who understands that failure to do so would cause their blood to be on his hands (Ezek. 33:8–9).

I never cease to lament over those who refuse to heed the warnings. It is an unceasing burden of my heart. My only respite is found in a clear conscience combined with the ministry of the Spirit in His Word. This is why it is so important to know with certainty that I have done all I can do to sound the trumpet of truth without compromise, and with this assurance comes the reward of a clear conscience, despite the response of the people. While I grieve over those who simply refuse to hear and believe, I know in my heart that as a faithful watchman on the wall I have done all that I could do. Every minister of the gospel must learn to live with the sad reality that not all will come to repentance. God made this clear in His words to Ezekiel:

> But as for you, son of man, your fellow citizens who talk about you by the walls and in the doorways of the houses, speak to one another, each to his brother, saying, "Come now and hear what the message is which comes forth from the LORD." They come to you as people come, and sit before you as My people and hear your words, but they do not do them, for they do the lustful desires expressed by their mouth, and their heart goes after their gain. Behold, you are to them like a sensual song by one who has a beautiful voice and plays well on an instrument; for they hear your words but they do not practice them. So when it comes to pass—as surely it will—then they will know that a prophet has been in their midst.
> (Ezek. 33:30–33)

Notwithstanding the response of the wicked, the role of the watchman is clear, as the apostle Paul stated to the elders in Ephesus in Acts 20:25–27: "And now, behold, I know that all of you, among whom I went about preaching the kingdom, will no longer see my face. Therefore, I testify to you this day that I am innocent of the blood of all men. For I did not shrink from declaring to you the whole purpose of God." Indeed, a pure conscience is an immense treasure, as the persecuted Reformers and Puritans attested from firsthand experience. To this end, the seventeenth century Scottish minister and pastor, David Dickson (1583–1663), described it this way:

It sweetneth evils to a man, as trouble, crosses, sorrows, afflictions. If a man have true peace in his conscience, it comforteth him in them all. When things abroad do disquiet us, how comfortable it is to have something at home to cheer us? So when trouble and afflictions without turmoil vex us and add sorrow to sorrow, then to have peace within, the peace of conscience, to allay all and quiet all, what a happiness is this? When sickness and death cometh, what will a good conscience be worth then? Sure, more than all the world besides. . . . The conscience is God's echo of peace to the soul: in life, in death, in judgment it is unspeakable comfort.[89]

In similar fashion, when Paul was about to retire from the field of battle, he could do so with heartfelt joy, having received the blessed reward of a clear conscience. Knowing he was about to receive the eternal reward of Christ's perfected righteousness, he was therefore able to say with peaceful assurance,

> I have fought the good fight, I have finished the course, I have kept the faith; in the future there is laid up for me the crown of righteousness, which the Lord, the righteous Judge, will award to me on that day; and not only to me, but also to all who have loved His appearing.
> (2 Tim. 4:7–8)

A clear conscience is therefore a blessed prize to possess in life and in death as we anticipate the greatest prize of all: *the spiritual vision of God's revelation of Himself in the eternal state.*

The Eternal Rewards of the Warrior Preacher

The ultimate reward of eternal life in the presence of God is awarded to all believers and is sometimes characterized in the New Testament as a wreath awarded to a victorious athlete (1 Cor. 9:25; 2 Tim. 4:8; 1 Thess. 2:19; 1 Peter 5:4; James 1:12; Rev. 2:10). This future reward will include the inheritance of the saints (Col. 1:12), the ultimate blessing of beholding the glory of Christ (John 17:24), and enjoying God forever in a realm of sinless perfection and unimaginable splendor.

---

89 David Dickson, *Therapeutica Sacra: The Method of Healing the Diseases of the Conscience Concerning Regeneration* (1664), 4.

But Scripture also speaks of *degrees of rewards* for believers that will be granted when Christ returns, as Jesus declared in Revelation 22:12: "Behold, I am coming quickly, and My reward *is* with Me, to render to every man according to what he has done." The biblical use of the term *reward* carries the idea of *a divine repayment for doing good or evil*, which is how various Hebrew words translate the term in the Old Testament. My primary emphasis, however, is on God's reward for righteous motives, thoughts, attitudes, and outward service devoted to God (especially as it relates to a faithful preacher of the Word). We see this, for example, in Proverbs 11:31: ". . . the righteous will be rewarded in the earth," and in Proverbs 13:13: "But the one who fears the commandment will be rewarded." David says, "Moreover, by them [i.e., the judgments revealed in Scripture] Your servant is warned; in keeping them there is great reward" (Ps. 19:11).

The ultimate reward of eternal life in the presence of God is awarded to all believers and is sometimes characterized in the New Testament as a wreath awarded to a victorious athlete.

The New Testament uses the term "reward" (*misthos*) twenty-nine times, which means essentially the same thing as the Old Testament concept, namely, a "wage" or "recompense," as in 1 Corinthians 3:14 where Paul says, "If any man's work which he has built on it remains, he will receive a reward." John MacArthur offers helpful insight regarding the dynamics surrounding this future judgment:

> How are these rewards determined? Our *works* will be tested for this very purpose. In that day when we stand before the judgment seat of Christ, the whole "edifice" of our earthly works will be tested by the fire of God. Some impressive superstructures will be reduced to rubble, because they are built only for show—not out of lasting material. Like sets on a movie lot, these "buildings" may be magnificent and *appear* genuine even on close inspection, but the fire will test them for what they are made of not for what they look like. All the wood, hay and stubble will be burned away. Scripture promises, "If any man's work abide which

he hath built thereupon, *he shall receive a reward*" (1 Cor. 3:14; emphasis added). What about the person whose works are burned up? "He shall suffer loss: but he himself shall be saved; yet so as by fire" (v. 15). That evokes the notion of someone who is pulled from a burning building alive. He may be unharmed by the fire, but the smell of smoke is all over him—he has barely escaped destruction.[90]

While it is manifest in Scripture that good works contribute nothing to our justification—which is entirely of grace purchased by the merit of Christ alone—nevertheless, we cannot deny that *saints will be judged by their works and awarded varying degrees of glory and service in heaven according to them*. Wayne Grudem documents numerous passages in Scripture that either teach or imply varying degrees of rewards for believers.[91] We should therefore be motivated by rewards like Moses who "[considered] the reproach of Christ greater riches than the treasures of Egypt; for he was looking to the reward" (Heb. 11:25). Jesus also promised that those who suffer for His sake will be rewarded, saying, "Be glad in that day and leap for joy, for behold, your reward is great in heaven" (Luke 6:21). The concept of eternal rewards centers on the nature of our service to Christ throughout eternity and should therefore be a great motivator for every believer, especially the warrior preacher! Every faithful shepherd should be motivated by the promise that that "when the Chief Shepherd appears, [he] will receive the unfading crown of glory" (1 Peter 5:2).

It is important to understand, however, that *we do not pursue eternal rewards to elevate ourselves to some perceived superior status in heaven, but to exalt the Lover our soul and enlarge our enjoyment of Him.* This will, in effect, increase the enjoyment of all the redeemed. Charles Hodge gives further clarity to this subject:

---

90   John F. MacArthur, *The Glory of Heaven: The Truth About Heaven, Angels and Eternal Life* (Wheaton, IL: Crossway Books, 1996), 101.

91   Wayne Grudem, *Systematic Theology: An Introduction to Biblical Doctrine* (Grand Rapids, MI: Zondervan Publishing House, 1994), 1144. Passages include: 1 Cor. 3:12–15; 2 Cor. 5:10; Luke 19, 17, 19. See also Dan. 12:2; Matt. 6:20–21; 19:21; Luke 6:22–23; 12:18–21, 32, 42–48; 14:13–14; 1 Cor. 3:8; 9:18; 13:3; 15:19, 29–32, 58; Gal. 6:9–10; Eph. 6:7–8; Col. 3:23–24; 1 Tim. 6:18; Heb. 10:34, 35; 11:10, 14–16, 26, 35; 1 Peter 1:4; 2 John 8; Rev. 11:18; 22:12; *cf.* also Matt. 5:46; 6:2–6, 16–18, 24; Luke 6:35.

Although Protestants deny the merit of good works, and teach that salvation is entirely gratuitous, that the remission of sins, adoption into the family of God, and the gift of the Holy Spirit are granted to the believer, as well as admission into heaven, solely on the ground of the merits of the Lord Jesus Christ; they nevertheless teach that God does reward his people for their works. Having graciously promised for Christ's sake to overlook the imperfection of their best services, they have the assurance founded on that promise that he who gives to a disciple even a cup of cold water in the name of a disciple, shall in no wise lose his reward. The Scriptures also teach that the happiness or blessedness of believers in a future life will be greater or less in proportion to their devotion to the service of Christ in this life. Those who love little, do little; and those who do little, enjoy less. What a man sows that shall he also reap. As the rewards of heaven are given on the ground of the merits of Christ, and as He has a right to do what He will with his own, there would be no injustice were the thief saved on the cross as highly exalted as the Apostle Paul. But the general drift of Scripture is in favor of the doctrine that a man shall reap what he sows; that God will reward every one according to, although not on account of his works.[92]

Concluding Words of Exhortation and Encouragement

It is crucial for every minister of the gospel to remember that his service is rendered in the sight of God, and as such he is exhorted to "keep the commandment without stain or reproach until the appearing of our Lord Jesus Christ" (1 Tim. 6:13–14). He is to remain faithful to the revealed Word of God, as Paul charged Timothy, knowing that Christ will return and judge him accordingly. Christ Himself will one day evaluate the character and conduct of every believer, *but there will be a stricter judgment for those He called to function in a teaching and preaching capacity* (James 3:1). However, His reward will be great for those who were "not ashamed of the

92   Charles Hodge, *Systematic Theology, Vol. III* (Grand Rapids, MI: 1940), 244–5.

testimony of our Lord" but were willing to "[suffer] for the gospel according to the power of God" (2 Tim. 1:8). We find much comfort in Jesus' promise, "Truly I say to you, there is no one who has left house or wife or brothers or parents or children, for the sake of the kingdom God, who will not receive many times as much at this time and in the age to come, eternal life" (Luke 18:29).

The vast majority of pastors and church leaders I have counseled over the years struggle with fear, and many allow themselves to be ruled by it. As a result, they function in the power of the flesh, rather than the Spirit. They refuse to preach certain doctrines or make specific biblical applications as they relate to the culture or politics because it might cost them their job. If that is you, *I lovingly but forthrightly call you to repentance*. You are a *man-pleaser* instead of a *God-pleaser*, and as a result—whether you realize it or not—you preach a truncated and watered-down gospel that cannot save. I offer you the words of a true warrior preacher in this regard:

> As we have said before, so I say again now, if any man is preaching to you a gospel contrary to what you received, he is to be accursed! For am I now seeking the favor of men, or of God? Or am I striving to please men? If I were still trying to please men, I would not be a bond-servant of Christ. (Gal. 1:9–10)

The pulpit is no place for cowards, charlatans, entrepreneurs, or entertainers. If you fall into one of these categories, I plead with you to either repent or resign!

The pulpit is no place for cowards, charlatans, entrepreneurs, or entertainers. If you fall into one of these categories, I plead with you to either *repent* or *resign!* Like perhaps never before in redemptive history, the church is in desperate need of men of uncommon, Spirit-empowered valor to combat Satan's fury in these final days before our Lord's return. We need *warriors* not *wimps*! We need men who will unflinchingly preach the unvarnished gospel and all the doctrinal truths of Scripture—including the ones that are unpopular. The fears of dehumanizing despotism, once considered the exaggerated musings of a dystopian imagination, are now becoming a reality as the world continues to sink into an abyss of evil. It is manifest to every true Christian that we live in an age worse than Sodom and Gomorrah, and like those ancient idolaters, this world will also be judged.

Yes, those who dare say, "Thus says the Lord!" will suffer persecution, but they will also be protected and "kept from the evil one" by the Father (John 17:11–15). For every warrior preacher reading this volume—and for every man desiring to be one—I want to encourage you with the promises of Scripture. When your tour of duty is over, you will not only receive your *inheritance*, as will all believers (Rev. 5:4–5), but you will also receive other rewards commensurate with your faithfulness in service (Luke 19:15–19) and suffering for the King of glory (Matt. 5:11–12). Indeed, the faithfulness of your witness for Christ will determine your eternal capacity to reflect the glory of God, as Daniel reveals: "Those who have insight will shine brightly like the brightness of the expanse of heaven, and those who lead the many to righteousness, like the stars forever and ever" (Dan. 12:3).

I trust this will motivate your heart. And once again I challenge you to *know your enemy, put on your armor, get proficient with your weaponry, develop a warrior's mindset, grow in godly character, and pursue the rewards of faithfulness* that Christ will bestow upon you to the praise of His glory. May these sacred endeavors be the great passion and earnest prayer of every man of God who has been called and gifted to stand in a pulpit and proclaim the unsearchable riches of Christ until He comes. May He come quickly!

Chapter 6 Questions

1. Do you contemplate the subject of eternal rewards during seasons of discouragement?

2. How will you be remembered when the Lord takes you home?

3. Describe the temporal blessings God has bestowed upon you and state why they are so precious to your soul.

4. Do you enjoy sweet fellowship with God through the study of His Word?

5. Do you work hard at preaching and teaching or are other aspects of ministry a greater priority?

6. How would you describe the fruit that your life is bearing for the glory of Christ and what must you do to bear more fruit?

7. Do you have a clear conscience before God as it relates to fulfilling the divine mandates of your calling regarding evangelism, discipleship, preaching the Word, and shepherding the flock of God?

8. Do you pursue eternal rewards, not to elevate yourself to some perceived superior status in heaven, but to exalt Christ and enlarge your enjoyment of Him in heaven?

Appendix 1:
War! War! War!

A Sermon Delivered on Sabbath Morning, May 1, 1859, by the Rev. C. H. Spurgeon, at the Music Hall, Royal Surrey Gardens

FIGHT THE LORD'S BATTLES[93]

---

93 Adapted from *The C. H. Spurgeon Collection*, Version 1.0, Ages Software. *"Fight the Lord's battles."* 1 Samuel 18:17. The New Park Street Pulpit 1, NO. 250

We shall not take these words in their literal application, as coming from the lips of Saul, when he gave David his elder daughter, Marab, to wife; but we shall accommodate the passage and use it as an exhortation given to the church of Christ and to every soldier of Jesus—"Fight the Lord's battles." If this exhortation is not found in the same words, coming from the lips of Jesus, nevertheless, the whole tenor of the Word of God is to the same effect—"Fight the Lord's battles."

At the present crisis, the minds of men are exceedingly agitated with direful prospects of a terrible struggle. We know not whereunto this matter may grow. The signs of the times are dark and direful. We fear that the vials of God's wrath are about to be poured out and that the earth will be deluged with blood. As long as there remains a hope, let us pray for peace, no, even in the time of war let us still beseech the throne of God, crying that He would "send us peace in our days."

> If this exhortation is not found in the same words, coming from the lips of Jesus, nevertheless, the whole tenor of the Word of God is to the same effect—"Fight the Lord's battles."

The war will be looked upon by different persons with different feelings. The Italian will consider all through the controversy, his own country. The Sardinian will be looking continually to the progress or to the defeat of his own nation—while the German, having sympathy with his own race, will be continually anxious to understand the state of affairs. There is one power, however, which is not represented in the congress and which seems to be silent because the ears of men are deaf to anything that it has to say. To that power all our sympathies will be given and our hearts will follow it with interest. And all through the war, the one question that we shall ask, will be, "How will *that* kingdom prosper?"

You all know to which kingdom I refer—it is the kingdom of Jesus Christ upon earth. That little one which is even at this time growing and which is to become a thousand; which is to break in pieces all the monarchies of earth and to seat itself upon their ruins, proclaiming universal liberty and peace under the banner of Jesus Christ. I am sure that we shall think far more of the interests of religion than of anything else and our prayer will be, "O Lord, do what You will with the earthen pitchers of men's monarchies, but let Your kingdom come and let Your will be done on earth, even as it is in heaven!"

While, however, we shall anxiously watch the contest, it will be quite as well if we mingle in it ourselves. Not that this nation of England should touch it—God forbid! If tyrants fight, let them fight. Let free men stand aloof. Why should England have anything to do with all the coming battles? As God has cut us off from Europe by a boisterous sea, so let us be kept apart from all the broils and turmoil into which tyrants and their slaves may fall. I speak now, after a *spiritual* manner, to the church of Christ. I say, "Let us mingle in the fray; let us have something to do. We cannot be neutral—we never have been—our host is always in hostility to sin and Satan. My voice is still for war." The senate of Christ's church can never talk of peace, for thus it is written—"The Lord will have war with Amalek from generation to generation."

This will bring us to the text; and here I shall consider, first of all, *the Lord's battles*. We are not to fight our own; secondly, *the Lord's soldiers;* and thirdly, *the King's command*, "Fight the Lord's battles."

(I) The Lord's Battles

I. First, THE LORD'S BATTLES, what are they? Not the garment rolled in blood, not the noise and smoke and din of human slaughter. These may be the *devil's* battles, if you please, but not the Lord's. They may be days of God's vengeance, but in their strife the servant of Jesus may not mingle. We stand aloof. Our kingdom is not of this world—else would God's servants fight with sword and spear! Ours is a *spiritual* kingdom and the weapons of our warfare are not carnal, but spiritual and mighty through God, to the pulling down of strongholds.

What are God's battles? Let us here carefully distinguish between the battles of God and our own. Oh, my brothers and sisters in Christ, it is not your business to fight your own battles, not even in defense of your own character. If you are maligned and slandered, let the slanderer alone! His malignity will but be increased by any attempt that you shall make to defend yourself. As a soldier of Christ you are to fight for your *Master,* not *for yourself.*

You are not to carry on a private warfare for your own honor, but all your time and all your power is to be given to His defense and His war. You are not to have a word to speak for yourselves. Full often, when we get into little tempers and our blood is roused, we are apt to think that we are fighting the cause of the truth of God when we are really maintaining our own pride! We imagine that we are defending our Master, but we are defending our own little selves—too often the anger rises against an adversary not because his words reflect dishonor upon the glorious Christ, but because they dishonor us! Oh, let us not be so little as to fight our own battles! Depend upon it, the noblest means of conquest for a Christian in the matter of slander and falsehood is to stand still and see the salvation of God! Sheathe your own sword, put away all your own weapons when you come to fight your own battle and let God fight for you and you shall be more than conqueror!

> You are not to have a word to speak for yourselves.
> Full often, when we get into little tempers and our
> blood is roused, we are apt to think that we are
> fighting the cause of the truth of God when we are
> really maintaining our own pride!

Again, we must remember that there is such a thing as fighting the battles of our own sect, when we ought to be fighting God's battles. We imagine that we are maintaining the church when we are only maintaining our section of it. I would always be very tender of the honor of the Christian body to which I belong, but I would rather see *its* honor stained than that the glory of the entire church should be dimmed.

Every soldier ought to love the peculiar legion in which he has enlisted, but better to see the colors of that legion torn to tatters, than to see the old standard of the cross trampled in the mire! Now

I trust we are ready to say of our own denomination, "Let its name perish, if Christ's name shall get glory thereby." If the extinction of our sect should be the conquest of Christ and the promoting of His kingdom, then let it be wiped out of the book of record and let not its name be heard any more!

We should, I say, each of us, defend the body to which we belong, for we have conscientiously joined it believing it to be the nearest to the old standard of the church of Christ and God forbid that we should leave it for a worse. If we see a better, then would we sacrifice our prejudices to our convictions, but we cannot leave the old standard so long as we see it to be the very standard which floated in the hands of Paul and which was handed by him through many generations—through Chrysostom to Augustine—from Augustine to Calvin and so on through the glorious race of mighty men who have not been ashamed of the gospel of Christ Jesus. But yet, I say let our name and let our sect and let our denomination be absorbed and let it sink—so that the battle of the Lord may but be well fought and the time of Christ's triumph hastened!

"Fight the *Lord's* battles." Then what are these? These are battles with sin and battles with error and battles with war and battles with worldliness! Fight these, Christian, and you shall have enough to do!

The Lord's battles are first of all with sin. Seek grace to fight that battle in your own heart. Endeavor by divine grace to overcome those propensities which continually push you towards iniquity. Wrestle on your knees against your besetting sins. As habits appear, endeavor to break them by the battle-ax of strong resolution wielded by the arm of faith. Take all your lusts, as they bestir themselves, to the foot of the cross and let the blood of Jesus fall upon those vipers and they will die!

The blood of Christ shall spill the blood of sin—the death of Christ shall be the death of iniquity—the cross of Christ shall be the crucifixion of transgression! Labor to drive the Canaanites out of your hearts; spare none! Let no petty lust escape. Put down pride and sloth and lust and unbelief and you have now a battle before you which may fill your hands and more than fill them! Oh, cry unto God for strength and look unto the hills from where comes your help and then fight on! And as each sin is overcome, each evil habit broken off, each lust denied—go on to the rooting up of another and the destruction of more of them—until all being subdued, body soul and spirit shall be consecrated to Christ as a living sacrifice, purified by His Holy Spirit!

And while this battle is being fought, yes, and while it is still fighting, go out and fight with other men's sins. Smite them first with the weapon of holy example. Be yourselves what you would have others be! Be clean that bear the vessels of the Lord. Be clean yourselves before you can hope to be the purifiers of the world. And then, having first sought the blessing of God, go out into the world and bear your witness against sin.

The Lord's battles are first of all with sin. Seek grace to fight that battle in your own heart. Endeavor by divine grace to overcome those propensities which continually push you towards iniquity.

Let your testimony be unflinching. Never let a sin pass under your eyes without rebuke. Slay utterly young and old—let not one escape! Speak sometimes sternly if the sinner is hardened in his sin. Speak gently if it is his first offense, seeking not to break his head but to break the head of his iniquity—not to break his bones or wound his feelings –but to cut his sin in two and leave his iniquity dead before his eyes. Go forth where sin is the most rampant. Go down the dark alley; climb the creaking staircase; penetrate the dens of iniquity where the lion of the pit lies in his death lair and go and pluck out of the mouth of the lion two legs and a piece of an ear, if that is all which you can save! Count it always your joy to follow the track of the lion, to beard him in his den and fight him where he reigns most secure. Protest daily, hourly—by act, by word, by pen, by tongue—against evil of every kind and shape!

Be as a burning and shining light in the midst of darkness and as two-edged swords in the midst of the hosts of sin! Why, a true Christian who lives near to God and is filled with grace and is kept holy, may stand in the midst of sinners and do wonders! What a marvelous feat was that which Jonah did! There was the great city of Nineveh, having in it six score thousand souls that knew not their right hand from their left and one man went against it—Jonah—and as he approached it, he began to cry, "Yet forty days and Nineveh shall be overthrown." He entered the city—perhaps he stood aghast for a moment at the multitude of its population, at its richness and splendor—but again he lilted up his sharp shrill voice, "Yet forty days and Nineveh shall be overthrown." On he went and the crowd increased around him as he passed through each street, but they heard nothing but the solemn monotony, "Yet forty days and Nineveh shall be overthrown." And yet again, "Yet forty days and Nineveh shall be overthrown." And on he went, that solitary man, till he caused convulsion in the midst of myriads, and the king on his throne robed himself in sackcloth and proclaimed a fast, a day of mourning and of sadness! Yet on he went, "Yet forty days and Nineveh shall be overthrown." "Yet forty days and Nineveh shall be overthrown," till all the people bowed before him, and that one man was the conqueror of the thousands!

Ah, believer, if only you will go out and do the same! If only you will go into the streets, the lanes, the byways, the houses, and into the privacies of men and still, with this continued cry against sin and iniquity, say to them, "Look unto the cross and live! Look unto the cross and live." Though there were but one earnest man in London who would continue that monotony of, "Look unto the cross and live," from end to end, this city would shake and the great leviathan metropolis would be made to tremble! Go forth, then, believer, and cry against sin with all your might!

And even so must we cry against *error*. It is the preacher's business, Sabbath after Sabbath, and weekday after weekday, to preach the whole gospel of God and to vindicate the truth of God as it is in Jesus from the opposition of man. Thousands are the heresies which now beset the church of Christ. O children of God, fight the Lord's battles for the truth of God! I am astonished and yet more astonished when I come to turn it over, at the lack of earnestness that there is in the Protestantism of the present age! How do you imagine that Cardinal Wiseman pays for all his splendors and that the Romish church is supported? Fools and slow of heart, *you* find them much of their wealth! If he is to preach in any place, who is it that crowds the chapel full and pays for admission? The Protestants! And the Protestantism of England is the paymaster of the Pope!

I am ashamed that sons of the Reformers, who have Smithfield still in their midst unbuilt upon, should bow themselves before the beast and give so much as a single farthing to the shrine of Satan's first-born son! Take heed to yourselves, you Protestants, lest you be partakers of her plagues! Touch her not, lest you be defiled! Give a drachma to her, or a grain of incense to her censors—you shall be partakers of her adulteries and partakers of her plagues! Every time you pass the house of Popery, let a curse light upon her head—thus said the Lord—"Come out of her, My people, that you be not partakers of her sins and that you receive not of her plagues, for her sins have reached unto heaven and God has remembered her iniquities. Reward her even as she rewarded you and double unto her double according to her works—in the cup which she has filled, fill to her double. How much she has glorified herself and lived deliciously, so much torment and sorrow give her, for she said in her heart, "I sit a queen and am no widow and shall see no sorrow. Therefore shall her plagues come in one day, death and mourning and famine, and she shall be utterly burned with fire—for strong is the Lord God who judges her" (Rev. 18:4–8).

It is all very well with that church when it is separated from her heretical sons and a great gulf fixed--but all that helps to bridge that gulf must mar her glory and destroy her power! We must have no truce, no treaty with Rome! War! War to the knife with her!

How soft some men's minds are growing—how effeminate in the battle! I hear then speaking of Puseyism—and what is that but Popery made worse than it was before, by being more despicable and deceivable than even Popery itself? Do you not hear men talk of the Puseyites in these days and say, "Ah, well, they differ a little from us." Does not the evangelical party in the Church of England seem at the present moment to make common cause and party with the Puseyite? Else how is it that the great preaching has been alternatively conducted by High and Low Church? It is all very well with that church when it is separated from her heretical sons and a great gulf fixed—but all that helps to bridge that gulf must mar her glory and destroy her power! We must have no truce, no treaty with Rome! War! War to the knife with her! Peace there cannot be! She cannot have peace with *us*—we cannot have peace with *her*. She hates the true church, and we can only say that the hatred is reciprocated! We would not lay a hand upon her priests. We would not touch a hair of their heads. Let them be free. But their *doctrine* we would destroy from the face of the earth as the doctrine of Satan! So let it perish, O God, and let that evil thing become as the fat of lambs. Into smoke let it consume—yes, into smoke let it consume away!

We must fight the Lord's battles against this giant error, whichever shape it takes. And so must we do with every error that pollutes the church. Utterly slay it! Let none escape! "Fight the Lord's battles." Even though it is an error that is in an Evangelical Church, yet must we smite it.

> And as soon as we perceive an error, though it is but as the shadow of one, let us root it out and drive it from us, lest it plague the whole body and put leprosy into the entire fabric of the church! No peace with sin! No peace with lies!

I love all those who love the Lord Jesus Christ, but, nevertheless, I cannot have any truce, any treaty with many errors that have crept into the church, nor would I have you regard them with complacency. We are one in Christ— let us be friends with one another. But let us never be friends with one another's error! If I am wrong, rebuke me sternly. I can bear it and bear it cheerfully—and if you are wrong; expect the same measure from me and neither peace nor parley with your mistakes. Let us all be true to one another and true to Christ. And as soon as we perceive an error, though it is but as the shadow of one, let us root it out and drive it from us, lest it plague the whole body and put leprosy into the entire fabric of the church! No peace with sin! No peace with lies! War, war, war without deliberation—war forever with error and deceit!

And yet again—it is the Christian's duty always to have war with *war*. To have bitterness in our hearts against any *man* that lives is to serve Satan. We must speak very harshly and sternly against error and against sin, but against men we have not a word to say, though it were the Pope himself—I have no enmity in my heart against him as a man, but as *anti-Christ*. With men the Christian is one. Are we not every man's brother? "God has made of one flesh all people who dwell upon the face of the earth." The cause of Christ is the cause of humanity! We are friends to all and are enemies to none. We do not speak evil, even of the false prophet himself, as a *man*, but as a false prophet—we are his sworn opponents!

Now, Christians, you have a difficult battle to fight because as you fight with all evil and hostility between man and man—you are to be *peacemakers*. Go wherever you may, if you see a quarrel, you are to abate it. You are to pluck firebrands out of the fire and strive to quench them in the waters of loving kindness. It is your mission to bring the nations together and weld them into one. It is yours to make man love man; to make him no more the devourer of his kind. This you can only do by being the friends of purity. Peace with error is war with man—but war with error is peace with man. Smite error, smite sin and you have done your best to promote happiness and union among mankind. Oh, go, Christian, in the Spirit's strength and smite your own anger—put that to the death! Smite your own pride—level that and then smite every other man's anger. Make peace wherever you can—scatter peace with both your hands. Let this be the very air you breathe! Let nothing drop from your lips but words of healing; words of tenderness; words which shall abate the strife and noise of this poor distracted world. And now, you have a battle before you—a battle against sin and against error and then, also, a battle against strife—the battle of love.

(II) The Lord's Soldiers

II. And now, FOR THE LORD'S SOLDIERS—who are they who are to fight the Lord's battle? Not everybody. The Lord has His army, His church—who are they? The Lord's soldiers are all of His own choosing. He has chosen them out of the world. And they are not of the world, even as Christ is not of the world. But if you want to know the Lord's soldiers, I will tell you how you may ascertain whether you are one.

When the Lord Jesus enlists a soldier in His church, the first thing He does with him is He tells him that he must first take off every rag of the old garments that he was desirous to wear. "Now," says Jesus to him, "your rags must be relinquished. Your sins and your self-righteousness must both be forsaken. Here is the uniform—here is the inner garment of My imputed righteousness and here is the outward garment of divine sanctification. Put on these and you are Mine. But, in your own robes I will have nothing to do with you—you shall still continue an heir of wrath and I will not enlist you among the heirs of grace." As soon as a man has his rags taken off, Christ has enlisted him!

The next thing he is required to do is to wash. He is washed, from head to foot, in a matchless bath of blood. And when washed, he is arrayed and clothed upon with the righteousness of Jesus Christ. This done, he is taken into the midst of the army and introduced to his comrades and he is led to love the whole army. "Well," says one, "I love my own rank." Do you? Then you do not belong to God's army if you do not love the other ranks, too! He who is a true soldier of Christ wears His uniforms and he loves the whole army. He keeps to his own regiment and he likes its banner—the flag that has braved so often the battle and the storm. Still, he loves the whole army, however much the colors may differ. He loves all them who serve the Lord Jesus Christ. "By this also you shall know whether you are His disciples, if you love one another, even as Christ has loved you."

Once brought into the army, there is one mark whereby you may know Christ's soldier, namely, that he is not his own. If you meet him, he will say, "From head to foot I belong to my Captain, every inch of me. And what is more, I have given up goods and chattels, wife and children, time and talents, *everything* for Him! I am not my own, I am bought with a price." He is a consecrated man.

Come, then, put these questions to yourselves. Have you been washed in the blood of Christ? Do you boast in the imputed righteousness of Christ? And are you clothed about with the sanctification of His Spirit? Have you given up everything for His cause? For the love you bear His name, are you willing to live or willing to die—as He shall please—if you may but promote His honor? Well, then, you are His soldier and, therefore, I shall not need to draw any further lines of distinction. But go to the third point, which is—

(III) The Exhortation

III. THE EXHORTATION—"Fight!" "Fight the Lord's battles." If you are the soldier of the heavenly King, "To arms! To arms!" "Fight the Lord's battles."

Here I would observe that there are some people who are very fond of looking on, but not fighting! Perhaps five out of every six of our churches do little but look on. You go to see them and you say, "Well, what is your church doing?" "Well, we bless God; we are doing a great deal! We have a Sabbath school with so many children. Our minister preaches so many times and so many members have been added to the churches. The sick are visited. The poor are relieved." And you stop them and say, "Well, friend, I am glad to hear that you are doing so much. But which work is it that *you* take? Do you teach in the Sabbath school?" "No." "Do you preach in the street?" "No." "Do you visit the sick?" "No." "Do you assist in the discipline of the church?" "No." "Do you contribute to the poor?" "No." Yet I thought you said you were doing so much! Stand out, Sir, if you please—you are doing nothing at all—you should be ashamed!

Your Master does not say, "Look on at the Lord's battles," but, "Fight" them!

Your Master does not say, "*Look on* at the Lord's battles," but, "Fight" them! "Ah," says one, "but then, you know, I contribute towards the support of the ministers—*he* has to do all that other stuff." Oh, I see you have made a mistake! You thought that you belonged to the English government and not to Christ's government! You have been paying for a substitute, have you? You are not going to fight in person? You are paying to keep a substitute to fight for you? Ah, you have made a great mistake here! Christ will have *all* his soldiers fight! Why, I am not kept to do the fighting for you—I will endeavor to encourage you and nerve you for the battle—but as to doing your duty, no, thank you.

The Romanist may believe that his priest does the work for him; I do not believe any such thing in my case, nor in the case of your ministers. Christ did not serve you by proxy, and you cannot serve Him by proxy! No, "He His own self bore our sins in His own body," and you must work for Christ in your own body, your own self, with your own heart and with your own hands! I hate that religion which another man can do for you! Depend upon it, it is good for nothing! True religion is a personal thing.

O soldiers of the heavenly King, leave not your lieutenants and your officers to fight alone! Come on with us! We wave our swords in front. Come soldiers, on! We are ready to mount the call, or lead the forlorn hope. Will you desert us? Come up the ladder with us! Let us show the enemy what Christian blood can do and at the sword's point let us drive our foes before us! If you leave us to do all, it will all be undone—we all need to do something—all to be laboring for Christ. Here, then, is the exhortation to each individual Christian—"Fight the Lord's battles."

And now, I will read you the martial code—the rules which Christ, the Captain, would have you obey in fighting His battles.

REGULATION I.—NO COMMUNICATION NOR UNION WITH THE ENEMY! "You are not of the world." No truce, no league, no treaty are you to make with the enemies of Christ! "Come out from among them and be you separate, and touch not the unclean thing."

⌘

REGULATION II.—NO QUARTER TO BE GIVEN OR TAKEN! You are not to say to the world, "There! Believe me to be better than I am"— and do not ever believe the world to be better than it is. Do not ask it to excuse you. Do not excuse it. No parley with it whatever. If it praises you, do not care for its praise. If it scorns you, laugh in its face. Have nothing to do with its pretended friendship! Ask nothing at its hands; let it be crucified to you and you to it.

⌘

REGULATION III.—NO WEAPONS OR AMMUNITION TAKEN FROM THE ENEMY ARE TO BE USED BY IMMANUEL'S SOLDIERS, BUT ARE TO BE UTTERLY BURNED WITH FIRE! If you beat them and you find their guns lying on the ground, spike them and melt them! Never fire them off—that is to say, never fight Christ's battles with the devil's weapons. If your enemy gets angry, do not get angry with him. If he slanders you, do not slander him. One of the devil's long guns is slander—spike it and melt it—do not attempt to use it against the enemy! All kinds of bitterness—these are firebrands of death which Satan hurls against us—never hurl them back at him. Remember your Master. "When He was reviled He reviled not again." Never meddle with the enemy's weapons, even if you can. If you think you can crush him by his own mode of warfare, do not do it. It was all very well for David to cut off Goliath's head with his own sword, but it would not have done for him to try that until he had first of all split his head open with a stone. Try to get a stone out of the brook of truth and throw it with the sling of faith, but have nothing to do with Goliath's sword! You will cut yourself with it, and get no honor.

⌀

REGULATION IV.—NO FEAR, TREMBLING, OR COWARDICE! "The children of Ephraim, being armed, turned their backs in the day of battle," but Christ wants no cowardice of you. Fear not! Remember, if any man is ashamed of Christ in this generation, of him will Christ be ashamed in the day when He comes in the glory of His Father and all His holy angels. "I say unto you, fear not him who can kill the body, but after that has no more that he can do; but fear Him who is able to cast both body and soul into hell. I say unto you, fear Him."

⌀

REGULATION V.—NO SLUMBERING, REST, EASE, OR SURRENDER! Be always at it, all at it, constantly at it, with all your might at it. No rest. Your resting time is to come, in the grave. Be always fighting the enemy. Ask every day for grace to win a victory and each night sleep not unless you can feel that you have done something in the cause of Christ—have helped to carry the standard a little further into the midst of the enemy's ranks. Oh, if we did but attend to these regulations how much might be done! But because we forget them, the cause of Christ is retarded and the victory is afar off.

⌀

And now, before I send you away, I would call out Christ's soldiers and drill them for a minute or two. I see sometimes the captains marching their soldiers to and fro and you may laugh and say they are doing nothing. But mark, all that maneuvering; that forming into squares and so forth, has its practical effect when they come into the field of battle. Allow me, then, to put the Christian through his postures.

The Christian's Best Postures

The first posture the Christian ought to take and in which he ought to be very well practiced, is this—DOWN UPON BOTH KNEES, HANDS UP, AND EYES UP TO HEAVEN! No posture like that. It is called the posture of prayer. When Christ's church has been beaten every way else, it has at last taken to its knees, and then the whole army of the enemy has fled before us, for on its knees Christ's church is more than conqueror! The praying legion is a legion of heroes. He who understands this posture has learned the first part of the heavenly drill.

ℒ

The next posture is—FEET FAST, HANDS STILL, AND EYES UP! A hard posture that, though it looks very easy. "Stand still and see the salvation of God." I have known many men who could practice the first position who could not practice the second. Perhaps that was the hardest thing that the children of Israel ever did. When they had the sea before them and Pharaoh behind them, they were commanded to stand still. You must learn to stand still when you are provoked, to be silent when you are mocked, to wait under adverse providences and still believe that in the darkest hour the sun is not dead, but will shine out again. Patient waiting for Christ's coming—may we all learn this!

ℒ

Another posture is this—QUICK MARCH, CONTINUALLY GOING ONWARD! Ah, there are some Christians who are constantly sleeping on their guns—they do not understand the posture of going onward. Quick march! Many Christians seem to be better skilled in the goose-step of lifting up one foot after another, and putting them down in the same place, rather than going onwards! Oh, I wish we all knew how to progress—to "grow in grace and in the knowledge of our Lord and Savior Jesus Christ." Never think you are doing anything unless you are going forward—have more love, more hope, more joy—and extend your sphere of usefulness. Soldiers of Christ, quick march! "Speak to the children of Israel, that they go forward." Let them not go back. Let them not stand still. On, on, on, soldiers of Christ! Go forward!

$\mathscr{Q}$

Another posture is one that is very hard to learn, indeed. It is what no soldier, I think, was ever told to do by his captain, except the soldier of Christ—EYES SHUT, AND EARS SHUT, AND HEART SHUT! That is when you go through Vanity Fair. Eyes shut, so as not to look upon temptation. Ears shut, so as not to regard either the praise or the scoffs of the world. And heart shut against evil, with the great stone of precept. "Your Word have I hid in my heart, that I might not sin against You." Roll a stone at the door of your heart so that sin may not come out of it. That is a hard posture. But you will never fight the battles of the Lord till you know how to maintain that.

$\mathscr{Q}$

And then there is another posture—FEET FIRM, SWORD IN HAND. EYES OPEN; LOOKING AT YOUR ENEMY—WATCHING EVERY FEINT THAT HE MAKES, AND WATCHING, TOO, YOUR OPPORTUNITY TO LET FLY AT HIM, SWORD IN HAND! That posture you must maintain every day. Guard against the darts of the enemy. Hold up your shield and be ready to run on him and give him a deadly wound! I need not explain that. You who have to do with business, you who are in the ministry—you who are serving God as deacons and elders— you know how often you have to ward off the darts and look well at your enemy and meet him sword in hand, ready to rush in whenever your time shall come. Let no opportunity—let no occasion pass by! Wound your enemy whenever you can. Slay sin, slay error and destroy bitterness as often as you have opportunity to do so!

$\varnothing$

There is one other posture, which is a very happy one for the child of God to take up and I would have you remember today. HANDS WIDE OPEN, AND HEART WIDE OPEN, WHEN YOU ARE HELPING YOUR BRETHREN—a hand ready to give whatever the church needs and an eye ready to look up for help when you cannot give help with your hand and ready to guide the hand whenever help is needed. And a heart open to hear the tale of another's needs, to "rejoice with them who rejoice and weep with them who weep."

$\varnothing$

Above all, the best posture for Christ's church is that of PATIENT WAITING FOR THE ADVENT OF CHRIST—a looking for His glorious appearance, who must come and will not tarry, but who will get unto Himself the victory!

$\varnothing$

Now, if you will go to your houses and if divine grace shall help you put yourselves through this form of drill, you will be mighty in the day of battle to put down the enemy.

And now, allow the word of exhortation, very brief, but hot and earnest. O Christian brothers and sisters, the more you think of it, the more will you be ashamed of yourselves and of the present church— that we do so little for Christ!

Some 1800 years ago there was a handful of men and women in an upper room. And that handful of men and women were so devoted to their Master, and so true to His cause, that within a hundred years they had overrun every nation of the habitable globe! Yes, within fifty years they had preached the gospel in every land! And now look at this great host gathered here today. Probably there is not less than two or three thousand members of Christian churches, besides this mixed multitude—and now what will *you* do in fifty years? What does the church do in any year of its existence? Why, hardly anything at all!

I sometimes wonder how long God will allow the church to be cooped up in England. I fear that we shall never see the world converted till this country is invaded. If it should ever happen that our hearths and homes should be invaded and that we should be scattered—north, south, east and west, all through the world—it will be the grandest thing that ever happened for the church of Christ! I would go down on my knees and pray night and day that it may not happen for the nation's sake, but nevertheless, I sometimes think that the greatest disaster that can ever occur to our nation, will be the only way in which Christ's church will be spread!

Look at it. Here you have your churches in almost every street and despite the destitution of London, it is not destitute if you compare it with the nations of the world. Oh, ought we not, as ministers of Christ, pour out in legions? And ought not our people go everywhere in the habitable world, in ones and twos and threes, preaching the gospel? But would you have us leave wife and house and children? I would not have you do it, but if you would do it, then would Christ's power be seen and then would the might of the church return to it once again! They were men without purse or scrip that went everywhere preaching the Word—and God was with them and the world heard them and was converted.

Now, we cannot go if we are not sent and perhaps, it is only reasonable that flesh and blood should not ask more. But still, if the life of God were in the church, it would never stay in England for long! It would send forth its bands and legions, rolling along in one tremendous stream—a new crusade would be preached against the heathen nations, and the sword of the Lord and of Gideon would smite the stoutest of our foemen, and Christ would reign, and His peaceful kingdom then would come!

Oh that the church had power with men and power with God! Dear brothers and sisters, look out and see what you can do, every one of you! Do something today! Do not let this Sunday go without every one of you trying to be the means of winning a soul to God! Go to your Sunday schools this afternoon. Go to your preaching stations. Go to your tract district, each one in his sphere. Go to your families, your mothers, fathers, brothers, sisters—go home and do *something* today! "Fight the Lord's battles." You can do nothing of yourselves. But God will be with you—if you but have the will to serve Him, He will give you the power! Go today and seek to heal some breach; to put away some enmity; to slay some sin, or to drive out some error! And God being with you, this shall be a happier day to your soul and a holier day to the world, than you have seen in all your experience before!

I will have one blow, and then you may go. Sinner, I remember that you are here this morning as well as the saint. Sinner, you are not Christ's soldier. You are a soldier of Satan! You will have your pay soon, man, when you have worn your sword out, and worn your arm out in fighting against Christ. You shall have your pay. Look at it and tremble! "The wages of sin is death," and damnation, too! Will you take these two, or will you now renounce the black old tyrant, and enlist under the banner of Christ?

O that God would give you the earnest money of free grace, and enlist you now as a soldier of the cross! Remember, Christ takes the very dregs to be His soldiers. Every man who was in debt and every man who was discontented came to David, and he became a captain over them. Now, if you are in debt this morning to God's law and cannot pay; if you are discontented with the devil's service; jaded and worn out with pleasure—come to Christ, and He will receive you, make you a soldier of the cross, and a follower of the Lamb! God be with you and bless you, from this day forth, even forever! Amen.

Appendix 2:
Encourarging Words to
Warrior Preachers' Wives

Older women likewise are to be reverent in their behavior, not malicious gossips nor enslaved to much wine, teaching what is good, so that they may encourage the young women to love their husbands, to love their children, to be sensible, pure, workers at home, kind, being subject to their own husbands, so that the word of God will not be dishonored.

TITUS 2: 3–5

I have had the privilege of counseling many couples in various capacities of pastoral leadership. It is always a bittersweet experience because of the unique challenges they face in church ministry—challenges that are far greater for true warrior preachers and their wives, given the great opposition they face from both inside and outside their church. Considering these difficulties, I wish to offer a few words of encouragement to warriors' wives, who, unhappily, can sometimes feel discouraged, disillusioned, and even underappreciated.

It is important to understand that there are no specific instructions to a pastor's wife found in Scripture, nor are there any references to her character, qualifications, gifts, or responsibilities to be fulfilled, as if she were an *ex officio* part of the pastoral office. But there are specific directives for all Christian women which would obviously apply to all Christian wives, whether they are married to a pastor or a man in some other vocation. She should therefore never be encumbered with obligatory ministerial duties within the church as if she is the unpaid counterpart of her husband's ministry—sadly, a burden many churches place upon her. In biblical terms, her role and responsibilities are no different than any other woman in the church and can best be summarized in Titus 2:3–5:

> Older women likewise are to be reverent in their behavior, not malicious gossips nor enslaved to much wine, teaching what is good, so that they may encourage the young women to love their husbands, to love their children, to be sensible, pure, workers at home, kind, being subject to their own husbands, so that the word of God will not be dishonored.

The typical pastor's wife serves in obscurity. In many cases, she is seldom seen or even acknowledged; nevertheless, *her influence on her husband and her ministry to him and the church are immeasurable.* She is not only his helper, but also his soul-mate and spiritual counterpart—the joy of his heart and treasure of his soul.

Every married man who faithfully serves Christ is deeply humbled by the gift of his wife, and their marriage will illustrate the oneness of covenantal love between Christ and His bridal church. The husband's loving headship will picture Christ's loving headship over His bride, and the wife's joyful submission to her husband will picture the church's joyful submission to her Lord. Together, their lives become a living sermon for all to behold. And when these realities are honored in the bond of holy matrimony between one man and one woman (Gen. 2:23–24; Eph. 5:31–33), Christ is exalted, the union is blessed, and the congregation they serve will benefit in a myriad of ways that are often intangible. Who can measure the benefits of a couple who model Christ's love for His church in their marriage?

Every pastor's wife is fully aware of the many battles that must be fought, and she knows better than anyone that her husband doesn't fight them alone.

However, even the most Christ-honoring marriages will struggle. Sin is always present in and around us, and Satan works overtime to destroy godly leaders who endeavor to thwart his diabolical purposes. Every pastor's wife is fully aware of the many battles that must be fought, and she knows better than anyone that her husband doesn't fight them alone. Without fail, the godly couples that I have counseled over the years will give many examples of the heartaches they have jointly experienced and the countless ways God has met them at their point of need, drawing them ever closer to Him and therefore closer to each other. Sadly, however, couples with weak marriages tend to crumble under the weight of life's inevitable burdens, especially those afflictions that must be borne in service to Christ in His church.

Considering these challenges, I wish to offer three brief reminders to warrior preachers' wives that I trust will be encouraging; they are as follows:

1. Be Content
2. Be Committed
3. Be Chaste

While each category is worthy of far more discussion than is possible in this brief appendix, perhaps they will provide the necessary impetus for further consideration and meditation.

1. Be Content
with God's sovereign call upon your life to be a pastor's wife

I encourage you to remember that the mystical oneness in the covenant of marriage is the result of a supernatural bonding: "For this reason a man shall leave his father and mother and shall be joined to his wife, and the two shall become one flesh" (Eph. 5:31). The oneness of this bond is so powerful and so intimate that both the husband and the wife share the triumphs and trials of each other's life. God created both male and female to be in relationship with one another. For this reason, after God created Adam, He said, "It is not good that the man should be alone; I will make him a helper fit for him" (Gen. 2:18). This is God's design. This is His sovereign plan for every godly wife.

> *I encourage you to remember that the mystical oneness in the covenant of marriage is the result of a supernatural bonding.*

Therefore, please understand that *out of all the women God has created, He has specifically chosen you to be one with your husband in every expression of covenantal oneness—spiritually, physically, and emotionally.* Though God has called you to serve in his shadow and therefore in obscurity before the eyes of a watching world, you are God's choice servant. Neither your husband's headship over you nor his function in Christian ministry diminishes your worth in the slightest. Together, you reflect the relationship that exists within the Trinitarian Godhead—the kind of functional submission that is manifest in Christ's relationship to the church and His heavenly Father in His work of redemption.

Furthermore, like your husband, you are a steward who is to be found trustworthy (1 Cor. 4:2). Think of it this way: *God has called and equipped you to co-labor with the husband He has chosen for you.* Your value to him personally and to the body of Christ is therefore tantamount to a vital organ within the physical body; *it may never be seen, but the body cannot function effectively without it.* As you faithfully serve in your God-ordained role as a wife (and perhaps, a mother), God is pleased, your marriage and family are blessed, and the church will be doubly blessed by your example. Your role is vital in his life, in the life of your family, and the church. In fact, your husband cannot "be one who manages his own household well, keeping his children under control with all dignity" (1 Tim. 3:4)—one of the qualifications of an elder—apart from your help.

So, be content and rejoice in God's sovereign purpose for you as a warrior preacher's wife (and perhaps the mother of his children). For indeed, all that God does is perfect and unfathomably good! Trust Him in this. For this reason, the psalmist gives this magnificent exhortation: "O taste and see that the LORD is good; how blessed is the [woman] who takes refuge in Him" (Psalm 34:8)!

2. Be Committed
to a personal pursuit of holiness

I have witnessed many pastors and church leaders fail miserably in their ministry because of an ungodly wife. Perhaps such wives were unregenerate, or maybe they were simply immature babes in Christ like those Paul described in 1 Corinthians 3 who were ruled by their flesh more than the Spirit, "men of flesh . . . infants in Christ" (1 Cor. 3:1). Either way, a worldly wife will destroy a man's ministry, marriage, and family; moreover, she will forfeit God's blessing in her life and find herself languishing in a desert of divine chastening. May I gently challenge you to examine your heart in this regard, as I must examine my own on a routine basis.

Remember this: sinful attitudes are well concealed in the recesses of our heart. They will only be exposed by the light of the Word and the power of the Spirit, and this must be your passionate prayer and the priority of your life. Although sin will inevitably manifest itself in our interpersonal style of relating to God and others, nevertheless, it is often considered to be right and therefore justified (Prov. 14:12).

For example, a controlling woman who embraces the unbiblical ideologies of modern evangelical feminism will see nothing wrong with her antipathy towards the authority of Scripture and her unwillingness to submit to the loving leadership of her husband or the elder authority God has placed over her in the church. The enemy will therefore seize upon her rebellion by carefully concealing snares in the well-worn paths of her habitual sinfulness. It is therefore in the regions of the heart where our greatest battles must be fought. It is here where we must be committed to a personal pursuit of holiness.

Devote yourself to piety in every facet of your life.
Guard your heart and be an example to your husband,
to your children, and to your friends.

Even though you are married to a pastor, without a zeal for godliness, the lusts of your flesh and the temptations of the world will gradually enslave you once again into the very corruptions of character and conduct from which you have been delivered (Rom. 6:11–14). Said simply, *unless you commit yourself to walking by the Spirit, you will carry out the desire of the flesh* (Gal. 5:15). Given the target on your husband's back—and indirectly on yours as well—you simply must learn to hate hypocrisy in your own life more than what you see in others and you must learn to despise all that is linked to the world (1 John 2:15). It is incumbent upon all believers to "fear this honored and awesome name, the LORD your God" (Deut. 28:58), for "the eye of the LORD is on those who fear Him, on those who hope for His lovingkindness" (Ps. 33:18).

I humbly challenge you to "discipline yourself for the sake of godliness" (1 Tim. 4:7). Devote yourself to piety in every facet of your life. Guard your heart and be an example to your husband, to your children, and to your friends. And with the psalmist, say, "I have chosen the faithful way; I have placed Your ordinances before me. I cling to Your testimonies; O LORD, do not put me to shame! I shall run the way of Your commandments, for You will enlarge my heart" (Ps. 119:30–32). For indeed, "godliness actually is a means of great gain, when accompanied by contentment" (1 Tim. 6:6).

3. Be Chaste—
Modest and discreet in dress, reflecting a godly demeanor

The wife of a warrior preacher must share his commitment to moral purity. Her priority will therefore be one of spiritual adornment, rather than physical adornment. Every godly woman must restrain her fleshly desire to draw attention to herself—a sinful lust that is typically manifested in immodest and ostentatious attire and demeanor. The contemporary literature describing the sensual and flamboyant manner of dress of courtesans and harlots in first-century Rome explains why the apostle Paul had to address this issue in the early church. Evidently some of the Christian women allowed their hearts to be conformed to the world, and like the courtesans and harlots, adorned themselves in similar fashion—a disgrace that is far too common in churches today. For this reason, Paul gave this exhortation: "I want women to adorn themselves with proper clothing, modestly and discreetly, not with braided hair and gold or pearls or costly garments, but rather by means of good works, as is proper for women making a claim to godliness" (1 Tim. 2:9–10).

The wife of a warrior preacher must share his commitment to moral purity. Her priority will therefore be one of spiritual, rather than physical adornment.

It is important for the wife of every pastor and church leader to have a heart so committed to honoring Christ that her inward beauty will naturally manifest itself in her modest and discreet attire and her godly, feminine demeanor. How a woman dresses and conducts herself reflects the propriety and priority of her heart. The more flesh a woman reveals on the outside, the less she has to offer on the inside. The more attention she seeks externally, the less joy she has in Christ internally. While there is nothing wrong with a Christian woman having an interest in beauty and adornment—if it is modest and discreet—Paul's exhortation is against an excessive preoccupation with external physical appearances resulting in provocative attire, all of which are motivated by a heart that wishes to flaunt sensuality and wealth, and not honor Christ.

True beauty will be self-evident in women who are Spirit-controlled. Vanity, immodesty, or any kind of provocative dress or deportment will have no place in the heart of a woman who has cultivated a reverence for God and finds her joy in Christ and in the husband He has given her. While it is rare, it is refreshing to see a Christian woman whose very appearance is a living sermon, a testimony to her purity and devotion to Christ. She understands Peter's admonition to wives when he said,

> . . . you wives, be submissive to your own husbands so that even if any of them are disobedient to the word, they may be won without a word by the behavior of their wives, as they observe your chaste and respectful behavior. Your adornment must not be merely external—braiding the hair, and wearing gold jewelry, or putting on dresses; but let it be the hidden person of the heart, with the imperishable quality of a gentle and quiet spirit, which is precious in the sight of God. For in this way in former times the holy women also, who hoped in God, used to adorn themselves, being submissive to their own husbands.
> (1 Peter 3:1–5)

Such a wife is a rare blessing, "for her worth is far above jewels. . . . Charm is deceitful and beauty is vain, but a woman who fears the LORD, she shall be praised" (Prov. 31:10, 30). Knowing full well our culture's disdain for God's sacred instructions to women and wives, I encourage the wife of every pastor and church leader to embrace these great truths with all your heart, for the glory of Christ and the blessings that will be yours as a result of faithful obedience.

A Final Word of Encouragement

I join many other men in giving thanks to God for a wife who is a living example of all that has been expressed in this brief appendix. The depth of her godliness is an inspiration to me and all who know her—I can look into her eyes and never see bottom. Indeed, she is the most tangible expression of God's grace in my life, a helpmate in every expression of the word. And as such, I am even more devoted to Peter's admonition, to "live with your [wife] in an understanding way, as with someone weaker, since she is a woman; and show her honor as a fellow heir of the grace of life, so that your prayers will not be hindered" (1 Peter 3:7).

Without a wife who is *content, committed,* and *chaste,* the effectiveness of a man's ministry will always be hindered, and the joy of marriage will always be diminished. But with such a wife, the opposite will be true. Moreover,

> Her children rise up and bless her;
> Her husband also, and he praises her, saying:
> "Many daughters have done nobly,
> But you excel them all."
> (Prov. 31:28–29)

I humbly challenge you, if you are a wife, to dedicate yourself to these ends, not only for the temporal blessings that will be yours because of your humble obedience to Christ, but for the sake of His kingdom to which you belong and which you are building with your husband. And I wish to thank each godly wife of every warrior preacher for the shining light of Christlikeness that you emanate in this dark world. Your faithfulness and beauty do not go unnoticed, nor is your contribution to the church unseen. You are a blessing to us all, and for that we are eternally grateful. To be sure, your reward will be great.

Soli Deo Gloria!

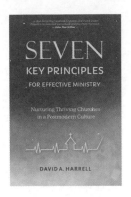

Seven Key Principles for Effective Ministry
Nurturing Thriving Churches in a Postmodern Culture
David A. Harrell

Trade Paperback, 192pp
ISBN: 9781633421301
Published by Shepherd Press

A book that exhorts and encourages Christian ministers and leaders to be committed to the principled model for successful ministry that God has established through the teaching of the New Testament.

"Dave Harrell outlines with unusual clarity the essential features of authentic church ministry. . . . Prepare to be instructed, encouraged, and powerfully motivated."—JOHN MACARTHUR

"It is refreshing to have such a clear, direct, and powerful book."
—SHANNON HURLEY

". . . succinctly summarizes the essential principles of authentic biblical ministry."—PHIL JOHNSON

"Here is a book worth reading and passing on to those just starting the journey of church leadership and ministry."
—CONRAD MBEWE

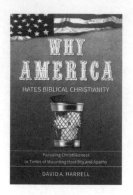

Why America Hates Biblical Christianity
Pursuing Christlikeness inTimes of Mounting Hostility and Apathy
David A. Harrell

Trade Paperback, 224pp
ISBN: 9781633422377
Published by Shepherd Press

"Dave Harrell skillfully shows from Scripture how true followers of Christ should respond—and why we must remain steadfast—even as the moral fabric of American society is unraveling all around us."
—DR. JOHN MACARTHUR

". . .clear, insightful, encouraging analysis of our culture's spiritual meltdown, and our duty as Christians to respond with courage and conviction. I'm certain you will be emboldened and uplifted by this excellent book." —PHIL JOHNSON

"This book is well written, well researched, and engaging. It is easy to read while covering matters that are heart-wrenching for Christians who long for the United States of America to return to her Christian roots. This is a book which will be instructive and inspirational for all God-fearing Christians." —DR. DEWEY ROBERTS

Compact Expository Pulpit Commentary Series
A Series of Eight Mini Books
4.25 x 7 inch small format
David A. Harrell

Approximately 96pp each
Published by Great Writing Publications
www.greatwriting.org

Finding Grace in Sorrow: Enduring Trials with the Joy of the Holy Spirit, ISBN 9781734345285

Finding Strength in Weakness: Drawing Upon the Existing Grace Within, ISBN 9781734345247

Glorifying God in Your Body: Seeing Ourselves from God's Perspective, ISBN 9781735949116

God, Evil, and Suffering: Understanding God's Role in Tragedies and Atrocities, ISBN 9780960020362

God's Gracious Gift of Assurance: Rediscovering the Benefits of Justification by Faith, ISBN 9781734345216

Our Sin and the Savior: Understanding the Need for Renewing and Sanctifying Grace, ISBN 9781734345209

The Marvel of Being in Christ: Adoring God's Loving Provision of New Life in the Spirit, ISBN 9781734345230

The Miracle of Spiritual Sight: Affirming the Transforming Doctrine of Regeneration, ISBN 9781734345292

Shepherd's Fire Media is positioned to be an oasis and central go-to resource for materials—whether in print, digital, or audio/video format—to be accessed by a global audience, and therefore become a major publisher devoted to strengthening and encouraging biblical preachers who are currently engaged in the battle for truth.

www.shepherdsfiremedia.org